Friedrich Engels and Modern Social and Political Theory

FRIEDRICH ENGELS AND MODERN SOCIAL AND POLITICAL THEORY

Paul Blackledge

SUNY
PRESS

Published by State University of New York Press, Albany

© 2019 State University of New York

For information, contact State University of New York Press, Albany, NY
www.sunypress.edu

Library of Congress Cataloging-in-Publication Data

Names: Blackledge, Paul, 1967– author.
Title: Friedrich Engels and modern social and political theory / Paul Blackledge.
Description: Albany : State University of New York Press, 2019. | Includes
  bibliographical references and index.
Identifiers: LCCN 2018059663 | ISBN 9781438476872 (hardcover : alk. paper) |
    ISBN 9781438476889 (pbk. : alk. paper) | ISBN 9781438476896 (ebook)
  Subjects: LCSH: Engels, Friedrich, 1820–1895. | Social history—19th century. |
    Socialism—History—19th century. | Communism—History—19th century. |
    Political science—Philosophy—History—19th century.
Classification: LCC HX276.E6 B55 2019 | DDC 300.1—dc23
LC record available at https://lccn.loc.gov/2018059663

10 9 8 7 6 5 4 3 2 1

To Kristyn, Johnny, Matthew, Kate, and Jack, with love

Contents

Contents

Acknowledgments

Some of the arguments presented in this book were first rehearsed in articles published in the journals *Critique, Science and Society, Socialism and Democracy, Social Theory and Practice*, and *War and Society* and in the edited collections *The Oxford Handbook on Karl Marx* and *Marx and Contemporary Critical Theory: The Philosophy of Real Abstraction*. Thanks to the editors and referees of these publications for forcing me to sharpen up my ideas. Thanks also to the numerous others who have helped along the way. These include Sue Abbott, Jeff Abrams, Simone Abram, Yunus Bakhsh, Colin Barker, Ron Beadle, Lori Beckett, Andrius Bielskis, Sue Birch, Ian Birchall, Vicky Blake, Ann Blair, Tim Briggs, Geoff Brown, Adrian Budd, Tony Burns, Phil Cardew, Janet Carr, Tony Collins, Catherine Connolly, Suzanne Corazzi, Nick Cox, Jon Dart, John Davies, Jonathan Davies, Jennifer Dods, Pete Dwyer, Sandra Falshaw, Ziyun Fan, Anne Foley, Dana Foote, John Bellamy Foster, John Green, Robert Hayes, Christian Høgsbjerg, Oriel Kenny, Mumtaz Khan, Farzad Khosrowshahi, Sarah Kingston, Kelvin Knight, Buket Korkut Raptis, Eleni Leontsini, Anna Liddle, George Lodorfos, Jonathan Long, Lesley McGorrigan, James McGrath, Jo McNeill, Hugh Meyer, Richard Miles, Joanna Moncrief, Carlo Morelli, Ryan Morris, Bob Mouncer, Jeff Nicholas, Brendon Nichols, Jane Nolan, Mark Oley, Dorron Otter, Annemarie Piso, Michael Rinella, Ruth Robbins, Jeannie Robinson, Stephen Robson, Helen Rodgers, Ted Sarmiento, Sean Sayers, Darren Shaw, Sue Sherwin, Alan Smith, Karl Spraklen, Jacqueline Stephenson, Louisa Tamplin, Dan Taylor, Lisa Taylor, Briony Thomas, Terry Thomas, Vikki Tommy-Knight, Lee Tucker, Lise Vogel, Jennifer Walker, Jayne-Louise Watkins, Colin Webster, Phil Webster and Terry Wrigley. Finally, my wife and children continue to inspire me. This book is dedicated to them.

Introduction

Marx, Engels, Marxism

As we approach the bicentenary of his birth, Friedrich Engels's reputation as an original thinker is, among Anglophone academics at least, at its nadir. The main reason for this unfortunate state of affairs is undoubtedly political. Despite the recent global economic crisis and associated increases in inequality that have tended to confirm Marx and Engels's general critique of capitalism, Marxism is an optimistic doctrine that has not fared well in a context dominated by working-class retreat and demoralization (Barker, et al. 2013, 5, 14, 25). But if this context has been unpropitious for Marxism generally, criticisms of Engels's thought have a second, quite separate, source. Over the course of the twentieth century, a growing number of commentators have claimed that Engels fundamentally distorted Marx's thought, and that "Marxism" and especially Stalinism emerged out of this one-sided caricature of Marx's ideas (Levine 1975, xv; xvii; Bender 1975, 1–52; Carver 1981, 1983, 1989; Claeys 2018, 219–228; Jordan 1967, 332–333; Liedman 2018, 497; Rockmore 2018, 73; Sperber 2013, 549–553; Stedman Jones 2016, 556–568; Thomas 2008, 35–49; Tucker 1961, 184; Walicki 1995, 121).

While the claim that Engels distorted Marx's ideas has roots going back to the nineteenth century (Rigby 1992, 4), 1956 was a pivotal moment after which it increasingly became a dominant theme within the secondary literature (Rees 1994). When a New Left emerged in response to Khrushchev's Secret Speech, the Russian invasion of Hungary, and the Anglo-French-Israeli invasion of Egypt, it attempted to renew socialism through a critical reassessment of Marxism. Engels's contribution to Marxism became a focal point in the ensuing debate. Though a small minority among this milieu attempted to rescue Engels's and Lenin's reputations alongside that of Marx from any association with Stalin's counterrevolution, a much larger group concluded that the experience of Stalinism damned the entire Marxist tradition all the way back to Marx. Between these two poles, a third grouping counterposed Marx's youthful "humanistic" writings to Engels's "scientific" interpretation of Marxism (Blackledge 2014b).

Drawing on a one-sided interpretation of Georg Lukács's early critical comments on Engels's concept of a dialectics of nature, this milieu gravitated to the view that Engels was Marx's greatest mistake. Thus, by 1961, George Lichtheim could take it for granted that whereas Marx had sought to transcend the opposition between idealism (autonomous morality) and materialism (heteronymous causation) through his concept of praxis, Engels had reduced Marxism to a positivistic form of materialism (Lichtheim 1964, 234–243). A few years later Donald Clark Hodges essentially endorsed the view among academics that "the young Marx has become the hero of Marx scholarship and the late Engels its villain" (Hodges 1965, 297). Similarly, in 1968, Alasdair MacIntyre wrote of, and rejected, Engelsian Marxism for its apparent conception of revolution as a quasi-natural event. Engels, according to this critique, believed that "we must await the coming of the revolution as we await the coming of an eclipse" (MacIntyre 1995, 95).

In what is probably the most uncharitable critique of Engels's thought, Norman Levine argues that while it is true that Marxism gave rise to Stalinism, twentieth-century Marxism is best understood as a form of "Engelsism," a bastardization of Marx's original ideas in which his sublation of idealism and materialism was reduced to a positivist, mechanical, and fatalistic caricature of the real thing. "There was," according to Levine, "a clear and steady evolution from Engels to Lenin to Stalin," and "Stalin carried this tradition of Engels and the Engelsian side of Lenin to its extreme" (Levine 1975, xv–xvi).

The rational core of the claim that Engels begat Marxism derives from the fact that Engels penned the most influential popularization of his and Marx's ideas: the ironically titled *Herr Eugen Dühring's Revolution in Science*. Universally known as *Anti-Dühring*, this book played a key part in winning the leadership of the German Social Democratic Party (SPD) to Marxism during the period of Bismarck's antisocialist laws (Mayer 1936, 224; Adamiak 1974). *Anti-Dühring* is also Engels's most controversial work. This is in large part because, as Hal Draper has pointed out, it is "the only more or less systematic presentation of Marxism" written by either Marx or Engels. Consequently, anyone wanting to reinterpret Marx's thought must first detach this book from his seal of approval (Draper 1977, 24). It is thus around *Anti-Dühring*, the shorter except from it, *Socialism: Utopian and Scientific*, and other related works, most notably *Ludwig Feuerbach and the End of Classical German Philosophy* and the unfinished and unpublished in his lifetime *Dialectics of Nature*, that debates about the relationship of Marx to "Engelsian" Marxism tend to turn.

In his contribution to this literature, John Holloway argues that while it would be wrong to overemphasize the differences between Marx and Engels, this is more to the detriment of the former—particularly the Marx of the 1859 preface to *A Contribution to the Critique of Political Economy*—than it is to Engels's advantage. According to Holloway, "Science, in the Engelsian tradition which became known as 'Marxism,' is understood as the exclusion of subjectivity" (Holloway 2010, 121). If Holloway is honest enough to recognize that Marx's ideas cannot easily be unpicked from those of Engels (Holloway 2010, 119), Paul Thomas wants to spare Marx from the consequences of similar criticisms of Engels: "Engels's post-Marxian doctrines owe little or nothing to the man he called his mentor." According to Thomas, the "conceptual chasm separating Marx's writings from the arguments set forth in *Anti-Dühring* is such that even if Marx was familiar with these arguments, he disagreed with" Engels's view that "human beings . . . are in the last analysis physical objects whose motion is governed by the same general laws that regulate the motion of all matter" (Thomas 2008, 39, 9, 43). Terrell Carver has produced what is probably the most comprehensive version of the divergence thesis. He argues that whereas Marx saw "science as an *activity* important in technology and industry," Engels viewed "its importance for socialists in terms of a *system* of knowledge, incorporating the causal laws of physical science and taking them as a model for a covertly academic study of history, 'thought' and, somewhat implausibly, current politics" (Carver 1983, 157).

Like Thomas, Carver disapproves of this approach and believes it separates Engels from Marx. Carver explains Marx's indulgence toward these alien ideas in very disparaging terms: "perhaps he felt it easier, in view of their long friendship, their role as leading socialists, and the usefulness of Engels's financial resources, to keep quiet and not interfere in Engels's work, even if it conflicted with his own" (Carver 1981, 76; cf. Carver 1983, 129–130; Thomas 2008, 48). Unfortunately, or so Carver suggests, Marx's silence about *Anti-Dühring* and related works allowed Engels's thought to take on the mantle of orthodoxy within, first, the Second International before subsequently becoming "the basis of official philosophy and history in the Soviet Union" (Carver 1981, 48; 1983, 97; cf. Rockmore 2018, 79). This was a disastrous turn of events, for Engels was either "unaware (or had he forgotten?)" that whereas *The German Ideology* had transcended the opposition between materialism and idealism, "his materialism . . . was close in many respects to being a simple reversal of philosophical idealism *and* a faithful reflection of natural sciences as portrayed by positivists" (Carver 1983, 116). In a nutshell, Carver, Holloway, Levine, Lichtheim, and Thomas are prominent proponents of what John Green calls a "new orthodoxy" that condemns Engels for having reduced Marx's conception of revolutionary praxis to a version of the mechanical materialism and political fatalism against which he and Marx had rebelled in the 1840s (Green 2008, 313; Stanley and Zimmermann 1984, 227).

Superficially, at least, the claim that Engels's *Anti-Dühring* is a mechanically materialist and politically fatalist text is an odd complaint. Engels's engagement with Dühring was explicitly intended as a defense of revolutionary political practice against the latter's moralistic reformism—and no less an interventionist Marxist than Lenin described it as "a handbook for every class-conscious worker" (Lenin 1963b, 24; Blackledge 2018b). More substantively, Engels's response to Dühring's criticism of Marx's deployment of Hegelian categories as a "nonsensical analogy borrowed from the religious sphere" (CW 25, 120) included a clear recapitulation of Marx's revolution in philosophy. Whereas Dühring claimed that Marx's use of the term "sublation" to explain how something can be "both overcome and preserved" was an example of "Hegelian verbal jugglery," Engels insisted that this term helped Marx synthesize the partial truths of older forms of materialism and idealism into a whole that transcended the limitations of these earlier perspectives (CW 25, 120). In fact, as we shall see later, the claim that *Anti-Dühring* represents a fundamental break with Marx's philosophy rests on an unconvincing caricature of Engels's arguments. Moreover, the related attempt to downplay the essential unity of Marx and Engels's thought cannot withstand critical scrutiny.

In the most detailed attempt to force a division between Marx and Engels, Carver claims that they neither spoke with one voice in "perfect agreement" nor did they embrace a simple division of labor such that obvious differences between their two voices can be dismissed as natural consequences of their engagements with different subject matters (Carver 1998, 173–174; 1983, xiii). Carver insists that the myth of a "perfect partnership" was invented by Engels after Marx's death to justify his own standing within the international socialist movement, and that, contra this myth, evidence for collaboration between the two friends is much less significant than is commonly supposed. He argues that Marx and Engels penned only three "major" joint works during their lifetimes, and of these *The Holy Family* included separately signed chapters while *The Communist Manifesto* was written by Marx alone after taking into consideration Engels's earlier drafts. Finally, *The German Ideology* remained unfinished and unpublished in their lifetimes and is in fact an opaque document that obscures more than it reveals of their early relationship—Carver labels it an "apocryphal" text that, as a book, "never took place." By contrast with the "perfect partnership" paradigm, Carver claims that it was only after Marx's death that Engels sought to, and largely succeeded in, "revoicing Marx" in his own words (Carver 1998, 161–172; 1983; 2010; Carver and Blank 2014, 2; Rockmore 2018, 96).

A problem with Carver's interpretation of the Marx-Engels relationship is signaled in Holloway's critique of Engels's thought noted earlier. As Holloway suggests, Marx, particularly the Marx of the 1859 preface, shared many of the assumptions that are typically associated with Engels's supposed distortion of his thought. A comparable point, though from the opposite perspective, was made forty years ago by Sebastiano Timpanaro. He argued that "everyone who begins by representing Engels in the role of a banalizer and distorter of Marx's thought inevitably ends by finding many of Marx's own statements too 'Engelsian'" (Timpanaro 1975, 77). Likewise, the best two existent studies of Engels's work, Stephen Rigby's *Engels and the Formation of Marxism* (1992) and Dill Hunley's *The Life and Thought of Friedrich Engels* (1991) both powerfully contribute to demolishing the divergence myth, but do so by arguing that Marx shared many if not all of the flaws usually associated with Engels's work. Rigby insists that "attempts to counterpose the views of Marx and Engels are essentially a strategy to forestall a confrontation with the problems which lie within Marx's works themselves" (Rigby 1992, 4, 8). Meanwhile, Hunley concludes that "in most respects the two men fundamentally agreed with each other" and their writings share similar contradictions between more and less powerful themes (Hunley 1991, 64, 126). In effect, Rigby and to a lesser extent Hunley conclude that Engels should not be seen as the fall guy in the history of Marxism because the defects associated with his ideas are also characteristic of Marx's thought.

Beyond the problem for the divergence thesis of the theoretical parallels between Marx's and Engels's works, Carver's account of the actual extent of collaboration between Marx and Engels is difficult to square with what we know of their relationship. In the first instance, Carver's defense of the divergence thesis depends on something of a straw man argument. Outside the quasi-religious ideologues of the old Soviet Bloc, where Marx and Engels's relationship was rather absurdly described as a "perfect whole" in which a "meeting in mind and spirit . . . worked together in harmony for forty years" (Gemkov et al. 1972, 6; Ilyichov et al. 1974, 10; Stepanova 1985, 45–79), the "perfect agreement" thesis is uninteresting because it is obviously untrue—and Engels certainly did not make any such claim. Any reasonable attempt to reaffirm the uniquely close bond between Marx and Engels from the 1840s until Marx's death in 1883 in no way implies that there were no disagreements or fallouts nor differences in tone, emphasis, and even substance across their writings over this period. Not only would it be utterly bizarre if there were no such differences, but it is possible to locate such differences internal to the works of both Marx and Engels themselves (and to the works of any other interesting thinker!).

Second, Carver is wrong to dismiss the importance of the intellectual division of labor that undoubtedly characterized Marx and Engels's relationship. It is a fact that Engels tended, as Hal Draper points out in his superb study of Marx and Engels's politics, to handle "popularised expositions, 'party' problems, and certain subjects in which he was particularly interested or expert" (Draper 1977, 23). And while it is true that this division of labor between the two founders of the Marxist tradition was in no sense absolute, once properly understood this fact actually serves to reinforce the claim of a high degree of collaboration between the two men. The extensive correspondence between them, especially in the period when Engels worked in Manchester while Marx lived in London (before and after this separation they had much more opportunity simply to talk to each other), evidences a profound intellectual dialogue over a vast range of subjects from which both learned and through which they both honed their arguments.

Third, the division of labor between these two friends reflected the fact that Engels was the intellectually stronger of the two men in a number of areas. In the 1970s Perry Anderson rightly challenged the already "fashionable" tendency "to depreciate the relative contribution of Engels to the creation of historical materialism" by making the "scandalous" but nonetheless valid point that "Engels's *historical* judgements are nearly always superior to those of Marx. He possessed a deeper knowledge of European history, and had a surer grasp of its successive and salient structures."

Anderson was well aware of the "supremacy of Marx's overall contribution to the *general theory* of historical materialism" but was justifiably keen to distance himself from the typically crude criticisms associated with the anti-Engels literature (Anderson 1974, 23).

Fourth, Carver's assessment of the degree of formal collaboration between Marx and Engels is simply disingenuous. Beside the three "major" works he mentions in his discussion of their supposed noncollaboration, Marx and Engels coauthored numerous important, theoretically informed political interventions throughout their lives. They also corresponded on numerous issues, and readers of their correspondence can often find Engels's influence on subsequent texts written by Marx (Hunley 1991, 127–143). It is typical that one of Marx's most famous aphorisms about history repeating itself, "the first time as tragedy, the second as farce," was borrowed from Engels (CW 38, 505), while much of the substance, for instance, of Marx's justly famous *Critique of the Gotha Programme* drew on similar arguments put forth previously by Engels (CW 45, 60–66). Indeed, once we take seriously their joint political writings alongside their voluminous correspondence it quickly becomes obvious just how implausible is Carver's suggestion that their common project was Engels's invention.

The closest thing to hard evidence for Marx's corroboration of the divergence thesis is a jokey letter he wrote to Engels on August 1, 1856. Carver emphasizes how, in this letter, Marx complains about a journalist writing of the two of them as if they were one (Carver 1998, 165). The writer in question was Ludwig Simon, an émigré deputy from the Frankfurt Assembly of 1848–1849, who exhibited what Marx called an "exceedingly odd" tendency "to speak of us in the singular—'Marx and Engels says' etc." Now, outside of a cowritten text, this phrase is by any measure a grammatical oddity. Nonetheless, in joking about Simon's badly written "jeremiad"—Marx wrote to his old friend that he would "sooner swill soap-suds or hobnob with Zoroaster over mulled cow's piss than read through all that stuff"—Marx actually wrote of jokes that Engels had made during the revolution as if they belonged to the two of them "in the singular": "Even the jokes we cracked about Switzerland in the *Revue* 'fill him with indignation'" (CW 40, 63–64).

Despite Carver's claim that Marx "says nothing positive" in this letter "or elsewhere at any length about the parameters of separation and overlap between" himself and Engels, the fact is that Marx repeatedly used the terms "us," "our," and "we" when referring to his political and theoretical relationship with Engels. And while his comments on this relationship may not have been written "at length," the extant evidence overwhelmingly supports the claim that Marx believed that he and Engels had a unique intellectual and political partnership. Perhaps his most famous comment on the importance of his collaboration with Engels is to be found in his 1859 preface to *A Contribution to the Critique of Political Economy*:

> Frederick Engels, with whom I maintained a constant exchange of ideas by correspondence since the publication of his brilliant essay on the critique of economic categories . . . arrived by another road (compare his *Condition of the Working-Class in England*) at the same result as I, and when in the spring of 1845 he too came to live in Brussels, we decided to set forth together our conception as opposed to the ideological one of German philosophy, in fact to settle accounts with our former philosophical conscience. (CW 29, 264)

A year later, November 22, 1860, he reaffirmed and indeed strengthened this claim in a letter to Bertalan Szemere in which he insisted that Engels "must" be considered "my alter ego." As to Engels's intellectual abilities, Marx wrote to Adolf Cluss, October 18, 1853, that "being a veritable walking encyclopaedia," Engels is "capable, drunk or sober, of working at any hour of the day or night, [he] is a fast writer and devilish QUICK in the uptake" (CW 41, 215; CW 39, 391).

For her part, Marx's daughter Eleanor wrote that her father used to talk to Engels's letters "as though the writer were there," agreeing, disagreeing, and sometimes laughing "until tears ran down his cheeks." And of their friendship she wrote, "it was one which will become as historical as that of Damon and Pythias in Greek mythology" (Marx-Aveling n.d., 187, 189). Similarly, Marx's son-in-law Paul Lafargue reminisced that Marx "esteemed [Engels] as the most learned man in Europe" and "never tired of admiring the universality of Engels's knowledge and the wonderful versatility of his mind" (Lafargue n.d., 89–90). In fact, contra Carver's baseless and frankly defamatory suggestion that Marx kept quiet about his criticisms of Engels's work because of the "usefulness of Engels's financial resources," it is unimaginable that anyone but "the most learned man in Europe," and beside that one of the greatest revolutionary activists of the age, could maintain an equal partnership with a man of Marx's stature for some four decades. As Arthur writes, attempts to downplay Engels's influence on Marx are as unfair to Marx as they are to Engels: "Marx was never one to judge lightly the intellectual deficiencies of others, yet of all his contemporaries it was with Engels he chose to form a close intellectual partnership" (Arthur 1970, 14).

Marx's appreciation of the importance of his collaboration with Engels was reaffirmed in his largely forgotten book *Herr Vogt* (1860). In a comment on Engels's *Po and Rhine*, which, Marx wrote, was published "with my agreement" and which he described as providing a "scientific"—nasty Engelsian word this—"military proof that 'Germany does not need any part of Italy for its defence,'" he wrote that he and Engels generally "work[ed] to a common plan and after prior agreement" (CW 17, 114). Despite the facts that this unambiguous statement was made in print, and that it was highlighted by Draper in *Karl Marx's Theory of Revolution* (Draper 1977, 23), it tends to be ignored by those who aim to force divisions between Marx and Engels.

Nor did Marx's favorable comments on his collaboration with Engels end in 1860. Seventeen years later in a letter to Wilhelm Blos, November 10, 1877, he wrote of "Engels and I" and "us" when reviewing earlier political positions they had previously taken together (CW 45, 288). More importantly, in a letter to Adolph Sorge dated September 19, 1879—written shortly after the publication of *Anti-Dühring* and less than four years before his own death—Marx evidences the profound degree of collaboration between him and Engels. He wrote not only of making "provision" that Engels take care of "business matters and *commissions*" while he had been away on holiday, but also of Engels writing the now famous 1879 *Circular Letter* to the leadership of the SPD in both of their names and in which "our point of view is plainly set forth." Meanwhile he wrote of "our attitude," "our support," "we maintain," "Engels and I," "our complaint," "we differ from [Johan] Most," "our names," and against attempts to "rope us in" to supporting positions with which they disagreed. All of this while praising Engels's rebuttal, from their shared point of view, of reformist "partisans of 'peaceable' development." Engels, he wrote, "showed how deep was the gulf between [Höchberg—PB] and us" by giving him a "piece of his mind" (CW 45, 411–414; cf. CW 45, 392–394).

This letter and many others like it indicate that while it might be foolish to treat Marx and Engels in the singular, it is much more absurd to claim, as does Paul Thomas, that "there is no evidence for any joint doctrine outside of Engels's insistence that it was somehow—or had to be—'there'" (Thomas 2008, 39). This is simply untrue, and Thomas's denial of evidence from Marx for a joint doctrine with Engels suggests his research suffers from a problem he is eager to ascribe to others: "an astonishing ignorance of what Marx had written" (Thomas 2008, 3).

Of course, Thomas is not ignorant of what Marx had written. But why then continue to insist on the divergence thesis when the extant evidence, as Hunley points out, "should demonstrate to anyone not utterly blinded by ideology that Marx and Engels basically agreed with each other" (Hunley 1991, 145)? It does seem that the proponents of the divergence thesis are motivated more by ideology than by evidence. Indeed, Carver and Thomas argue not merely (and justifiably) that Marx's legacy should be disassociated from the inheritance of Stalinism but also (and unjustifiably) that it should similarly be disassociated from modern revolutionary politics (Thomas 2008, 1–8; Carver 1998, 111–112). Tom Rockmore's anti-Engelsian position is different from Carver's and Thomas's because he accepts that "Marx and Engels agree[d] politically," while insisting that they "disagree[d] philosophically" (Rockmore 2018, 4). Rockmore's argument benefits from recognizing, contra Carver's claim that Marx conceived the transition to socialism through "constitutional" and "peaceful" means (Carver 1998, 111–112), that Engels was right when he said in his eulogy to Marx that his collaborator was "above all else a revolutionist." Nonetheless, as we shall see, Rockmore is wrong about Marx and Engels's supposed philosophical disagreements.

Engels's own assessment of his part in the formulation of the theoretical foundation of their political perspective is famously, and unduly, self-deprecating. A year after Marx's death he claimed in a letter to Johann Philipp Becker, August 15, 1884, to have been merely "second fiddle" to Marx:

> my misfortune is that since we lost Marx I have been supposed to represent him. I have spent a lifetime doing what I was fitted for, namely playing second fiddle, and indeed I believe I acquitted myself reasonably well. And I was happy to have so splendid a first fiddle as Marx. But now that I am suddenly expected to take Marx's place in matters of theory and play first fiddle, there will inevitably be blunders and no one is more aware of that than I. And not until the times get somewhat more turbulent shall we really be aware of what we have lost in Marx. Not one of us possesses the breadth of vision that enabled him, at the very moment when rapid action was called for, invariably to hit upon the right solution

and at once get to the heart of the matter. In more peaceful times it could happen that events proved me right and him wrong, but at a revolutionary juncture his judgment was virtually infallible. (CW 47, 202)

Four years later in *Ludwig Feuerbach and the End of Classical German Philosophy* he elaborated on this modest appreciation of his contribution in print:

> Lately repeated reference has been made to my share in this theory, and so I can hardly avoid saying a few words here to settle this point. I cannot deny that both before and during my forty years' collaboration with Marx I had a certain independent share in laying the foundations of the theory, and more particularly in its elaboration. But the greater part of its leading basic principles, especially in the realm of economics and history, and, above all, their final trenchant formulation, belongs to Marx. What I contributed—at any rate with the exception of my work in a few special fields—Marx could very well have done without me. What Marx accomplished I would not have achieved. Marx stood higher, saw further, and took a wider and quicker view than all the rest of us. Marx was a genius; we others were at best talented. Without him the theory would not be by far what it is today. It therefore rightly bears his name. (CW 26, 382)

It would, of course, be foolish to deny Marx's greater part in his collaboration with Engels. But this fact is hardly surprising given that even in his youth one of his contemporaries, Moses Hess, felt justified in describing Marx thus:

> he is a phenomenon . . . the greatest—perhaps the only genuine—philosopher of the current generation. When he makes a public appearance, whether in writing or in the lecture hall, he will attract the attention of all Germany. . . . He will give medieval religion and philosophy their *coup de grâce*; he combines the deepest philosophical seriousness with the most biting wit. Imagine Rousseau, Voltaire, Holbach, Lessing, Heine and Hegel fused into one person—I say fused not juxtaposed—and you have Dr Marx. (Hess qtd. in Wheen 1999, 36–37)

To say that Engels (or anyone other than a latter-day Aristotle) failed to match the intellectual level of someone who could reasonably be described in these terms is not particularly illuminating. It is much more interesting to recognize, with Anderson, that Engels had significant intellectual strengths and that he made a number of important contributions to his and Marx's joint theoretical perspective.

Indeed, Marx was the first to recognize Engels's strengths and to disabuse him of his uncalled-for humility. For instance, in a letter of July 4, 1864, he wrote: "As you know. First, I'm always late off the mark with everything, and second, I inevitably follow in your footsteps" (CW 41, 546). As we shall see later, this assertion was especially true in the 1840s when Engels played not merely an important but also a leading role in their intellectual and political partnership. Thereafter, the two men worked closely together in a collaboration through which each learned from the other and both became considerably more than they would have been had they merely worked alone.

The divergence thesis, by contrast, tends to make far too much of relatively minor differences between the two men and, at worst, to invent differences where they do not exist to suit the particular predilections of each critic. Commenting on Levine's variant of this argument, Alvin Gouldner writes that "it is typical of Levine . . . that his formulations are not merely inexact but ludicrous" (Gouldner 1980, 283). He adds the idea that Engels initiated the vulgarization of Marx's ideas continues to hold sway "less because of its intellectual justification than because of the need it serves": the divergence myth effectively allows critics of Marxism to lay blame on Engels for whatever aspect of classical Marxism they want to reject (Gouldner 1980, 252). In effect this approach has informed a tendency to reimagine Engels, as Edward Thompson put it, as the "whipping boy" who has been saddled with any defect "that one chooses to impugn to subsequent Marxism" (Thompson 1978, 69). However, the anti-Engels literature is largely negative in scope and far from coherent. Because Engels's critics generally dump onto him whichever part of Marxism they dislike, they are inclined, as Dill Hunley points out, to contradict "one another and sometimes even themselves" (Hunley 1991, 55, 61). More to the point, what Chris Arthur calls the Engels-phobic literature tends to be so keen to denounce Engels that authors of this persuasion skirt over significant problems with their own arguments (Arthur 1996, 175).

This criticism is particularly true of attempts by Engels's critics to evidence some degree of coherence between his views and Stalin's debased version of Marxism. Carver and Thomas, for instance, share Levine's belief that Stalin's ideology can be derived from "Engelsism." As Carver wrote in 1981, "political and academic life in the official institutions of the Soviet Union . . . involves a positive commitment to dialectical and historical materialism that derives from Engels's work but requires the posthumous imprimatur of Marx" (Carver 1981, 74; Thomas 2008, 4). A couple of years later he wrote that "the tenets" of Engels's philosophical works were "passed on lectures, primers and handbooks, down to official Soviet dialectics" (Carver 1983, 97). However, though it has often been repeated that Stalin's interpretation of historical and dialectical material- ism (Histmat and Diamat, as they became known in the Soviet Union) derived from Engels's work, it is less often noted that Stalin's attempt to legitimize his counterrevolutionary regime by reference to Marxism and the October Revolution led him to gut Marx and Engels's thought of its revolutionary essence.

In respect to Engels's thought, Stalin explicitly rejected a number of key ideas that derived from his work. He expunged from official Soviet theory Engels's critique of the idea of socialism in one country, his view that socialism would be characterized by the withering away of the state, and his claim that the law of value would cease to operate in a social- ist society. In relation to philosophy, Stalin removed the concept of the "negation of the negation" from the account of dialectics that became orthodoxy in Russia in the 1930s (Evans 1993, 32, 39–40, 48, 52; Sandle 1999, 198–199; 2007, 61–67; Marcuse 1958). These parts of Engels's thought were not insubstantial aspects of his Marxism. As Alfred Evans points out in a claim that sits ironically beside the attempts by Carver and others to wrench Marx from Marxism so as to reimagine him as a theorist of constitutional and peaceful change, Stalin's "innovations" underpinned a reinterpretation of Marxism from which "any revolutionary implications for socialist development" was severed (Evans 1993, 52; Sandle 2007, 67). Stalin also acted to reify the historical schema presented in Marx's 1859 preface to his *Contribution to the Critique of Political Economy* so as to exclude from orthodoxy Marx and Engels's concept of an "Asiatic mode of pro- duction," through which they had aimed to make sense of oppressive class relations in societies without private property relations and which might easily be deployed to illuminate class relations in Soviet Russia (Marcuse 1971, 102–103; Blackledge 2006a, 78; 97; 110). If the political reasoning behind this decision is obvious enough, the fact that Stalin nonetheless felt compelled to invert Marx's account of the relationship between base and superstructure as outlined in this famous essay as he attempted to justify the role of the state in Soviet economic development illuminates the fact that he revised Marx and Engels's thought, not as part of a healthy developing tradition of inquiry but through the incoherent demands associated with the more mundane task of justifying the socialist credentials of "a nonsocialist society" (Marcuse 1971, 128; Pollock 2006, 172–173, 182).

As it happens, not only is Engels's thought incompatible with Stalinist ideology (Hunt 2009, 361–362), but his ideas can be and have been profitably mined to make sense of the counterrevolutionary essence of Stalinism (Cliff 1974, 165; CW 25, 266). In this sense at least, Stalin's revisions of Marxism reflect his better understanding of the critical and revolutionary implications of Engels's thought than is evident in the work of many of the anti-Engels faction: it is precisely because Engels's ideas were so critical and revolutionary that they were incompatible with Stalin's dictatorship. And if the revolutionary essence of Engels's thought helps explain why Stalin aimed to neuter his Marxism, the anti-Stalinist implications of his work are good reason why modern socialists should seek an honest reassessment of his contribution to social and political theory.

A similar point could be made in relation to Engels's much-maligned concept of a dialects of nature. Since the publication of Georg Lukács's *History and Class Consciousness* in 1923, a defining characteristic of the Western Marxist tradition has included a rejection of Engels's attempt to root Marxist theory in a dialectical understanding of nature (Foster et al. 2010, 218).

In *History and Class Consciousness*, Lukács suggested that Engels's unfortunate extension of the concept of dialectics from the social to the natural realms led him to ignore the "most vital interaction, namely the dialectical relation between subject and object in the historical process," without which "dialectics ceases to be revolutionary" (Lukács 1971, 3, 24n6). Interestingly, though Lukács's critique of Engels's thought has had a very strong influence on the anti-Engels literature, it was somewhat cursory: amounting to no more than a passing comment supported by a twelve-line footnote. Besides, this comment was balanced by other comments in the text that seemed much more compatible with Engels's arguments. For instance, where he wrote of "the necessity of separating the merely objective dialectics of nature from those of society" (Lukács 1971, 207). As it happens, within a couple of years of the publication of *History and Class Consciousness* Lukács did write much more substantially, and much more positively, about the idea of a dialectic in nature (Rees 2000, 19–21):

Self-evidently the dialectic could not possibly be effective as an *objective principle of development* of society, if it were not already effective as a principle of development of nature before society, if it did not already *objectively exist*. From that, however, follows neither that social development could produce no new, equally objective forms of movement, dialectical movements, nor that dialectical movements in the development of nature would be *knowable* without the mediation of the new social dialectical forms. (Lukács 2000, 102)

This passage is evidence that Lukács continued to reject philosophical reductionism, without collapsing, as Antonio Gramsci and Karl Korsch had warned was a possible consequence of rejecting the dialectic of nature, into "the opposite error . . . a form of idealism" (Gramsci 1971, 448; cf. Korsch 1970, 122; Lukács 1978, 7). Unfortunately, while Lukács, Gramsci, and Korsch differentiated between reductive and nonreductive interpretations of Engels's idea of a dialectic of nature, Engels's modern critics tend to be adamant that the concept of a dialectics of nature lends itself inevitably to mechanical materialism and positivism.

John Bellamy Foster has argued that this critique of Engels emerged out of a one-sided interpretation of what he calls the "Lukács problem." Whereas Lukács, in *History and Class Consciousness*, incoherently combined a denial that the dialectical method is applicable to nature because of the missing subjective dimension with a recognition of the existence of a distinct, objective, dialectics in nature, Western Marxism has tended simply to deny the existence of a dialectic in nature (Foster et al. 2010, 224). More specifically, Western Marxists have generally argued that Marx's understanding of dialectics assumed, contra Engels, what Foster calls "a social ontology cordoned off from nature" (Foster et al. 2010, 226). As we shall see, this claim not only contradicts what we know of Marx's generally supportive comments on Engels's work on the dialectics of nature, it also underpins a strong tendency toward forms of philosophical idealism. Consequently, rather than explore Marx's work for tools to help exculpate Marxism from the twin pitfalls of mechanical materialism on the one side and philosophical idealism on the other, Western Marxists have tended to lend their support to the project of driving a wedge between an idealist interpretation of Marx and a mechanically materialist interpretation of Engels (Foster et al. 2010, 226). By contrast with this approach, Foster, following Andrew Feenberg and Alfred Schmidt, has detailed how, through the concept of sensuous human activity, Marx's work provides the necessary tools to make sense of the dialectical relationship between nature and society. According to Foster, Marx's materialism assumes what he calls a form of "natural praxis" through which human sensuous practice is understood to be embodied in the sensuous world itself. Our perceptions of the world are rooted in our natural senses, but, contra empiricism, the senses through which nature becomes aware of itself are not merely passive recipients of information from the external world but are active and developing processes within the natural world whose development continues and deepens through humanity's productive interaction with nature. Foster insists that the concept of natural praxis is compatible with Engels's emergentist conception of reality while avoiding the pitfalls of reductionist readings of Engels's work (Foster et al. 2010, 215–247). Moreover, and much more interestingly, he argues that this conception of praxis coheres with contemporary ecological concerns. Prefiguring modern ecology's concern with humanity's oneness with nature, Engels's conception of a dialectics of nature opens a space through which ecological crises could be understood in relation to alienated nature of capitalist social relations. Because production is first and foremost a metabolic exchange with nature, alienated relations of production include an alienated relationship to nature itself. Consequently, the same forces that underpin capitalism's tendency to economic crises generate parallel tendencies to environmental crises. Marx and Engels's understanding of the unity of humanity and nature is thus suggestive of a revolutionary perspective that is simultaneously political, social, and ecological in scope: the socialist revolution would involve not merely a transformation of social and political relations, it would also necessarily involve a radical transformation of humanity's relationship to nature. The internal relationship between capitalist and ecological crises informs Foster's argument that Engels's claim that "nature is the proof of dialectics" can and should be revised to read that "ecology" has become "the proof of dialectics" (Foster et al. 2010, 240; 245). So, whereas Engels's critics have tended to reimagine Marx as merely a social theorist, Engels's philosophical writings illuminate the powerful ecological dimension of his and Marx's thought, and consequently the internal link between ecological concerns and anticapitalism.

Foster's argument powerfully illuminates my contention that it would be a grievous mistake to lose sight of Engels's fundamental, overwhelmingly positive and still relevant contribution to socialist theory and practice. His thought shares the central strengths of Marx's work, whose themes he often prefigured, while he made powerful and independent contributions to Marxism in his own right. And it is my belief that the left would benefit enormously from a serious reassessment of his work.

Alongside Marx, Engels worked a revolution in theory: the two of them famously synthesized French socialism, German philosophy, and English political economy into a new revolutionary perspective on society. This genuinely collaborative project was forged through the odd medium of a fragmentary manuscript that remained unpublished in their lifetimes and that has come down to posterity as *The German Ideology*. Though this text is problematic, its production nonetheless represents, as Marx wrote and Engels reinterated, a key moment of "self-clarification" through which their subsequent theoretical and practical project was framed. Commenting on this period in their lives, Karl Korsch writes:

> Marx and Engels during the next two years worked out in detail the contrast prevailing between their own materialist and scientific views and the various ideological standpoints represented by their former friends among the left Hegelians (Ludwig Feuerbach, Bruno Bauer, Max Stirner) and by the philosophical belles-lettres of the "German" or "true" socialists. (Korsch 2015, 77)

By contrast with both Marx's and Engels's retrospective assessments of the significance of the moment when they wrote the manuscripts that have come down to us as *The German Ideology*, it is a characteristic of the anti-Engels literature that it attempts to downplay the extent to which these manuscripts evidence a pivotal moment in the process of their intellectual self-clarification (Carver 1998, 106; Levine 1975, 117; Carver and Blank 2014, 140).

One problem with this line of argument is that even though *The German Ideology* never existed as a proposed book, Marx and Engels did work up their ideas into a form that they attempted to have published in 1845–1846 (Carver and Blank 2014, 7). And as Carver himself has pointed out, the sketch of Marx's method outlined in his 1859 preface closely follows the language of the chapter on Feuerbach in *The German Ideology* (Carver 1983, 71). More to the point, Chris Arthur argues that all the insights from their earlier writings are synthesized in these manuscripts through the idea that people make and remake themselves through their social and productive interaction with nature to meet their evolving needs

(Arthur 1970, 21; 2015). This perspective was both rooted in and oriented toward the new proletarian form of social practice, and as a philosophy of praxis it was first tested and deepened through a remarkable political intervention into the revolutionary events of 1848–1849.

The 1840s was a moment of great democratic expectation when the mismatch between Europe's existing institutions of power on the one hand and the new social reality of burgeoning capitalist development on the other informed a growing sense of radical change across the continent (Hobsbawm 1962, 366). If the defeat of this movement occasioned Marx and Engels's systematic reflections on their own practical and theoretical contributions to the movement, their subsequent work is best understood as extending and deepening the approach they forged in the 1840s: "1848" became the touchstone for everything else they wrote and did (Lenin 1962, 37). Subsequently, their unique and profound collaboration remained undiminished up until Marx's death in 1883, after which Engels continued their project both through his own political and theoretical works and by preparing for (re)publication a number of Marx's writings including, most importantly (and controversially), the second and third volumes of *Capital* (Thompson 1978, 69).

If the fundamentals of Marx and Engels's strategy were forged collaboratively in the mid-1840s, Engels was already moving in the direction of their joint project before he met Marx, and he subsequently made independent and important contributions to their collaborative work. Gareth Stedman Jones is right to point out that

> a number of basic and enduring Marxist propositions first surface in Engels's rather than Marx's early writings: the shifting focus from competition to production; the revolutionary novelty of modern industry marked by its crises of overproduction and its constant reproduction of a reserve army of labour; the embryo at least of the argument that the bourgeoisie produces its own gravediggers and that communism represents, not a philosophical principle, but "the real movement which abolishes the present state of things"; the historical delineation of the formation of the proletariat into a class; the differentiation between "proletarian socialism"; and small-master or lower-middle-class radicalism; and the characterisation of the state as an instrument of oppression in the hands of the ruling propertied class. (Stedman Jones 1977, 102; 1982, 317; cf. Cliff 2001)

This is an incredibly impressive list by any measure. Yet it does not tell the whole story. Beyond Engels's codiscovery of the working class as a potential revolutionary agent of change, he was the first socialist to recognize the importance of trade union struggle to the socialist project. He also laid the foundations for a historical understanding of the emergence of women's oppression and a unitary theory of its capitalist form. Alongside Marx, in *The German Ideology* he elaborated a materialist conception of history through a synthesis of the idea of practice with a historical conception of material interest, and shortly thereafter he penned the first work of "Marxist" history—instigating an immensely productive and influential tradition (Blackledge 2019a). In his drafts of what became *The Communist Manifesto* he applied the general perspective outlined in *The German Ideology* to the specific context of Germany in 1847, formulating a deeply democratic conception of socialism as a necessarily international movement—which incidentally showed that at its inception Marxism precluded Stalin's notion of socialism in one country. Furthermore, against the dominant socialist voices of his day, Engels recognized that the struggle for socialism was not a zero-sum game. He insisted that socialists should support bourgeois democratic movements while maintaining the political independence of the workers' party with a view to challenging the bourgeoisie for power immediately upon the defeat of absolutism. He deepened this theory of "revolution in permanence" through his involvement in the revolutions of 1848 when alongside Marx he played a key role as a journalist in raising the general strategic analysis outlined in *The Communist Manifesto* to the level of practice: extending, deepening, and shifting their perspective along the way. Subsequently, he played a role in the military struggle against Prussian absolutism. And after the defeat of this movement he focused much of his intellectual energies on developing a materialist analysis of military power—and in so doing, "The General," as he became known in the Marx household, became one of the nineteenth-century's greatest military thinkers (Hunley 1991, 21; Neumann and von Hagen 1986, 265). Though it has often been dismissed as a mere eccentricity, Engels's military writings were of the first importance to nineteenth-century revolutionary strategy and remain of interest to modern socialists despite the significance of changes to military power over the succeeding century.

Perhaps most importantly, Engels also won generations of socialists over to Marxism through his popularization of the Marxist method. And alongside his own and his collaborative works he also prepared the second and third volumes of Marx's *Capital* for publication—and though modern scholarship has picked holes in this project, he nonetheless performed a Herculean task in presenting these manuscripts as coherently as possible; the left has benefited enormously from his efforts (Moseley 2016).

There were, of course, numerous problems with Engels's contribution to the Marxist project: on reformism, value theory, nationalism, and the task of formulating a unitary theory of women's oppression, among other contributions, his thought suffered from important gaps and outright errors. But it would be wrong, indeed gravely so, to allow these weaknesses to cloud our judgment of Engels's contribution to Marxism. What Lenin once said of Rosa Luxemburg might equally be said of Engels: "eagles may at times fly lower than hens, but hens can never rise to the height of eagles." Luxemburg, like any truly original thinker, made important theoretical and political mistakes, yet she was an intellectual and political eagle (Lenin 1966, 210). I shall similarly argue that, whatever his weaknesses, Engels was an intellectual and political eagle whose writings remain of the first importance to those of us on the contemporary revolutionary left whose aim it is to avoid the limitations of reformism without collapsing into sectarianism while simultaneously forging an ethical and ecological socialism that escapes the moralistic "impotence in action" of so much modern leftist rhetoric (CW 4, 201; CW 5, 11).

1

Discovering the Working Class

Engels was born in Barmen, now Wuppertal, on November 28, 1820. His father was an affluent mill owner and an active member of the Pietist sect of Protestantism. Thanks to his mother, from whom, apparently, he "inherited his cheerful disposition" and his love of reading (Marx-Aveling n.d., 183), his was a comfortable but anti-intellectual childhood where his ability to constantly disappoint his father's hopes that he would cast aside his idealistic inclinations to focus on pursuing a successful career was balanced by love from his mother.

He was educated at a local Pietist school until he was fourteen. Here he mastered the Bible. After primary education, he entered the still nominally Pietist but more liberal gymnasium for a further three years' study. He left school with a good report card, but a year short of the necessary tenure to enable university entrance—his father was too pragmatically middle class to waste money on unnecessary classes. After school, he went to work in Bremen for his father's export agent and consul for the king of Saxony. Carver points out that Bremen, a large seaport, was a much more liberal and cosmopolitan environment than Barmen had been, and he describes Engels's period there as "intellectually and politically formative" (Carver 1989, 12). In Bremen Engels broadened his reading and began to write. Here too he came under the influence of the liberal Young Germany movement.

Prussia was an absolutist state with Lutheran coloring, and Young Germany's literary challenge to royal power informed a deeper rationalist critique of Pietism. It was thus that in 1839 Engels came into contact with the Young Hegelian milieu when he read David Strauss's pathbreaking *The*

Life of Jesus. Strauss's book had caused a stir on its publication four years earlier by decisively challenging the literal interpretation of the gospels. Reading Strauss placed Engels on a trajectory that quickly drew him into an increasingly close orbit around the radical Young Hegelian movement; indeed, shortly after reading Strauss, he moved on to Hegel's *Philosophy of History* and embraced pantheism.

After two and a half years in Bremen, Engels moved to Berlin, then the center of Young Hegelian radicalism. Nominally he was there as a volunteer with the Prussian artillery, but actually he used military service as a back-door entry into university life. This was a particularly interesting time to be a radical young student as Friedrich von Schelling had just arrived at the University of Berlin with a mission from the Prussian king to root out the (Young) Hegelians. Schelling had been a contemporary and friend of Hegel's (they had apparently shared a room at university) before relations between them became acrimonious as Hegel's fame grew while Schelling was reduced to a mere footnote in the intellectual movement from Kant to Hegel. Schelling's role in Berlin was simple: to defeat the Young Hegelians by demolishing their mentor. Alongside Engels the impressive list of attendees at Schelling's lectures speaks to the importance of this event: Mikhail Bakunin, Jacob Burckhardt, Alexander von Humboldt, and Søren Kierkegaard were all disappointed with the old professor after expecting intellectual fireworks. For his part, Engels took it upon himself to pen a series of critical journalistic pamphlets in which he defended Hegel against Schelling's philosophical defense of the Christian God. These pamphlets also contained an important admission: the Young Hegelians were, he wrote, atheists in all but name. Thus it was that, without fanfare, he announced the culmination of his own intellectual movement from liberal rationalist critique of Pietism through pantheism and on to atheism. This radical stance informed his embrace of "The Free," a group of radical Berlin intellectuals including Bruno and Edgar Bauer whose critique of absolutism and religion was leaning toward an abstract but vociferously expressed conception of communism (Carver 1989, 1–94).

It was as a communist that Engels first met Marx in November 1842. However, this meeting was, as he reported to Franz Mehring half a century later, a "distinctly chilly" affair. In the months prior to this meeting, Marx had, in Engels's words, "taken a stand against" Bruno and Edgar Bauer's Young Hegelian "hot air brand of communism, which was based on a sheer love of 'going to extremes.'" By contrast with their abstract and propagandistic politics, Marx wanted the newspaper he edited alongside Moses Hess, *Rheinische Zeitung*, to be a voice for much more concrete "political discussion and action." Unfortunately, because Engels "corresponded with the Bauers," Marx regarded him "as their ally" while the Bauers in turn caused Engels "to view Marx with suspicion" (CW 50, 503).

Despite this initial mutual mistrust, Engels's healthy tendency to youthful political excess was mediated from the start by the kind of "serious" and "sober-minded" work Marx demanded of the contributors to his newspaper and against the "frivolous" style of "political romanticism" he believed was compromising "the cause of the party of freedom" (CW 1, 287; Carver 1983, 23). Indeed, Engels had already distinguished himself from his peers by the thoughtful pen-portrait he made of the effects of "factory work" in his home district.

Engels's *Letters from Wuppertal*, published in a newspaper of the Young Germany movement, the *Telegraph für Deutschland*, when he was still only eighteen years old, in many ways prefigures the assessment of the negative consequences of industrialization he was to detail a few years later in *The Condition of the Working Class in England* (Marcus 1974, 77). He argued both that industrialization had led to the physical and moral "degradation" of workers and that religious Pietism played an important role in justifying this malign situation. He suggested that the Lutheran factory owners justified stern workplace discipline in exchange for a meager wage as a means of protecting workers from the evils of drink, while the workers did their best to cope with these dehumanizing conditions either by losing themselves in drink and licentiousness, or by internalizing religious fundamentalism as an emollient to salve the pain of their existence, or, more often, by hypocritically combining elements from both of these coping strategies (CW 2, 9–10). These letters were, as Carver observes, produced by a man with a sharp eye for detail and a "hunger for knowledge and hatred of dogmatism" (Carver 1983, 5). What is more, they were obviously produced by a serious student of German society who was aware both of his own strengths as a writer and of his weaknesses as a student of that about which he was writing. It was to remedy this failing that Engels announced, prior to his meeting with Marx, his intention to "devote more time to studying" (CW 2, 545; Carver 1989, 99).

The first substantial fruit of his renewed studies was his *Outlines of a Critique of Political Economy* (commonly known as the *Umrisse*)—written in October–November 1843 and published the following year. This "brilliant essay," as Marx subsequently called it (CW 29, 264), not only marked an important moment in Engels's evolution away from Young Hegelianism toward a more materialistic and realistic conception of revolutionary practice, it was also, as Samuel Hollander points out, "the founding document in the Marxian theoretical tradition" (Hollander 2011, 25; cf. Oakley 1984, 30–36). Indeed, the *Umrisse* was the first published critique of political economy by either man and the first to point toward a systematic critique of capitalism as a historical form—though it is probably true to say that Engels's essay paralleled Marx's independent realization, on the basis both of his critique of Hegel's theory of the state, his notes on Adam Smith and James Mill, and his examination of the Rhineland Parliament's proceedings on the theft of wood, that it was impossible to fully understand political questions independent of the underlying economic relations they express (Avineri 1968, 39; McLellan 2006, 47; Carver 1983, 32; CW 29, 261–262).

By the time of their next meeting in August 1844 Marx had read the *Umrisse* and exchanged (unfortunately lost) letters with Engels about the essay (Carver 1983, 37). From this moment onward the two men found themselves, as Engels put it some four decades later, in "complete agreement in all theoretical fields" (CW 3, 375–376; CW 26, 318). Their revolutionary perspective did not emerge, like Athena, fully formed at this moment. Rather, they began to articulate a common perspective through a process of both critical engagement with the works of the political economists and their socialist critics and practical work as active socialists.

This project was initially realized through the cowritten theoretical works *The Holy Family* and *The German Ideology* alongside a number of independently and cowritten shorter and more directly political interventions. Of these works, the closest to a common programmatic statement prior to the publication of *The Communist Manifesto* was Engels's *Principles of Communism* (October 1847)—itself a reworked version of his earlier *Draft of a Communist Confession of Faith* (June 1847). *The Communist Manifesto* itself, which closely followed the arguments of *Principles of Communism*, declared the solution to capitalism's ills to lie through the struggles of the new proletariat to overcome the inhumanity of bourgeois society. Engels's contribution to this claim should not be underestimated. He came to this conclusion over a pivotal three-year period between 1842 and 1845. This moment marked the point when he moved beyond the burgeoning literature mapping the horrific consequences of industrial capitalism for the new working class to recognize, through his relationship to Chartism, that workers were not merely victims of the new capitalist system but could also act as progressive agents of its overthrow. Engels first gestured toward this conclusion in a series of articles published in the *Rheinische Zeitung* in late 1842.

In *The English View of the Internal Crisis* (1842) he suggested that England's middle and upper classes viewed the Chartist call for universal suffrage as, in essence, a revolutionary demand because through it the "unpropertied . . . mass of proletarians" threatened their hold on power. In subsequent installments of the article published over the next two days he added that, though English industrial development had made the country rich, it had done so only at the cost of creating "a class of unpropertied, absolutely poor people." However, whereas Hegel had seen in this class mere victims of industrialization (Hegel 1952, 150), Engels argued that that summer's general strike was evidence not merely of this class's independent agency but also of their growing awareness that "only a forcible abolition of the existing unnatural conditions, a radical overthrow of the nobility and industrial aristocracy, can improve the material position of the proletarians." Interestingly, he also wrote that while "the Englishman's inherent respect for the law" was holding back the revolutionary implications of this process, the existence of economic crises would put unbearable stress on this ideological barrier to radical change: "revolution is inevitable for England" because "fear of death from starvation will be stronger than fear of the law." So, in stark contrast to Young Hegelian idealism, he concluded with the materialist claim that "it will be interests and not principles that will begin and carry through the revolution . . . the revolution will be social, not political" (CW 2, 368–374).

This germ of the idea of historical materialism was further deepened in his *Letters from London*, published the following May in the Zurich-based radical weekly *Schweizerischer Repulikaner*. Despite the defeat of the previous summer's general strike, he claimed that "[t]he democratic party in England is making rapid progress . . . despised and derided socialism marches forward calmly and confidently and gradually compels the attention of public opinion . . . a new party of countless numbers has taken shape in a few years under the banner of the People's Charter" (CW 3, 379). Subsequently, he reconstructed the moment when the English working class emerged as an independent political force at the 1843 Chartist Convention:

> The fruit of the uprising was the decisive separation of the proletariat from the bourgeoisie. The Chartists had not hitherto concealed their determination to carry the Charter at all costs, even that of a revolution; the bourgeoisie, which

now perceived, all at once, the danger with which any violent change threatened its position, refused to hear anything
further of physical force, and proposed to attain its end by
moral force, as though this were anything else than the direct
or indirect threat of physical force. This was one point of dissension, though even this was removed later by the assertion
of the Chartists (who are at least as worthy of being believed
as the bourgeoisie) that they, too, refrained from appealing to
physical force. The second point of dissension and the main
one, which brought Chartism to light in its purity, was the
repeal of the Corn Laws. In this the bourgeoisie was directly
interested, the proletariat not. The Chartists therefore divided
into two parties whose political programmes agreed literally,
but which were nevertheless thoroughly different and incapable
of union. At the Birmingham National Convention, in January,
1843, Sturge, the representative of the Radical bourgeoisie,
proposed that the name of the Charter be omitted from the
rules of the Chartist Association, nominally because this name
had become connected with recollections of violence during
the insurrection, a connection, by the way, which had existed
for years, and against which Mr. Sturge had hitherto advanced
no objection. The working-men refused to drop the name, and
when Mr. Sturge was outvoted, that worthy Quaker suddenly
became loyal, betook himself out of the hall, and founded a
"Complete Suffrage Association" within the Radical bourgeoisie.
So repugnant had these recollections become to the Jacobinical
bourgeoisie, that he altered even the name Universal Suffrage
into the ridiculous title, Complete Suffrage. The working-men
laughed at him and quietly went their way. From this moment
Chartism was purely a working-men's cause freed from all
bourgeois elements. (CW 4, 522–523)

These lines are taken from the young Engels's masterpiece: *The Condition
of the Working Class in England* (1845). Published when Engels was still
only twenty-four years old, this book has consistently, according to Eric
Hobsbawm, not only been "substantially accepted as standard," but it is
also "by far the best single book on the working class of the period"
(Hobsbawm 1964, 106; 1969, 17). What made Engels's book stand out
from the crowd was not merely his eye for illuminating detail but, more

importantly, his method for making sense of this detail (Rex 1969, 70). Though not explicitly stated in the book itself, Engels's approach was signaled in two earlier essays: the *Umrisse* and a positive yet critical review of Thomas Carlyle's *Past and Present: The Condition of England* (Hollander 2011, 25).

Writing some four decades later, Engels suggested the key lesson he learned in Manchester in the early 1840s was

> that the economic facts which have so far played no role or only a contemptible one in historiography are, at least in the modern world, a decisive historical force; that they form the basis for the emergence of the present-day class antagonisms; that these class antagonisms, in the countries where they have become fully developed by dint of large-scale industry, hence especially in England, are in their turn the basis for the forma- tion of political parties, party struggles, and thus of all political history. (CW 26, 317)

If his comments on the relationship between interests and principles quoted previously tend to confirm this general point, he first defended the analytical core of this claim in the *Umrisse*, in which he extended themes from Pierre-Joseph Proudhon's (anarchist) *What Is Property?* and (more significantly) John Watts's (Owenite socialist) *The Facts and Fictions of Political Economists* to fashion a revolutionary critique both of political economy and more importantly of capitalism itself (Claeys 1984).

Marx pointed to the methodological importance of this contribution to political economy a few months later. Whereas the political economists had taken the existence of "*private property* for granted," Proudhon's "great scientific advance" was to subject this concept to critical scrutiny. How- ever, Proudhon's critique of political economy was fundamentally limited because he failed to analyze "wages, trade, value, price, money, etc., as forms of private property in themselves." So, despite taking the first step in the critique of political economy, because Proudhon naturalized private property's many specifically capitalist forms, he failed to go beyond this first step: "his criticism of political economy" was essentially hidebound because it failed to escape "the standpoint of political economy." Engels's *Umrisse*, by contrast, pointed beyond the historical limits of political econ- omy because it deepened the critique of private property through a more general critique of its various forms (CW 4, 31–32).

Political economy, Engels argued, emerged in the eighteenth century alongside the growth of trade as the "science of enrichment" through which the previously dominant mercantilism was challenged in theory and practice. However,

> just as all the revolutions of this century were one-sided and bogged down in antitheses—just as abstract materialism was set in opposition to abstract spiritualism, the republic to monarchy, the social contract to divine right—likewise the economic revolution did not get beyond antithesis. The premises remained everywhere in force: materialism did not attack the Christian contempt for and humiliation of Man, and merely posited Nature instead of the Christian God as the Absolute confronting Man. In politics no one dreamt of examining the premises of the state as such. It did not occur to economics to question the *validity of private property*. (CW 3, 419)

And in a brilliant dialectical inversion, Engels showed that though Adam Smith's defense of free trade was a "necessary advance" beyond mercantilism's defense of monopolies, this critique was fundamentally limited by its continued naturalization of private property. Indeed, Engels claimed, private property was itself the most important form of monopoly. So, while the Smithians had fought for the destruction of "the small monopolies," they had created a world in which "the *one* great basic monopoly, property, may function the more freely and unrestrictedly" (CW 3, 421, 423). Consequently, political economy's claim to be in the general interest was a sham, for "only that view which rises above the opposition of the two systems, which criticises the premises common to both and proceeds from a purely human, universal basis, can assign to both their proper position" (CW 3, 421).

A number of commentators have taken this and similar humanistic statements from this period as clear evidence that Engels's critique of political economy did not evince a break with pre-Marxist forms of communism (Stedman Jones 1977, 91–92; 1982, 304–305). At one level this criticism is true enough. However, even at this point in his intellectual evolution there was a growing tension between the logic of his analysis of capitalism and crude humanistic morality. Engels argued not merely that private property was the basic form of monopoly but also that free trade acted against the formation of a general conception of good because it created "diametrically opposed interests" between a multiplicity of agents in the marketplace (CW 3, 422). It is not merely that capitalism is characterized by socially destructive forms of mutual distrust and fraud, but also that Adam Smith's attempted justification of this situation was more morally bankrupt than was mercantilism. For whereas, "[t]he mercantile system still had a certain artless Catholic candour and did not in the least conceal the immoral nature of trade," Adam Smith's critique of mercantilism paralleled Luther's critique of Catholicism: just as Luther stymied the humanism inherent in his overthrow of the external religiosity of Catholicism by internalizing faith as the "inner essence of man," so Smith exchanged Catholic candor for "Protestant hypocrisy" by embedding private property in our very essence (CW 3, 422–423). Unfortunately, by naturalizing private property, Smith naturalized the various dehumanizing forms through which it is expressed.

These contradictory consequences of private property underpin tendencies not merely to continuous conflict but also to crises that in turn fan the flames of these conflicts:

> as long as you continue to produce in the present unconscious, thoughtless manner . . . trade crises will remain; and each successive crisis is bound to become more universal and therefore worse than the preceding one; is bound to impoverish a larger body of small capitalists, and to augment in increasing proportion the numbers of the class who live by labour alone, thus considerably enlarging the mass of labour to be employed (the major problem of our economists) and finally causing a social revolution such as has never been dreamt of in the philosophy of the economists. (CW 3, 434)

So, according to Engels, private property is not merely the root cause of modern social contradictions; it also tends to push the conflicts attendant to these contradictions toward their revolutionary consummation. These conflicts would incline to increase in importance because, or so he believed, capitalist development would lead to the gradual disappearance of the middle classes that would be replaced by an increasingly large and, in response to economic crises, militant proletariat.

If these conflicts illuminated the morally bankrupt nature of capitalism, the response of the political economists to this situation was to legitimize this immorality by naturalizing it. This was particularly true of the work of the Reverend Thomas Malthus. While Smith, through his concept of an "invisible hand," attempted to justify individual selfishness and fraud as the means to general happiness, Malthus's work on population was notable less for its scientific rigor—Engels followed a line of socialist writers who illuminated the self-serving pseudo-scientific nature of Malthus's naturalization of capitalism's inability to meet basic human needs through his claim that population grew exponentially while food production only grew arithmetically—than for the way it illuminated both the barbaric essence of capitalism as a system that could not reproduce itself except by the constant dehumanization of the mass of the population and the intellectually moribund nature of political economy itself. The fact that even first-rate thinkers such as Ricardo should accept Malthus against all the evidence of science told Engels all he needed to know about the "hypocrisy, inconsistency and immorality" of the political economists as apologists for the status quo (CW 3, 420).

The essence of Engels's charge against capitalism was that private property gave rise to trade, which in turn bred "decidedly antagonistic" forms of "confrontation" (CW 3, 422). Political economy in turn naturalized this unnatural condition. In what he would later characterize as a contradiction between social production and individual appropriation (CW 25, 258), Engels highlighted the fact that capitalism was characterized by historically distinct forms of class conflict in a way that prefigured what John Bellamy Foster calls Marx's account of the "metabolic rift" between humanity and nature (Marx 1981, 949; Foster 2000, 105–110, 155–163):

> The immediate consequence of private property was the split of production into two opposing sides—the natural and the human sides, the soil which without fertilisation by man is dead and sterile, and human activity, the first condition of which is that very soil. Furthermore, we have seen how human activity in its turn was dissolved into labour and capital, and how these two sides antagonistically confronted each other. Thus, we already had the struggle of the three elements against one another, instead of their mutual support; now we have to add that private property brings in its wake the fragmentation of each of these elements. One piece of land stands confronted by another, one capital by another, one labourer by another. In other words, because private property isolates everyone in his own crude solitariness, and because, nevertheless, everyone

has the same interest as his neighbour, one landowner stands antagonistically confronted by another, one capitalist by another, one worker by another. In this discord of identical interests resulting precisely from this identity is consummated the immorality of mankind's condition hitherto; and this consummation is competition. (CW 3, 432)

Though Engels's focus on private property rather than production relations meant, as he subsequently would have been the first to acknowledge (CW 47, 158), that this essay did not as yet constitute a clear and fully thought out analysis of capitalism as a distinct mode of production, through his concrete analysis of the substance of modern social conflicts he nonetheless pushed the abstractly moral critique of private property a long way in the direction of the mature analysis of capitalism as a distinct mode of production that he and Marx first articulated in *The German Ideology* (Mandel 2015, 21). This intellectual movement was extended through his critical reading of Carlyle's romantic critique of capitalist industrialization: *Past and Present* (Levin 1999).

Published in the journal *Deutsch-Französisch Jahrbücher*, edited by Marx and Arnold Ruge, Engels's *The Condition of England* (1844) opened with praise for Carlyle as a "theoretician of the German type." However, Engels also made the point that Carlyle had failed to make good the promise of his theoretical insights because they were mixed rather than synthesized in his work with a countertendency toward superficial "empiricism" (CW 3, 467). Against empiricism, Engels was aware that facts must be chosen and interpreted and that "conclusions are nothing without the reasoning that has led up to them; this we have known since Hegel" (CW 3, 457). The problem with Carlyle's study was that while he powerfully described the essential soullessness of the modern condition, he misunderstood its cause. Carlyle embraced a relatively trivial explanation of the inhumanity of the modern world as a consequence of the rise of godlessness. Accordingly, he misconstrued part of the problem of modern life as itself the solution. Whereas Carlyle followed Ben Jonson in claiming that "man has lost his soul," Engels retorted that "in religion man has lost his own substance, has alienated his humanity, and now that religion, through the progress of history, has begun to totter, he notices his emptiness and instability. But there is no other salvation for him, he cannot regain his humanity, his substance, other than by thoroughly overcoming all religious ideas and returning firmly and honestly, not to "God," but to himself" (CW

3, 465). The moralistic humanism of this sentence cannot, however, be reduced to a simplistic rehearsal of the abstract humanism that, as we shall see, characterized the work of Ludwig Feuerbach and his True Socialist epigones. For Engels's essay on Carlyle includes the important suggestion that the moral and intellectual decline of the English "upper classes" left "only the workers, the pariahs of England, the poor" as the agents from which "England's salvation will come" (CW 3, 444–446). This class inflection to Engels's humanism set him apart from the German True Socialists for whom socialism was a rational moral corollary of humanism. It is not that he had already come to his mature political conclusions at this point—he had not. But neither was his work marred by a simple, Feuerbachian, belief that socialism was in the common, human interest. What Stephen Rigby wrote of Engels's *The Condition of the Working Class in England* is also true of this earlier essay: it is marked less by its utopian themes and more the degree to which his focus on the redeeming potential of the English workers' movement "anticipates the outlook which was to be developed in *The German Ideology* and *The Communist Manifesto*" (Rigby 1992, 51).

Among the earliest steps in the process by which he moved toward his mature conclusions was his detailed observations of English social conditions in his *Letters from London* (1843). Hal Draper suggests that, beyond the elements of abstract humanism, the most important political difference between these letters and *The Communist Manifesto* is that in the former Engels had yet to generalize his analysis of the revolutionary role of the proletariat from England to the Continent (Draper 1977, 155). But while he still believed that the middle classes could play a progressive role in Germany, if only they could be persuaded of the rationality of the case for socialism, his analysis of English social relations can be differentiated from his contemporaries by its rootedness in a much more concrete, and therefore much more practical, appreciation of the link between socialism and interests formed through existing social relations. It is important in this regard that, in sharp contrast to the abstract philosophizing of the Young Hegelian left in Germany, he praised the English socialists for being "far more principled and practical than the French." If there was a weakness with the practical character of English socialism, Engels commented, it stemmed from a certain ignorance of left-wing movements on the Continent. To counter this gap in their knowledge Engels set himself the task in 1843 of explaining to the English, who had come to socialism "practically by the rapid increase of misery, dehumanisation and pauperism," how the

French and German left had come to similar conclusions "politically" in the first instance and "philosophically" in the second (CW 3, 392–393).

Engels framed his account of the rise of modern socialism across the Continent against the background of Europe's dual revolution: England's industrial revolution on the one hand and France's political revolution on the other (Hobsbawm 1962). Writing on the *Progress of Social Reform on the Continent* for the Owenite newspaper *The New Moral World*, the twenty-three-year-old argued that though the French Revolution marked the emergence of democracy in Europe, it simultaneously revealed the contradictory essence of capitalist democracy: behind the "appearance of liberty" the social content of the new regime was the "reality of servitude." Engels believed that the instability of this contradiction must ultimately lead to its dissolution either in the direction of "undisguised despotism" (Napoleon) or "real equality—that is Communism" (Babeuf) (CW 3, 393). If Babeuf's Conspiracy of Equals had proved to be ultimately unsuccessful in the 1790s, Engels explained this failure in terms that prefigured, in more idealistic garb, the analysis of Thomas Müntzer he was to write a few years later in *The Peasant War in Germany*: it was a consequence of "the public mind" in France being "not yet far enough advanced" at the time (CW 3, 394). Subsequently, he argued that socialism had morphed through the "eccentric" but at times "brilliant" ideas of the Saint-Simonian "sect" through the much more "scientific" writings of Fourier—whose greatest contribution was to establish that the human essence is both social and active and thus includes general tendencies to association and to work (without compulsion), but whose thought was marred by a failure to call for the abolition of private property—and on to Proudhon's anarchism, which Engels praised for recognizing both that property is theft and that all kinds of government (democracy included) are "alike objectionable" (CW 3, 394–400). But if the heirs of Babeuf could thus teach the world that "democracy cannot give real equality," Engels nonetheless criticized the French for their tendency toward "secret associations" that he believed were "always contrary to common prudence, inasmuch as they make the parties liable to unnecessary legal persecutions" (CW 3, 397).

Engels argued that the flipside of France's political revolution was "a philosophical revolution in Germany." Beginning with Kant, and developing decisively through Hegel, this movement had by the 1840s, and aided by a relaxation of censorship that allowed the publication of various materials that would have been condemned as "treason" in France or "blasphemy" in England, morphed first into the atheism and republicanism of the

Young Hegelians before subsequently turning toward the "philosophical communism" of Ruge, Hess, Herwegh, and Marx. Engels highlighted the overlaps, rooted in a common "struggle . . . against religious prejudices," between this philosophical communism and the socialism of the English workers—whose practical bent he explained, in part, by reference to their "open struggle against the various churches" (CW 3, 385)—and argued that this overlap meant that whereas the German left had quickly discovered they knew more than their French teachers, "we shall have to learn a great deal . . . from the English socialists" whose "practice" placed them "a long way before us" (CW 3, 400–408).

So, Engels's youthful socialism inherited an anarchist inflection from Proudhon and a form of atheism from the German Young Hegelians. In relation to religion, Engels explained the hollowness of modern existence in terms of the "abstract subjectivity" characteristic of the "Christian-Germanic view of the world." He insisted that because this conception of subjectivity was abstract and one-sided it was "bound to turn at once into its opposite . . . the restoration of slavery in another form." If this renewed form of slavery initially took the form of serfdom, after the reformation it merely became "more inhuman and more universal" through the "Christian state [that] . . . arose from the ruins of feudalism." This state elevated "subjective and egoistical . . . interestedness to a general principle," which in turn took the form of "universal fragmentation" (CW 3, 475–476). But Engels's atheism did not lend itself to a form of mechanical materialism. He prefigured Marx's theses on Feuerbach when he claimed that eighteenth-century materialism was the mere inversion of idealistic subjectivism, whereas liberation necessitated a resolution of this antithesis between "necessity and freedom" through a really human conception of subjectivity (CW 3, 470–471). Moreover, despite the obvious limitations of his historical sketch, through this lens he began to unpack the social structure of England as a product of a history that synthesized Germanic (idealistic) with Romance (materialistic) elements culminating in the emergence of three-way class conflict between "the landed aristocracy, the monied aristocracy, and working-class democracy" (CW 3, 469–488). He unmasked the rights enshrined in the English constitution as a cover for the reality that "property," that is "inhumanity," ruled in England and that this was being challenged by working-class democracy or "socialism" (CW 3, 489–513).

This conclusion became all the more important when, in 1844, the Silesian weavers rose in struggle against their German masters. Engels's response was immediate and profound: in June 1844 he wrote in the Chartist newspaper *The Northern Star* that the Silesian weavers' movement represented concrete evidence that processes experienced in England were being reproduced in Germany: "the consequences of the factory system . . . for the working class are quite the same on the continent as they are in England: oppression and toil for the many, riches and wealth for the few" (CW 3, 531; 534). This insight informed his decision to write *The Condition of the Working Class in England* over the next few months (September 1844–April 1845). His reason for writing this book was rooted in his belief that the German left needed to learn from English social developments because the struggle of workers against inhumanity in England was of universal significance.

While returning to Germany to write *The Condition*, Engels stopped off in Paris to meet Marx. This was the moment, August 28, 1844, in the Café de la Régence, that history's most important intellectual and political partnership was inaugurated. Initially, the two men agreed to write a brief pamphlet together criticizing Young Hegelianism. This was subsequently published, under both of their names but with individually signed chapters, as *The Holy Family*. Engels stayed with Marx for ten days to write his "half" of the pamphlet—a brief, biting critique of the elitism of Bruno and Edgar Bauer. Marx's "half" grew like Topsy over the next couple of months to become about nine times the length of Engels's contribution. In the process Marx transformed a brief scornful pamphlet into a mess of a book—so much so that when he saw the finished product Engels commented that "the thing is too long. The supreme contempt we two evince towards the *Literatur-Zeitung* is in glaring contrast to the twenty-two sheets we devote to it" (CW 38, 28).

For the purposes of this book, two pivotal passages from Engels alongside one from Marx stand out as being of general significance. First, Engels opened the book with a powerful critique of the Bauer brothers' intellectual snobbery. Their thought, he wrote, was characterized by an elitist attitude toward the "masses" who they viewed as inert victims of the system and for whom they had "boundless pity" (CW 4, 9; Draper 1977, 221–224). Against this perspective, Marx insisted on the differential class experience of alienation:

> The propertied class and the class of the proletariat present
> the same human self-estrangement. But the former class feels
> at ease and strengthened in this self-estrangement, it recognizes

estrangement as its own power and has in it the semblance of a human existence. The class of the proletariat feels annihilated in estrangement; it sees in it its own powerlessness and the reality of an inhuman existence. It is, to use an expression of Hegel, in its abasement the indignation at that abasement, an indignation to which it is necessarily driven by the contradiction between its human nature and its condition of life, which is the outright, resolute and comprehensive negation of that nature. (CW 4, 36)

This passage points to the fact that even at his most Feuerbachian, Marx's "real humanism" was much more concrete than Feuerbach's abstract humanism (CW 4, 7; cf. Lobkowicz 1967, 251). What is more, Marx and Engels were beginning to draw the political consequences from this perspective. The proletariat was not a collection of mere victims of alienated relations but rather a real force through which these disparate elements were brought together through collective struggle to maintain their humanity against capitalist relations: "It is not a question of what this or that proletarian, or even the whole proletariat, at the moment *regards* as its aim. It is a question of *what the proletariat is*, and what, in accordance with this *being*, it will historically be compelled to do" (CW 4, 37). Finally, Engels insisted that this essentialist perspective should not be confused with some form of fatalistic teleology: proletarian agents were real agents because "[h]istory does nothing, it possesses no immense wealth, it wages no battles. It is man, real living man who does all that, who possesses and fights, "history" is not, as it were, a person apart, using man as a means to achieve its own aims; history is nothing but the activity of man pursuing his aims" (CW 4, 93). If history was thus made by real men and women, though structured through objective class relations, it stands to reason that theory, rather than looking down on practice with Olympian disdain, should aim to raise itself to the level of practice by striving adequately to conceptualize what Marx and Engels would later call "the *real* movement which abolishes the present state of things" (CW 5, 49).

This is precisely what Engels tried to do both in *The Condition of the Working Class in England* and his attempt, just prior to writing this book, to introduce a German audience, this time the readers of the True Socialist journal *Deutsches Bürgerbuch*, to material gleaned from the Owenite newspaper *The New Moral World* on concrete alternatives to capitalism. *Description of Recently Founded Communist Colonies Still in Existence* is an interesting essay both for the evidence of Engels's unsectarian approach to politics at this time alongside his evolving attempt to raise theory to the level of practice. On the one hand, despite the newspaper being set up by Christian sects, Engels did not let his atheism blind him to the practicality of the "communist" colonies he described:

> It is in any case obviously a matter of indifference whether those who prove by their actions the practicability of communal living believe in *one* God, in twenty or in none at all; if they have an irrational religion, this is an obstacle in the way of communal living, and if communal living is successful in real life despite this, how much more feasible must it be with others who are free of such inanities. (CW 4, 215)

On the other hand, his main concern was to show against the naysayers that, far from being an abstract utopia, communism "is not only possible but has actually already been realised in many communities in America and in one place in England" (CW 4, 214, 227). Whereas he and Marx were subsequently to dismiss such projects in *The Communist Manifesto* (CW 6, 517–518), this should not detract from the fact that his discussion of these colonies, just as much as his subsequent rejection of their model, stemmed from an admirable desire to theorize communism as a real practical movement. And if essays on these (doomed) reformist attempts to build alternatives to capitalism by bypassing it and the state represented his early attempt to theorize this movement, his *Speeches in Elberfeld*, delivered in February 1844 and republished later that year in the True Socialist *Rheinische Jahrbücher zur gesellschaftlichen Reform*, were the agitational flipside to this reformist and utopian propaganda. Aimed at "gentlemen," the key point he made in these speeches was that as capitalism creates a multiplicity of "divergent interests," the only hope to "avoid a violent and bloody overthrow of the social conditions" was the "peaceful introduction" on the basis of rational argument of "communism" (CW4, 245, 251, 263).

As we shall see, the conclusion of *The Condition of the Working Class in England* represented the final significant attempt to defend this line of argument against the logic of the evidence deployed within the book. And, as Engels acknowledged in his preface to the 1892 edition, he changed his mind because his old view was not adequate to reality. The problem with this abstract model of socialism was that it was politically "useless, and sometimes worse, in practice" (CW 27, 261).

2

Mapping the English Working Class

E ngels's *The Condition of the Working Class in England* was no academic treatise. Its intended audience was the German intellectual left, and its aim was to inform strategic thinking within the German socialist movement. It is also, as Draper and Wolf wrote, respectively, a "treasury of seedlings . . . of later Marxism" and a "milestone in social history" (Draper 1977, 183; Wolf 1987, 83). In the preface, Engels argued that developing a true grasp of the condition of the working class was imperative not merely because the modern proletariat experienced "the highest and most unconcealed pinnacle of the social misery existing in our day," but more so because the workers' movement "is the real basis and point of departure of all social movements of the present. . . . French and German working-class Communism are its direct, Fourierism and English Socialism, as well as the Communism of the German educated bourgeoisie, are its indirect products." Consequently, a "knowledge of proletarian conditions is absolutely necessary to be able to provide solid ground for socialist theories, on the one hand, and for judgments about their right to exist, on the other." More concretely, the conditions of the English working class were of particular importance because it was in England that these conditions took "their *classical form.*" Conversely, the theoretical nature of German socialism and communism meant the German left "knew much too little of the real world" and thus was "in need of a knowledge of the facts" (CW 4, 302–303).

Interestingly, the only portion of the original 1845 edition of the book to be published in English was its two-page dedication to the "Working Classes of Great Britain." Here, Engels wrote that he had forsaken "the company and the dinner-parties, the port-wine and champagne of the middle-classes" to devote "my leisure-hours almost exclusively to the inter-course with plain working men." He was both "glad" and "proud" to have done so because, by contrast with the "brutally selfish policy and general behaviour of your ruling middle-class," the workers evidenced "with all their faults" that they were indeed "members of the great and universal family of Mankind, who know their interest and that of all the human race to be the same." These lines continue to evidence a form of moralism, but it is a form of moralism very much with a class inflection. Indeed, he insisted that the middle classes were the "opponents" of the workers, and thus of the universal human interest, because they have "interests diametrically opposed to" those of the working class (CW 4, 297–298).

According to Engels, the English working class emerged as a corol-lary of the "invention of the steam engine and of machinery for working cotton." Interestingly, though he noted it was "well known" that these inventions gave rise "to an industrial revolution, a revolution which altered the whole of civil society," the concept of an industrial revolution had yet to be used either in English or German and was probably borrowed by him from the French literature of the time. What is undoubtedly true is Engels's next point: "the historical importance of" the industrial revolution "is only now beginning to be recognised" (CW 4, 307; Kellner 1999, 169).

Unlike Carlyle, who criticized industrial England from a romanticized view of the past, Engels anticipated the analysis of the peasantry made famous by Marx in the *Eighteenth Brumaire*. For all its evils industrializa-tion had succeeded in breaking with the vegetative state of the previous agricultural society that had reproduced "strong, well-built people" who were, nonetheless, "intellectually . . . dead" (CW 4, 309). This revolution was rapid and dramatic. In words that prefigured *The Communist Manifesto*'s famous image of capitalism as a system in which "all that is solid melts into air," Engels explained the industrial revolution as a "universal whirl of activity" into which "everything was drawn" (CW 4, 318).

> Sixty, eighty years ago, England was a country like every other, with small towns, few and simple industries, and a thin but *proportionally* large agricultural population. Today it is a country like *no* other, with a capital of two and a half million inhabitants; with vast manufacturing cities; with an industry that supplies the world, and produces almost everything by means of the most complex machinery; with an industrious, intelligent, dense

population, of which two-thirds are employed in trade and commerce, and composed of classes wholly different; forming, in fact, with other customs and other needs, a different nation from the England of those days. The industrial revolution is of the same importance for England as the political revolution for France, and the philosophical revolution for Germany; and the difference between England in 1760 and in 1844 is at least as great as that between France under the *ancien régime* and during the revolution of July. But the mightiest result of this industrial transformation is the English proletariat. (CW 4, 320)

The question of what was to become of this class underpinned, according to Engels, "all parliamentary debates of any importance" (CW 4, 322). Despite this fact, there existed no serious study of the English working class, and hence no serious awareness of "the deep wrath of the whole working-class . . . against the rich, by whom they are systematically plundered and mercilessly left to their fate, a wrath which . . . must break out into a revolution in comparison with which the French Revolution, and the year 1794, will prove to have been child's play" (CW 4, 323). Somewhat oddly, Engels's actual chapter on the industrial proletariat is scarcely three pages long—though it does invoke an interesting image of the degree of intelligence of the modern working class, "with the possible exception of the Irish" (I shall return to this theme of national characteristics in the discussion of nonhistoric peoples later), in "proportion to their relation to manufacture" with factory workers acting as the core of the labor movement by dint of their role in production (CW 4, 324). Indeed, he suggested that the new form of sociality associated with this class was the concrete alternative to the society "composed wholly of atoms" that does not "trouble itself" about the conditions of the poor (CW 4, 373).

So it was that Engels began to outline a historical form of humanism as embodied in workers' solidarity. And though this phenomenon was rooted in the changes wrought by industrialization, its social potential was realized through the concrete struggles of workers—in particular through their participation in trade unions: striking together for their interests nourished "the bitter hatred of the workers against the property-holding class" while simultaneously playing the part of "the military school of the working-men in which they prepare themselves for the great struggle which cannot be avoided" (CW 4, 508, 512). More specifically, unions fought against the forced competition between workers that is the mainspring of capitalism:

The active resistance of the English working-men has its effect in holding the money-greed of the bourgeoisie within certain limits, and keeping alive the opposition of the workers to the social and political omnipotence of the bourgeoisie, while it compels the admission that something more is needed than Trades Unions and strikes to break the power of the ruling class. But what gives these Unions and the strikes arising from them their real importance is this, that they are the first attempt of the workers to abolish competition. They imply the recognition of the fact that the supremacy of the bourgeoisie is based wholly upon the competition of the workers among themselves; i.e., upon their want of cohesion. And precisely because the Unions direct themselves against the vital nerve of the present social order, however one-sidedly, in however narrow a way, are they so dangerous to this social order. The working-men cannot attack the bourgeoisie, and with it the whole existing order of society, at any sorer point than this. If the competition of the workers among themselves is destroyed, if all determine not to be further exploited by the bourgeoisie, the rule of property is at an end. Wages depend upon the relation of demand to supply, upon the accidental state of the labour market, simply because the workers have hitherto been content to be treated as chattels, to be bought and sold. The moment the workers resolve to be bought and sold no longer, when, in the determination of the value of labour, they take the part of men possessed of a will as well as of working-power, at that moment the whole Political Economy of today is at an end. The laws determining the rate of wages would, indeed, come into force again in the long run, if the working-men did not go beyond this step of abolishing competition among themselves. But they must go beyond that unless they are prepared to recede again and to allow competition among themselves to reappear. Thus once advanced so far, necessity compels them to go farther; to abolish not only one kind of competition, but competition itself altogether, and that they will do. (CW 4, 507)

Engels was the first socialist to highlight the importance of trade unions to the struggle for socialism, and this fundamental insight was the concrete corollary of his historical humanism.

He developed his suggestion of a historical conception of human nature and thus of historical morality in his discussion of the relations between the sexes—in a section that anticipates his mature reflections on these issues in *The Origin of the Family, Private Property and the State*. Commenting on the movement of women into the factories, Engels noted the "wrath" felt by many (especially unemployed) working-class men at this reversal of roles and he condemns how "this condition which degrades, in the most shameful way, both sexes, and, through them, Humanity, is the last result of our much-praised civilisation." But rather than end his analysis at this descriptive and moralistic level, Engels extended it to claim that "we must admit that so total a reversal of the position of the sexes can have come to pass only because the sexes have been placed in a false position from the beginning. If the reign of the wife over the husband, as inevitably brought about by the factory system, is inhuman, the pristine rule of the husband over the wife must have been inhuman too." Engels postulated that family roles could be reversed, and indeed that the family could itself wither away altogether only because it is itself a product of history. Specifically, the modern family existed as a consequence of "private interest lurking under the cloak of a pretended community of possessions" (CW 4, 438–439).

If the dissolution of the family was one aspect of the increasing atomization of society under pressure of market forces, Engels extended arguments from the *Umrisse* to claim that "competition is the completest expression of the battle of all against all which rules in modern civil society," in which the proletarian is dehumanized while the bourgeoisie is enriched because of its "monopoly of all means of existence" (CW 4, 375–376). This is a system of "murder." Not in the trivial sense of individual capitalists murdering individual workers, but more profoundly as a society that functions such as to place workers "in such a position that they inevitably meet a too early and an unnatural death" (CW 4, 393). Against the moralism of the middle-class temperance and teetotal movements that emerged in the 1820s and 1830s, Engels insisted that in the barbaric conditions of poverty and insecurity in England at the time, drunkenness (and sexual license) were best understood not as vices but rather as a "necessary" and "inevitable effect" of these conditions (CW 4, 401, 423). Indeed, it was these social conditions that generated a sense of "demoralisation" among the working class (CW 4, 412; cf. Marcus 1974, 133).

Engels did not paint a one-sided picture of working-class demoralization. Rather he argued that it gave rise among the workers to what Carlyle called an increasingly "universal spirit" of "revolt against the upper classes, decreasing respect for what their temporal superiors command, decreasing faith from what their spiritual superiors teach." However, whereas Carlyle noted but did not condone this "fatal" behavior, Engels insisted that it was the basis for hope against the inhumanity of the capitalist system: "Carlyle is perfectly right as to the facts and wrong only in censuring the wild rage of the workers against the higher classes. This rage, this passion, is rather the proof that the workers feel the inhumanity of their position, that they refuse to be degraded to the level of brutes, and that they will one day free themselves from servitude to the bourgeoisie" (CW 4, 414). Engels reiterated a point that had come to characterize his analysis of the workers. Far from being mere victims of the system, they were potential agents of its overthrow and their own liberation. He argued, in contrast to the mean and selfish behavior of individual members of the bourgeoisie, that the workers tended to be much more "humane" in their interpersonal relations—and citing as authority for this claim no less than the Canon of Manchester (CW 4, 420, 501–502).

If this spirit of rebellion and interpersonal humanity was one side of the working class's response to demoralization (the other being drunkenness, etc.), the bourgeoisie tended to be wholly tied up in its own spirit of demoralization, which was manifested as an "incurably debased . . . selfish-ness" for which nothing existed save for "the sake of money." Infamously, Engels cited a conversation he had had with a member of the Manchester bourgeoisie shortly after arriving in the city. After Engels outlined the awful housing and social conditions endured by the Mancunian working class, the man responded with simple bluntness as he took his leave: "and yet there is a great deal of money made here; good morning, sir" (CW 4, 501–502).

Engels took this phrase to epitomize the attitude of the bourgeoisie to the dehumanizing consequences of poverty. He also insisted that this class defended and reproduced these debased and demoralized "interests with all the power placed at its disposal by wealth and the might of the state" (CW 4, 501). Though this claim did not rise to the level of theoretical sophistication characteristic of Marx's cotemporally produced critique of Hegel's theory of the state, it did prefigure the classical Marxist account of the modern state as a capitalist formation, while simultaneously open-ing a space for Engels to outline a sophisticated account of the process of working-class struggle against capitalism. Against simplistic models of this conflict that tend to find real movements wanting by contrast with some idealized simon-pure vision of a socialist labor movement, Engels traced the real movement of workers, warts and all. He insisted that not only strikes but also crime and machine breaking represented moments in the history of workers' struggles against their subjugation (CW 4, 502–503). If this account of the real movement was free of any attempt to romanticize crime, it was equally (and more importantly) free of the kind of pseudoradical moralistic critique of criminality that all too often lends itself to the justification of increased state power.

In addition, his discussion of the powers deployed by the bourgeoisie to maintain its rule includes an account not merely of the state as a capitalist institution but also of the law as "a rod which the bourgeois has prepared for" the workers (CW 4, 517). For example, he described the New Poor Law of 1834 as "the most open declaration of war of the bourgeoisie upon the proletariat" (CW 4, 570). Justified ideologically by Malthus's theory of population, the New Poor Law did in the 1830s what legislation on unemployment continues to do today: it blamed the poor for the crisis of capitalism.

Commenting on Malthus's theory of population, Engels wrote that Malthus had a point, but only under "existing conditions" (CW 4, 570). Whereas Malthus naturalized the existence of a surplus population, and thus of irredeemable poverty, Engels showed that the surplus—or the "reserve army of labour" as he termed it—was a product not of nature but of the capitalist trade cycle (CW 4, 384; Foster 2000, 109). And as with any other commodity, periods of boom would create conditions of relative scarcity followed by bust in which there would emerge a surplus. This situation was a characteristic of labor (power) as a commodity not of labor in itself, and insofar as the bourgeoisie accepted Malthus's theory—Engels pointed out that it was "the pet theory of all genuine English bourgeois" (CW 4, 570)—it reflected a desire to justify not merely its own selfish behavior, but more importantly its inability to develop a scientific understanding of social reality. Trapped within the standpoint of civil society, the bourgeoisie naturalized capitalist social relations and thus the position of the poor under capitalism. It was from this perspective that the workhouses—or Poor Law Bastilles as they were called in the workers' quarters—made sense as the rational response to poverty.

If the New Poor Law was an intense institutionalized form of class warfare, from the standpoint of civil society it appeared ideologically as a commonsense response to a natural problem. Contra this barbaric system, Engels pointed to the solidarity attendant to workers' struggles as the core of a concrete socialist alternative. Chartism was important to this process because the Chartists were the *real* vanguard of the labor movement. And though seemingly "harmless," Engels recognized that the social content of the six points of the People's Charter—universal male suffrage, annual Parliaments, payment of MPs, voting by ballot, equal electoral districts, and abolition of the property qualification—were, in that specific context with the attendant level of class consciousness among the workers, "sufficient to overthrow the whole English Constitution, Queen and Lords included" (CW 4, 518). If this important point is an example of Engels's approach, which is in fact the core of the scientific method, of looking beneath the appearance to the essence of a process, he also traced, as we noted earlier, the course by which Chartism had emerged as an alliance between workers and radical sections of the middle classes before these two groups separated as the struggle intensified. It was this process of separation, by which Chartism had become "a purely working men's cause freed from all bourgeois elements," that meant its social content was so much more radical than its nominal form (CW 4, 523). And it was this social content that so scared the bourgeoisie.

If, as Engels argued, the key strength of Chartism was its proletarian character—the Chartists were "genuine . . . representatives of their class"—the most important weakness of this movement was its relative theoretical backwardness. The socialists, by contrast, were "more far-seeing" but because they originated from among the middle classes, they had yet to "amalgamate completely with the working class." Engels welcomed the beginning of this process and asserted that "only" through the "union of Socialism with Chartism" would the "working-class be the true intellectual leader of England" (CW 4, 527). He also hinted that this process would not be quite as inevitable as traditional interpretations of his early thought have suggested. History, he suggested, was open: "When people are placed under conditions which appeal to the brute only, what remains to them but to rebel or to succumb to utter brutality?" (CW 4, 423–424) This sentence is reminiscent of his subsequent claim in *Anti-Dühring* that "if the whole of modern society is not to perish, a revolution in the mode of production and distribution must take place, a revolution which will put an end to class distinctions" (CW 25, 146). And if this line was famously picked up by Rosa Luxemburg, who referred to it when she asserted that the alternatives for humanity were "socialism or a regression into barbarism," the earlier line anticipates this argument and can certainly be read as an important call to arms (Luxemburg 1970c, 269).

Nonetheless, with hindsight, Engels did overstate his case. There was more than a tinge of fatalism about his belief in the eventual triumph of socialism. On rereading the book two decades later, Marx bemoaned nostalgically to him: "With what zest and passion, what boldness of vision and absence of learned and scientific reservations, the subject is still attacked on these pages! And then the very illusion that, tomorrow or the day after, the result will actually spring to life as history lends the whole thing a warmth, vitality and humour with which the later 'gray on gray' contrasts damned unfavourably" (CW 41, 469). Engels similarly commented in the preface to the 1892 edition that the book bore "the stamp of youth with its good and faulty features" (CW 27, 257).

Among the "faulty features" of *The Condition of the Working Class in England*, probably the least coherent and most obviously "pre-Marxist" was the concluding suggestion that the rise of communism among the Chartist leadership would hopefully militate against the probability of bloody revolution that followed from the main argument of the book. That a revolution was on its way, Engels took as read—the only question was whether English capitalism would survive one or more periods of crisis before its triumph. But because communism was an ideology of "humanity and not the workers alone," it "stands above the breach between bourgeoisie and proletariat." Consequently, the communists could, if strong enough, act as a brake on proletarian tendencies toward "vengeance": "The revolution must come; it is already too late to bring about a peaceful solution; but it can be made more gently than that prophesied in the foregoing page." Indeed, communism was the only hope for the bourgeoisie: otherwise the *Times'* prophesy of a proletarian Terror on a par with Robespierre's "war to the palaces, peace unto cabins" would be the future of the English middle classes (CW 4, 579–583). Fortuitously, as he wrote to Marx in October 1844, German workers would follow their English counterparts in recognizing not only that it was forlorn to protest at their condition of life through individual acts of violence but also that "their general capacity as human beings" could best be realized through communism (CW 38, 5).

The incoherent concluding section of *The Condition of the Working Class in England* neatly illuminates the contradictory nature of Engels's thought at the time. While his analysis of the facts of the English experience pointed forcefully toward the necessity of revolution, his "communism" remained a free-floating ideology of peaceful reform through persuasion.

Interestingly, as he was writing *The Condition of the Working Class in England* he read an early review copy of Max Stirner's *The Ego and*

His Own, within which Stirner turned Feuerbach's arguments against his system. Stirner showed that Feuerbach's moralism assumed a conception of "man" that was just as unworldly as the idea of God he sought to demolish. Writing to Marx in November 1844, Engels suggested that if their humanism was to navigate this critique of the wraithlike character of Feuerbach's "man," then they too must start their analysis "from the Ego, the empirical flesh-and-blood individual" (CW 38, 12). Their subsequent critique of the Young Hegelian milieu that has come down to posterity as *The German Ideology* was written through a lens very much influenced by Stirner's book, even if, in the end, it was utterly scathing of his method and conclusions. Stirner's egoistic individual was just as much of a false abstraction as was Feuerbach's "man" (Lefebvre 2009, 62).

Unfortunately, though *The German Ideology* was their most substantial genuinely collaborative work, they could not find a publisher for it in 1846—after which it was famously left to the "gnawing criticism of the mice" (Carver and Blank 2014, 7; CW 29, 264). It is also a problematic work. The form that eventually was published was cobbled together from various unfinished manuscripts intended for publication as separate journal articles written between November 1845 and August 1846. It is fragmentary and unfinished (Carver and Blank 2014). Nonetheless, *The German Ideology* remains an invaluable resource for anyone wanting to understand Marx and Engels's thought, for it was through writing these manuscripts that they achieved a degree of what Marx was later to call "self-clarification," and the manuscript itself, as Chris Arthur has written, offers "page after page [of] astonishing insights" (CW 29, 264; CW 26, 519; Arthur 2015).

3

A New Theoretical Foundation

The German Ideology

Intellectual development is always a process and *The German Ideology* was in many ways merely a moment in the process of Marx and Engels's intellectual development. Nevertheless, it would be foolish to deny the importance of this "breakthrough" moment when their new perspective in its essentials came to fruition—and it did so in response to the rigmarole of German theory in general and of Stirner's proto-Nietzschean anarchism in particular (Arthur 1970, 21). Unfortunately, the fact that *The German Ideology* is a biting, polemical engagement with the Young Hegelians means that it is a difficult read for anyone not au fait with ideas circulating in that milieu in the mid-1840s. Even so, anyone reading the section on Feuerbach will be struck not merely by its brilliance but also by just how far it prefigures so much of Marx and Engels's mature work. And though the section on Stirner is overlong and windy, it represents the moment at which they extricated their vision of communism as a movement emergent within capitalism from the moralism that had previously been its weakest aspect.

That Engels was independently moving in the direction of this critique is evident from a number of sources at the time. First, and in contrast with those who have portrayed him as a one-sided critic of utopian socialism, he wrote a wonderful introduction to a piece by Fourier on trade. Second, he penned a brief critical note on Feuerbach. As to Fourier, Engels compared him favorably to those on the German intellectual left who were picking up his theories and transforming his rich passionate condemnation of existing society into "the bad, abstract, unintelligible and clumsy form in which they have expressed these ideas" (CW 4, 614). Yes, Engels accepted, Fourier had allowed speculation about the future to get the better of him, but the great strength of his work—and Marx made a similar point at about the same time (CW 4, 597)—was the power of his condemnation of the oppression experienced by the mass of the population in the past and present:

> It is true that Fourier did not start out from the Hegelian theory and for this reason unfortunately could not attain knowledge of absolute truth, not even of absolute socialism. It is true that owing to this shortcoming Fourier unfortunately allowed himself to be led astray and to substitute the method of series for the absolute method and thereby arrived at such speculative constructions as the conversion of the sea into lemonade, the *couronnes boréale* and *australe* the anti-lion, and the conjunction of the planets. But, if it has to be, I shall prefer to believe with the cheerful Fourier in all these stories rather than in the realm of the absolute spirit, where there is no lemonade at all, in the identity of Being and Nothing and the conjunction of the eternal categories. French nonsense is at least cheerful, whereas German nonsense is gloomy and profound. And then, Fourier has criticised existing social relations so sharply, with such wit and humour that one readily forgives him for his cosmological fantasies, which are also based on a brilliant world outlook . . . Fourier's eccentricities, which are, after all, products of genius, are no excuse for the boring so-called systematic expositions of arid German theory. Fourier speculatively constructs the future, after correctly understanding the past and the present; German theory first of all arranges past history according to its liking and then prescribes to the future, too, what direction it should take. (CW 4, 614–615, 642)

Fourier's main weakness, as Engels was later to detail, was his inability to grasp the movement from the evils of the present to the freedom of the future because he wrote before the existence of the modern labor movement (CW 25, 20). Engels, by contrast, was blessed to be young at the moment of birth of the German labor movement: a moment he traced in the Chartist *Northern Star* in September 1845 (CW 4, 645–648).

When read in the context of his own critique of the limitations of Feuerbach's moralistic "passive adoration of nature"—which he contrasted negatively with Fourier's biting critique of morality as "powerlessness set in motion"—the scene was set for the revolution in thought to which he and Marx had been tending over the previous few years (CW 5, 11; cf. CW 4, 201).

Like Marx's *Theses on Feuerbach*, Engels's critique of Feuerbach's passive adoration of nature is predicated upon an active conception of subjectivity or "human sensuous activity, practice" as Marx called it (CW 5, 6). Engels shared with Marx an understanding of human agency as a form of praxis in which agents partake in "free, universal, creative and self-creative activity" (Petrovi 1991, 435). However, whereas the concepts of practice, technique, and theory had been understood by Aristotle to refer to distinct areas of human life—the first to relations between people, the second to the human ability to produce, and the third to the passive contemplation of reality—in *The German Ideology* Marx and Engels extend Kant's and Hegel's criticisms of these distinctions to argue that both theory and technique were rooted in practice. Marx and Engels's novel conception of praxis therefore sublated earlier divisions between practice, theory, and technique (Liedman 2018, 175–176).

But whereas the conception of subjectivity outlined in Marx's *Theses on Feuerbach* was somewhat one-sided, Engels's notes on Feuerbach pointed to the material basis for a conception of practice through the mediating factor of human need (CW 5, 11–12). This insight was of the first importance to the new materialist conception of history that Marx and Engels articulated through a synthesis of the concepts of material interest and practice on the pages of *The German Ideology* (Osbourne 2005, 36–38).

Marx and Engels argue in *The German Ideology* that humans make and remake themselves through labor to meet their evolving needs: it is through social, conscious productive interaction with nature to meet their needs that our ancestors in an important sense made themselves human (Childe 1966). As Ollman points out, because Marx and Engels insisted that nature and society are internally related, they understood that "an examination of any aspect of either involves one immediately with aspects of the other" (Ollman 1976, 53). One consequence of this approach is that, though Marx and Engels accept that we have a nature made up of needs and capacities, by contrast with crude materialists who posit this essence as a simple transhistorical fact, they insist that it is not fixed because these needs and capacities are not fixed; our nature evolves because these needs and capacities develop through our active interaction with nature. And whereas their German counterparts tended to ignore the material determination of action, they insisted that

> the first premise of all human existence and, therefore, of all history, the premise, namely, that men must be in a position to live in order to be able to "make history." But life involves before everything else eating and drinking, housing, clothing and various other things. The first historical act is thus the production of the means to satisfy these needs, the production of material life itself. . . . The second point is that the satisfaction of the first need . . . leads to new needs; and this creation of new needs is the first historical act. . . . The third circumstance which, from the very outset, enters into historical development, is that men, who daily re-create their own life, begin to make other men, to propagate their kind: the relation between man and woman, parents and children, the *family*. The family, which to begin with is the only social relation, becomes later, when increased needs create new social relations and the increased population new needs, a subordinate one (except in Germany), and must then be treated and analysed according to the existing empirical data, not according to "the concept of the family," as is the custom in Germany. (CW 5, 41–43; CW 45, 108; cf. Geras 1983)

This passage marks the point of synthesis between the concepts of practice and material need that came to constitute a core feature of Marxism. And because need is a social concept that nonetheless has natural roots, this was the point where they highlighted the unity (not identity) between natural and social history:

> We know only a single science, the science of history. One can look at history from two sides and divide it into the history of nature and the history of men. The two sides are, however, inseparable; the history of nature and the history of men are dependent on each other so long as men exist. The history of nature, called natural science, does not concern us here; but we will have to examine the history of men, since almost the whole ideology amounts either to a distorted conception of

this history or to a complete abstraction from it. Ideology is itself only one of the aspects of this history. (CW 5, 28–29)

This argument, though deleted for editorial reasons from the second clean copy of Marx and Engels's text, informs their famous claim that definite individuals at a specific moment in time had differentiated themselves from nature by consciously transforming their environment in order to meet their (initially natural) needs: "Men can be distinguished from animals by consciousness, by religion or anything else you like. They themselves begin to distinguish themselves from animals as soon as they begin to *produce* their means of subsistence, a step which is conditioned by their physical organisation. By producing their means of subsistence men are indirectly producing their material life" (CW 5, 31). Consequently, rather than follow modern political theory from Hobbes and Locke onward in positing abstract "man" as the starting point of their analysis, Marx and Engels took a lead from Stirner when they wrote that their study proceeds from the standpoint of definite individuals in definite social relations: "The premises from which we begin are not arbitrary ones, not dogmas, but real premises from which abstraction can only be made in the imagination. They are the real individuals, their activity and the material conditions of their life, both those which they find already existing and those produced by their activity" (CW 5, 31). The human essence is thus on their account a historical rather than ideal abstraction: at any particular juncture, it is the "sum of productive forces, capital funds and social forms of intercourse" (CW 5, 54).

Though too often dismissed as the background noise to history, the mere "reproduction of the physical existence *of* the individuals," human productive interaction with nature is rather "a definite form of activity of these individuals, a definite form of expressing their life, a definite *mode of life* on their part" (CW 5, 31). More specifically, by contrast with traditional elitist ideologies that tend to denigrate practice as the poor cousin to theory's pure universality, Marx and Engels insist that our consciousness is profoundly shaped by the way we produce to meet our needs.

In direct contrast to German philosophy which descends from heaven to earth, here it is a matter of ascending from earth to heaven. That is to say, not of setting out from what men say, imagine, conceive, nor from men as narrated, thought of, imagined, conceived, in order to arrive at men in the flesh;

but setting out from real, active men, and on the basis of their real life-process demonstrating the development of the ideo-logical reflexes and echoes of this life-process. The phantoms formed in the brains of men are also, necessarily, sublimates of their material life-process, which is empirically verifiable and bound to material premises. Morality, religion, metaphysics, and all the rest of ideology as well as the forms of consciousness corresponding to these, thus no longer retain the semblance of independence. They have no history, no development; but men, developing their material production and their material intercourse, alter, along with this their actual world, also their thinking and the products of their thinking. It is not con-sciousness that determines life, but life that determines con-sciousness. For the first manner of approach the starting-point is consciousness taken as the living individual; for the second manner of approach, which conforms to real life, it is the real living individuals themselves, and consciousness is considered solely as *their* consciousness. (CW 5, 36–37; cf. CW 29, 263)

Marx and Engels argue that production has both natural and social aspects. Production includes not only our work on nature to meet our needs but also the social relations that spring from working together to that end:

The production of life, both of one's own in labour and of fresh life in procreation, now appears as a twofold relation: on the one hand as a natural, on the other as a social relation— social in the sense that it denotes the co-operation of several individuals, no matter under what conditions, in what manner and to what end. It follows from this that a certain mode of production, or industrial stage, is always combined with a certain mode of co-operation, or social stage. (CW 5, 43)

They labeled the totality of these relations a "mode of production" and periodized history according to changes in the mode of production (CW 5, 43). Marx and Engels's conception of a mode of production as a totality is neither a vacuous claim about the interconnectedness of everything nor a suggestion that appearances can simply be reduced to essence. Rather, it was in the first instance a "scientific hypothesis" about how the world works (Vygodski 1973, 16). The scientific nature of this hypothesis is apparent once we recognize with Bertell Ollman that Marx and Engels considered the whole to be constituted through its internal relations, and the focus of their work was on the painstaking reconstitution of the whole as a concrete totality (Ollman 1976, 34; Marx 1973, 101). Marx and Engels may well have agreed with Hegel that the truth is the whole, but they insisted that the process of reproducing the whole as a concrete totality of many determinations was an arduous and ongoing scientific process.

If capitalism is indeed a total system, it is not constituted through the simple realization of transhistorical human characteristics—to truck, barter and exchange, and such like. Rather, it is best understood as the latest of these "definite" "modes of production" (CW 5, 32–37). It was through the concept of mode of production that Marx and Engels overcame some of the weaknesses with Engels's *Umrisse*. Whereas that earlier text had one-sidedly detailed only the destructive consequences of private property, *The German Ideology* outlined a more dialectical and historical view of private property: it had a history—having evolved through "tribal," "ancient communal," "feudal," and into its present capitalist form—and through its history these specific forms had played positive and negative parts at specific junctures: most recently, capitalist private property had fostered the social development necessary for the transition to socialism before itself becoming a fetter on further development (CW 5, 33, 48).

This conception of private property marked a step beyond the approach taken in the *Umrisse* because it recognized the historical and sometime positive function of private property. However, when compared with Marx's later conception of social determination, it remains analytically weak. For whereas Marx would subsequently insist that production determines exchange and distribution, in this earlier text Marx and Engels view production and exchange as codetermining distribution, which in turn determines them: "Industry and commerce, production and the exchange of the necessities of life in their turn determine distribution, the structure of the different social classes and are, in turn, determined by it as to the mode in which they are carried on" (CW 5, 40). This supposedly dialectical but in fact merely mutually interactive approach was reproduced three decades later in *Anti-Dühring*: "Political economy, in the widest sense, is the science of the laws governing the production and exchange of the material means of subsistence in human society. . . . [E]ach has, also to a great extent, its own special laws. But on the other hand, they constantly determine and influence each other to such an extent that they might be termed the abscissa and ordinate of the economic curve" (CW 25, 135). As John Weeks argues, by comparison with Marx's mature work this approach remains relatively superficial. As we shall see later, this seemingly minor difference in conceptualizing capitalism had an important consequence: Engels never fully understood Marx's value theory (Weeks 1981, 61–62).

Nonetheless, the analysis of private property in *The German Ideology* did constitute a profound theoretical breakthrough. It allowed Marx and Engels to grasp capitalism as a historical mode of production with dominant progressive and reactionary characteristics at different moments in its history. Additionally, they understood this dialectical account of capitalism to be a specific example of a more general historical law whereby social change through revolutions occurs when social relations that had previously fostered social development subsequently come to fetter that development: "The contradiction between the productive forces and the form of intercourse, which . . . has occurred several times in past history . . . necessarily on each occasion burst out in a revolution" (CW 5, 74; cf. CW 29, 263). They argued that though private property had previously played a progressive historical role, the crises and social conflicts that it now engendered meant that this was no longer the case. This claim was a double-edged sword: although socialism was now moving onto the agenda, this movement was only possible because of economic growth that had previously been fostered by private property relations. Consequently, any attempt to bypass this earlier stage of history would be disastrous for the socialist project: the "development of productive forces . . . is an absolutely necessary practical premise, because without it privation, *want* is merely made general, and with *want* the struggle for necessities would begin again, and all the old filthy business would necessarily be restored" (CW 5, 49). More concretely, they insist that it is "only with large-scale industry [that] the abolition of private property becomes possible" (CW 5, 64).

Socialism, on this account, far from being an abstract, transhistorical moral ideal, is best understood as a historically concrete form offered as a solution by definite historically constituted individuals to historically specific problems. Feuerbach could understand none of this because he assumed two related myths: a transhistorical human essence alongside a transhistorical natural world (CW 5, 40–41). This mistake meant that insofar as he "is a materialist he does not deal with history, and as far as he considers history he is not a materialist. With him materialism and history diverge completely" (CW 5, 41).

Marx and Engels's new approach to human history—historical materialism, though neither this term nor its synonym, the materialist conception of history, were used at this juncture—amounted to a real transcendence (sublation) of existing forms of materialism and idealism by which they were able to conceive definite historically determined individuals as real agents of change (Blackledge 2002; 2006a; 2019a): "Men make their own history, but they do not make it just as they please; they do not make it under circumstances chosen by themselves, but under circumstances directly encountered, given and transmitted from the past" as Marx famously put it (CW 11, 103). This sublation of materialism and idealism into a new approach to history nonetheless remained a form of materialism because it recognized that priority should be assigned to satisfying our needs: as Chris Arthur writes, "*in the first instance* material circumstances condition us, however much we revolutionise those conditions later" (Arthur 1970, 23).

By contrast with the fatalism of earlier mechanical forms of materialism, because Marx and Engels aimed to grasp real historical change, theirs was a form of "practical materialism" focused on "revolutionising the existing world, of practically coming to grips with and changing the things found in existence." Far from being mechanical and fatalistic, this form of materialism had at its center what Roy Bhaskar calls "human transformative agency" (CW 5, 38; Bhaskar 1989, 125; Bhaskar 1993, 94; Foster 2000, 2). Indeed, Marx and Engels claimed that in the modern world practical materialism was a synonym for communism because only those intent on the revolutionary reconstruction of existing social relations can transcend the sterile opposition between the old mechanical materialism, which accepted reality as a pregiven and immutable fact, and its idealist (moralist) other, which responded to the evils of the world with "impotence in action" (CW 4, 201; cf. Blackledge 2008b, 126). Conversely, practical materialism assumes the existence of agents already challenging the status quo: "The existence of revolutionary ideas in a particular period presupposes the existence of a revolutionary class" (CW 5, 60). In the modern world, or so Marx and Engels claimed, this was the working class, and they framed their political activity in relation to its real struggles against capitalism.

The profound political implications of this perspective were first elaborated in relation to Max Stirner's anarchist critique of True Socialism. True Socialism was the name taken by a movement of German intellectuals in the 1840s who sought to overcome the "crudities" of English and French class-based socialism through an appeal to the rationality of the general idea of socialism (Wood 1986; Gilbert 1981). In the words of one of their number, Hermann Semmig: "It seems that the French do not understand their own men of genius. At this point German science comes to their aid and in the shape of socialism presents the most reasonable social order, if one can speak of a superlative degree of reasonableness" (CW 5, 458). The True Socialists developed what they believed were the socialist implications of Feuerbach's humanism. Feuerbach rejected the egoistic conception of individualism, arguing that "man is conscious of himself not only as an individual, but also as a member of the human species" and that "God is really the perfected idea of the species viewed as an individual" (McLellan 1969, 92). Extending this claim, the True Socialists argued along lines that were very close to Engels's conception of communism in *The Condition of the Working Class in England*. Socialism, they claimed, was in the general human interest irrespective of class and other antagonisms. As we have suggested, Stirner highlighted the profound weaknesses with this type of moralism (McLellan 1969, 131), and it was through answering his criticisms of True Socialism that Marx and Engels moved beyond the limitations of their earlier politics.

Stirner argued that all political systems, conservative, liberal, socialist, or whatever, led in practice to authoritarian suppression of the individual ego. Even revolutions, by claiming to be in the common interest, involved the suppression of individual egoism. Consequently, Stirner conceived "self-liberation" to be possible only through an act of rebellion rather than revolution. He extended this argument into a rejection of the state and the suggestion that "political liberty" amounts to nothing less than the "individual's *subjugation* in the state" (Stirner 2005, 9, 106, 196, 255). In a comment on the French Revolution that he believed to have general salience, he suggested that this upheaval was not directed against "*the establishment*, but against the *establishment in question*, against a particular establishment. It did away with *this* ruler, not with *the* ruler." That the French Revolution ended in reaction should therefore come as no surprise: for it is in the nature of revolutions that one authority is merely exchanged for another (Stirner 2005, 110). "Political liberalism's" embrace of the postrevolutionary state revealed its authoritarian implications, implications which were also inherent in socialism and communism (ideologies he subsumed under the heading "social liberalism"), for these too would merely repeat the transference of power from one authority to another (Stirner 2005, 122, 130). Even the "humane liberalism" of the best of the Young Hegelians was suspect because it too saw the egoism of others as a weakness while denying it in itself. From the abstract claim that "*freedom can only be the whole of freedom, a piece of freedom is not freedom*" (Stirner 2005, 160), Stirner concluded that because all moral approaches preached self-sacrifice in the name of some metaphysical notion—god, man, the state, class, nation, and so on—they were equally the enemies of freedom. If "the road to ruin is paved with good intentions," the correct egoistic response was not revolution in the name of some "good" but a simpler rebellion of the ego against authority (Stirner 2005, 54, 75). Communism was not so much a radical alternative to the status quo as its latest moralistic variant (Stirner 2005, 18, 164, 258).

Against Stirner's claim that socialists had embraced a static model of human essence that provided them with a moral basis for criticizing existing society, Marx and Engels argued that the modern world is characterized by both egoistic and more social forms of individualism. Morality, as it was understood by Stirner, was an essential authoritarian characteristic only of communities made up of the former. By assuming the universality of egoism, Stirner naturalized capitalist social relations in a way that made it impossible for him to comprehend the concept of workers' solidarity except as a top-down imposition on otherwise free individuals. Conversely, Marx and Engels recognized that egoistic individualism was a new social form bound up with the rise of capitalism and that solidarity had become a real need and desire for workers as they strove to challenge the inhumanities of this system. So, contra True Socialism, Marx and Engels concluded that socialism should be understood as a real movement among workers rather than an abstract moral ideal imposed upon them. Consequently, they argued that "communists do not preach morality" (CW 5, 247). They criticized the moralism of the True Socialists, because they believed its tendency to abstract the human essence from its real manifestation in history acted as a barrier to the real diffusion of socialist consciousness within the working class.

> If, then, the theoretical representatives of the proletariat wish their literary activity to have any practical effect, they must first and foremost insist that all phrases are dropped which tend to dim the realisation of the sharpness of this opposition, all phrases which tend to conceal this opposition and may even give the bourgeois a chance to approach the communists for safety's sake on the strength of their philanthropic enthusiasms. (CW 5, 469)

Thus it was that they broke with their previously held moralistic model of communism. And rather than criticize the existing social order from some abstract moral standpoint outside history, from now on they insisted that the standpoint of critique was the point of view of real struggles against capitalism: "We call communism the *real* movement which abolishes the present state of things. The conditions of this movement result from the now existing premise" (CW 5, 49). Hence, as Draper points out, from here on in Marx and Engels tended to use the term "workers' power" rather than socialism or communism to describe the goal for which they fought (Draper 1978, 24).

And if this new standpoint allowed them to clarify what they were for, it also illuminated what they were against. Not merely capitalism but also the ideological and political forms through which it was reproduced. Obviously, Adam Smith, despite his insights, developed an ideology that helped justify capitalism, while Malthus took this approach to its brutal limits. On the left, anarchism and True Socialism, despite their superficial radicalism, acted as barriers to the diffusion of a culture of workers' solidarity against capitalism. This is why Marx and Engels insisted on ideologically combating their influence within the workers' movement.

Nonetheless, the key prop of the capitalist system was political rather than ideological: the modern state. Against those who posited the state as an institution where social antagonisms within nations were overcome, Marx and Engels insisted that states were, in their modern form, capitalist institutions rooted in the historical emergence of "civil society": "To this modern private property corresponds the modern state, which, purchased gradually by the owners of property by means of taxation, has fallen entirely into their hands through the national debt, and its existence has become wholly dependent on the commercial credit which the owners of property, the bourgeois, extend to it, as reflected in the rise and fall of government securities on the stock exchange" (CW 5, 90). Consequently, the modern state is best understood as a capitalist state, and insofar as it posits itself as the repository of communal life in the modern world, because it is rooted in but does not overcome the separation of individual interests through capitalist relations of production, it represents an "illusory communal life" (CW 5, 46).

The power of Marx and Engels's antistatism immunized them against Stirner's crude anarchism because it did not conflate the real community emerging through workers' struggles with the false, alienated community of the state. More generally, they were keenly aware, by contrast with Stirner's abstract conception of freedom, that "individuals obtain their freedom in and through their association." Indeed, humanity's natural sociality coupled with the historical extension and deepening of the division of labor meant that freedom is only possible within a community, and this community will be of a definite kind at any specific point in history (CW 5, 78). In the modern world, real community can only emerge in opposition both to the "illusory community" of the state and to its underlying conditions.

> [T]he proletarians, if they are to assert themselves as individuals, have to abolish the hitherto prevailing condition of their existence (which has, moreover, been that of all society up to then), namely, labour. Thus they find themselves directly opposed to the form in which, hitherto, the individuals, of which society consists, have given themselves collective expression, that is, the state; in order, therefore, to assert themselves as individuals, they must overthrow the state. (CW 5, 80)

And because the modern state is rooted in the capitalist mode of production in which social production is mediated through market relations that act as an alien power over us, the realization of freedom can only come through communism or "the abolition of private property," which is identical to the suppression of this alien power.

> Only this will liberate the separate individuals from the various national and local barriers, bring them into practical connection with the production (including intellectual production) of the whole world and make it possible for them to acquire the capacity to enjoy this all-sided production of the whole earth (the creations of man). *All-round* dependence, this primary natural form of the *world-historical* co-operation of individuals, will be transformed by this communist revolution into the control and conscious mastery of these powers, which, born of the action of men on one another, have till now overawed and ruled men as powers completely alien to them. (CW 5, 51–52)

The pressures tending toward revolution remained, as they had been in the *Umrisse*, capitalism's propensity to crisis alongside its fragmentation of society into divergent and increasingly polarizing interests that workers were becoming conscious of—though these pressures have been reframed in a new language. In the first instance class is defined not simply through objective interests as in *The Holy Family* but also through consciousness gained through struggle—if for no other reason than that outside these broader conflicts the competition between workers would prevail over their common interests: "The separate individuals form a class only insofar as they have to carry on a common battle against another class; in other respects they are on hostile terms with each other as competitors" (CW 5, 77; on Marxist class theory, see Das 2017 and Blackledge 2011b). Secondly, the conflicts attendant to private property that underpin the tendency to revolution are explained in terms of the growing clash between the development of the forces of production and existing "means of intercourse" (what would later be clarified as relations of production [CW 5, 52; CW 29, 263]).

More importantly, the process of revolution is conceived both as a clash with the existing state and as a profoundly democratic movement from below:

> Both for the production on a mass scale of this communist consciousness, and for the success of the cause itself, the alteration of men on a mass scale is necessary, an alteration which can only take place in a practical movement, a revolution; revolution is necessary, therefore, not only because the ruling class cannot be overthrown in any other way, but also because the class overthrowing it can only in a revolution succeed in ridding itself of all the muck of ages and become fitted to found society anew. (CW 5, 52–53)

Part of the "muck of ages" that workers had to discard to win their freedom was the dominant ideology: "The ideas of the ruling class are in every epoch the ruling ideas: i.e., the class which is the ruling *material* force of society is at the same time its ruling *intellectual* force" (CW 5, 59). If the dominance of these ideas meant that workers were no gods, this did not imply that Marx and Engels shared with Auguste Blanqui a conception of revolution as a temporary dictatorship of the elite over backward masses. Their theory of revolution had at its core the self-transforming activity of workers in struggle: it was only through the experience of revolutionary struggle that workers would be able to cast off these ideas and realize their own concrete form of freedom through a democratic movement from below. By contrast with old forms of materialism that posited the transformation of people as a passive response to changes in their environment, Marx and Engels's new revolutionary theory conceived socialism as issuing through proletarian self-emancipation. In Marx's words:

> The materialist doctrine concerning the changing of circum-stances and upbringing forgets that circumstances are changed by men and that it is essential to educate the educator himself. This doctrine must, therefore, divide society into two parts, one of which is superior to society. The coincidence of the changing of circumstances and of human activity or self-changing can be conceived and rationally understood only as revolutionary practice. (CW 5, 4)

Engels made the same point in a more concrete register during the rev-olutions of 1848:

> The people that has fought on the barricades and has been victorious is entirely different from the people that on March 18 marched to the palace to be enlightened, by means of cavalry attacks, about the significance of the concessions it had received. It is able to achieve things of a quite different nature and it confronts the Government in an entirely different way. The most important achievement of the revolution is the revolution itself. (CW 7, 78; Draper 1978, 75)

This idea of working-class self-emancipation framed Engels's politics for the rest of his life.

4

The Communist Manifesto

A Strategy for the Left

If Marx and Engels's concrete conception of freedom was far removed from the ahistorical abstractions of egoistic individualism, so too was their understanding of internationalism. Commenting on the Festival of Nations organized by radical Chartists in London in August 1845 to celebrate a democratic tradition going back to the French Revolution, Engels wrote that in contrast not only to "old instinctive national egoism" on the one hand and "hypocritical private-egotistical cosmopolitanism of free trade" on the other, internationalism had become for the workers' movement a real need. This need had nothing to do with the fatuous idea of brotherly love preached by the True Socialists or Kantian "fantasies" of "perpetual peace." Working-class internationalism was much more mundane and much more real: "while all such chimerical sentimentalities become completely irrelevant, the proletarians of all nations, without too much ceremony, are already really beginning to fraternise under the banner of communist democracy." The social basis for this fraternization was simple shared interests as realized through common struggle: "proletarians in all countries have one and the same interest, one and the same enemy, and one and the same struggle" (CW 6, 3–6).

So, against the national antagonisms' characteristic of modern social relations, Engels insisted that "[t]he great mass of proletarians are, by their very nature, free from national prejudices and their whole disposition and movement is essentially humanitarian, anti-nationalist. Only the proletarians can destroy nationality, only the awakening proletariat can bring about fraternisation between the different nations." Though Engels would have undoubtedly moderated the excessive optimism of this statement in later life, this essay marked the birth of the idea of proletarian internationalism as a scientific rather than purely moral concept. Engels's key historical point was that while the idea of a fraternity of nations had emerged under the banner of democracy at the time of the French Revolution, subsequently democracy morphed through French communism and English Chartism to become a *social* and not merely political movement: "democracy nowadays is communism" and communism is not an abstract moral absolute but is a real, interested "proletarian principle" (CW 6, 5–6).

This democratic and internationalist conception of politics underpinned Marx and Engels's political practice in the revolutionary wave of 1848–1849, but it did not lead them to embrace a crudely uniform conception of working-class politics. Capitalism's uneven spread across Europe implied that the concrete form taken by the struggle for freedom would be nationally specific. This point was brought home very clearly in an unfortunately incomplete pamphlet *On the Constitutional Question in Germany* (1847)—sometimes translated as *The Status Quo in Germany*—penned by Engels a few months prior to the publication of *The Communist Manifesto* (CW 6, 75–91; cf. CW 38, 117).

This pamphlet, which was described by Iring Fetscher as "one of the most brilliant criticisms of the (German) bureaucracy and political backwardness to be written by a revolutionary intellectual in the nineteenth century" (Henderson 1976, 98; cf. Hamilton 1991, 126), was occasioned when the Prussian king summoned a diet to raise taxes in response to growing economic hardship. The king needed money from the bourgeoisie in the diet, and they demanded liberal reforms in return. Parallels with the moment when Louis XVI called the Estates General easily sprang to mind, and Engels's goal in the pamphlet was to orient the left in this context. Against the dominant faux radicalism among sections of German communism that dismissed the conflict between the bourgeoisie and the absolutist state, Engels argued that a serious political orientation on the situation in Germany demanded a break with the ultra-leftist criticisms of the French Revolution that underpinned this abstentionist position. The True Socialists confused two very distinct though similar propositions about this world historic event. They argued that the victory of the bourgeoisie over absolutism in France had, for the mass of workers, led to a new form of exploitation. However, Engels insisted that it was utterly mistaken to reduce this truism to absurdity by claiming that the French Revolution amounted *merely* to this change in the form of exploitation.

The problem with this latter perspective was not academic: "True Socialism was reactionary through and through," or so Engels argued, because it "managed to use the most revolutionary propositions that have ever been framed as a protective wall for the morass of the German status quo" (CW 6, 77). Because the True Socialists dismissed the positive aspects of capitalist development, they were unable to grasp that the workers had a dog in the fight between the liberal bourgeoisie and the absolutist state. Marx and Engels's new theory of history helped immunize them against this type of posturing. Against True Socialism's "sovereign disdain" for these struggles, Engels insisted that socialists should orient themselves toward "practical, tangible results" that would come from the victory of the bourgeoisie over the nobility and, as he and Marx wrote elsewhere, expand the "elbow-room" within which the working class could grow to maturity (CW 6, 76; CW 26, 512, 306, 42, 552, 11, 162).

According to Engels, at the summit of contemporary German society the nobility exhibited a degenerate decline characterized by corruption, wasteful luxury spending, and petty squabbling. Unfortunately, the local-ism and narrow horizons of both the petty bourgeoisie and the peasantry meant that neither of these classes was able to offer an alternative national leadership to the nobility. Equally, the working class was too weak and undeveloped to present a viable national alternative to the status quo. By contrast with the local nature of petty bourgeois production, the admittedly weak bourgeoisie tended toward national production and an alternative national outlook: "the nobility is too much in decline, the petty bourgeoisie and peasants are, by their whole position in life, too weak, the workers are still far from sufficiently mature to be able to come forward as the ruling class in Germany. There remains only the bourgeoisie" (CW 6, 84). Engels claimed that the barriers the bureaucratic state apparatus had put in the way of national capitalist development meant that the bourgeoisie would be "compelled to break the power of the indolent and pettifogging bureaucracy" (CW 6, 88). Consequently, the bourgeoisie is "the only one that at present has a chance of success" (CW 6, 86). So, and in contrast to the True Socialists' abstention (and sometimes worse) from the struggle between the bourgeoisie and the princes, Engels insisted that the left should throw its lot in with the bourgeoisie in its struggle against the "status quo." For though he could agree in the abstract with the True Socialists that the bourgeoisie was the "natural enemy" of the workers' movements, he nonetheless insisted that the left should not abstain from the struggles of this class against the princes because "the German status quo is still more our enemy, because it stands between the bourgeoisie and us, because it hinders us from coming to grips with the bourgeoisie" (CW 6, 77).

This sophisticated political perspective informed Marx and Engels's practice in the coming revolutionary storm. What is more, it was deepened in a brief piece Engels wrote on *Protective Tariffs or Free Trade System*. Here he argued that with the victory of the bourgeoisie over the princes, the protective tariffs they would be compelled to introduce to foster growth in competition with England would mark an attack on private property itself, and this would simultaneously take the form of the transparent exploitation of the workers. Consequently, rather than act as mere cheer-leaders to the bourgeoisie, the workers would be "compelled" to move into conflict with the bourgeoisie immediately upon their victory over the princes: "The bourgeoisie will and must fall to the ground before the proletariat, just as the aristocracy and the absolute monarchy have received their *coup de grâce* from the middle class" (CW 6, 95). At this juncture Engels wrote *A Communist Confession of Faith*, in effect the first draft of *The Communist Manifesto*. In 1846 Marx and Engels had formed the Communist Correspondence Committee in Belgium with a view to creating a point of contact between various sections of the revolutionary left across Europe. One of the groups they contacted was the League of the Just, an organization of mainly émigré German Communists whose leadership had moved from Paris to London in 1846. Sensing an impending revolutionary moment in Germany, one of the first acts of the London leadership of the league was to send an address to all its branches asking for members to contribute to the formulation of a "simple communist confession of faith to serve as a guide for all"—this didactic style was common to Catholic and Protestant churches and would be easily rec-ognized within the workers' movement. A conference to frame policy was set for May 1847 (it eventually took place in June), with a view to thrashing out this new perspective. In January 1847 Joseph Moll was sent by the league's leadership with invitations for Marx and Engels in Brus-sels and Paris, respectively, to join their organization and this discussion. In the event, Engels attended the conference for the Communist Cor-respondence Committee (Marx, pleading poverty, did not travel), where he played a key role winning an argument that he and Marx had been pursuing with the league for the previous year. In fact, he was pushing at an open door as the league's leadership had already begun moving in the direction of his and Marx's politics (CW 26, 320). This was the moment when the league, formally at least, turned away from its previous abstract and sectarian methods toward his and Marx's politics. At the conference the league dropped its previous conspiratorial methods, changed its name to the Communist League, and replaced its slogan "All Men Are Brothers" with "Proletarians of All Countries, Unite"—subsequently, and rather famously, picked up and used in *The Communist Manifesto* (Hammen 1969, 160–161; McLellan 2006, 157; CW 6, 707, 585).

Engels's contribution to this process was fundamental, and he was tasked with penning the league's new program: *A Communist Confession of Faith*—which he drafted on the final day of the conference. This document added meat to the bones of his earlier argument that the aims of the communists were: "1. to ensure that the interests of the proletariat prevail, as opposed to those of the bourgeoisie; 2. to do so by abolishing private property and replacing same with community of goods; 3. to recognise no means of attaining these aims other than democratic revolution by force" (CW 38, 82). Within *A Communist Confession of Faith* he defined communism as a system of social organization in which "every member of [society] can develop and use all his capabilities and powers in complete freedom and without thereby infringing the basic conditions of this society." This social system would be realized by the abolition of private property and through "enlightening and uniting the proletariat." After a brief résumé of the history of the emergence of the proletariat and its differences from previously exploited classes, Engels insisted that communism was no transhistorical ideal but had "only arisen since machinery and other inventions made it possible to hold out the prospect of an all-sided development, a happy existence, for all members of society." He also argued that communism could not be won through conspiracies, because "revolutions are not made deliberately and arbitrarily but that everywhere and at all times they are the necessary consequence of circumstances." Though this statement appears to read as a form of mechanical materialism justifying political fatalism, it is better understood as part of his and Marx's critique of the idea that communism is a top-down ideology introduced by a conspiracy of intellectuals *for* the workers. His stress on the material roots of revolutionary politics, by contrast, underpinned their view of communism, as he put it in his critique of Karl Heinzen, as "the theoretical expression of the position of the proletariat in [the class] struggle and the theoretical summation of the conditions for the liberation"

(CW 6, 303–304). As to the coloration of a future communist society, he suggested that it would mark a profound change with existing social relations. So, just as the family, for instance, had morphed through various forms in the past, the abolition of private property would likely "have a most important influence on it." Similarly, nationalities will "supersede themselves" and religion would become "superfluous" (CW 6, 96–103).

Engels further deepened these arguments a few months later in *Principles of Communism*, effectively the second draft of what was to become *The Communist Manifesto*. This new essay included a reworking of the definition of communism more clearly as a working-class form: communism was "the doctrine of the conditions for the emancipation of the proletariat." He also elaborated on his hopes for a peaceful revolution:

> It is to be desired that [a peaceful revolution] could happen, and Communists certainly would be the last to resist it. The Communists know only too well that all conspiracies are not only futile but even harmful. They know only too well that revolutions are not made deliberately and arbitrarily, but that everywhere and at all times they have been the necessary outcome of circumstances entirely independent of the will and the leadership of particular parties and entire classes. But they also see that the development of the proletariat is in nearly every civilised country forcibly suppressed, and that thus the opponents of the Communists are working with all their might towards a revolution. Should the oppressed proletariat in the end be goaded into a revolution, we Communists will then defend the cause of the proletarians by deed just as well as we do now by word. (CW 6, 341, 349–350)

Clearly, despite the obvious line of continuity between these words and his closing arguments of *The Condition of the Working Class in England*, over the intervening couple of years Engels had developed a much richer understanding of the class basis of communism and of both the likelihood of violence from the counterrevolution and the consequent requirement of violence to defend the revolution. This much more concrete conception of communism informed his critique of other forms of socialism. First among these were the "reactionary socialists" who criticized capitalist development from the perspective of earlier feudal and patriarchal relations. Though this was understandable, and sometime insightful—one thinks of Engels's earlier comments on Carlyle—Engels argued that this form of socialism was irredeemably reactionary and consequently that communists should "strongly oppose it." Secondly, there were "bourgeois socialists"—effectively reformists—whose utopian aim was the preservation of "present society" while removing "the evils bound up with it." Like the reactionary socialists, Engels believed that this group must "be continuously fought by the Communists, since they work for the enemies of the Communists and defend the society which it is the Communists' aim to destroy." Finally, the "democratic socialists" shared with the communists a desire to "abolish the misery of present society" but without a full understanding either of the nature of this situation or the alternative to it. In a typically unsectarian gesture toward the relationship of communists to the real movement from below, Engels suggested that though communists should maintain their political independence from this grouping, by contrast with the other two they should learn to work with them to specific ends (CW 6, 355–356). Engels differentiates other parties within the socialist milieu not by what they said—the three other socialist tendencies overlapped at this level—but by what they did and the forces they represented. Principally because the democratic socialists represented part of the real movement against the prevailing state of things, Communists should learn to work with them.

Engels's politics differed from alternative voices on the left through the clarity of his analysis of the relation of communism to existing social conditions. Whereas industrialization had begun to create the circumstances necessary to overcome general want, capitalist social relations meant that this occurred in a way that brutalized workers while simultaneously giving rise to trade crises. These crises were evidence that, despite its historically progressive role, "competition and in general the carrying on of industrial production by individuals have become a fetter upon large-scale industry." If the existence of crises showed that it was necessary to supersede capitalism, the proletariat, which had emerged alongside and in proportion to capitalist development, felt the negative consequences of these crises most directly: its "whole existence depend[s] on the demand for labour, hence, on the alternation of times of good and bad business, on the fluctuations resulting from unbridled competition." To resist this condition, "association" had ceased to be an abstract moral imperative for workers and had instead become a real and urgent need. Association was not merely a form of rebellion against alienation but more positively the concrete solution to the contradiction between the social nature of capitalist production and its individual appropriation. Accordingly, the proletariat was best understood as at once a precondition and a result of capitalist development, while its collective struggles against the consequences of its exploitation and dehumanization marked an immanent alternative to capitalism. Hence, Engels insisted that the first aim of the revolution would be to "inaugurate a *democratic constitution* and thereby, directly or indirectly, the political rule of the proletariat" (CW 6, 350).

The "impending proletarian revolution" would not, however, inaugurate an immediate general change in economic conditions. Rather, it would "transform existing society only gradually" because private property could only be fully abolished when "the necessary quantity of the means of production has been created." The uneven development of capitalism also implied that the attitude of communists to other parties beyond the workers' movement would "differ from country to country." Specifically, in Germany, "[t]he Communists must . . . take the side of the liberal bourgeois against the governments but they must ever be on their guard against sharing the self-deceptions of the bourgeois or believing their false assurances about the benefits which the victory of the bourgeoisie will bring to the proletariat" (CW 6, 357). Despite this commonality of short-term interest between the bourgeoisie and the proletariat in the struggle against the status quo in Germany, the morrow of the bourgeois revolution would signal "the turn for the fight between bourgeois and proletarians" (CW 6, 357). So, while the German workers should support their bourgeoisie in the oncoming struggle against absolutism, they should do so without illusions and while maintaining their political independence.

The idea that the workers should engage in a common struggle alongside the German bourgeoisie was rooted in what Engels believed to be the shared interests of these two classes in overcoming the localism and parochialism of both the German princes and the petty bourgeoisie through a struggle to realize the potential of large-scale capitalist production to create a unified German state. But because capitalist production had long since expanded beyond national frontiers, a unified democratic Germany was not Engels's final strategic goal. The international expansion of the means of production meant that it would be impossible to overcome the contradictions of capitalism in a single country: "Large-scale industry, already by creating the world market, has so linked up all the peoples of the earth, and especially the civilised peoples, that each people is dependent on what happens to another." Consequently, the struggle for communism was necessarily an international conflict.

Further, in all civilised countries large-scale industry has so levelled social development that in all these countries the bourgeoisie and the proletariat have become the two decisive classes of society and the struggle between them the main struggle of the day. The communist revolution will therefore be no merely national one; it will be a revolution taking place simultaneously in all civilised countries, that is, at least in England, America, France and Germany. In each of these countries it will develop more quickly or more slowly according to whether the country has a more developed industry, more wealth, and a more considerable mass of productive forces. It will therefore be slowest and most difficult to carry out in Germany, quickest and easiest in England. It will also have an important effect upon the other countries of the world, and will completely change and greatly accelerate their previous manner of development. It is a worldwide revolution and will therefore be worldwide in scope. (CW 6, 352)

This theme was classically elaborated in *The Communist Manifesto*, "the most influential single piece of political writing since the French Revolution's *Declaration of the Rights of Man and the Citizen*" (Hobsbawm 1998, 4). Though the *Manifesto* was nominally cowritten by Marx and Engels—and Marx always insisted on its status as a joint work—Engels was not even in the same city as Marx at the time of its composition and very probably played no direct part in this process (Draper 2004, 9). Nonetheless, the degree of continuity between the *Manifesto* and Engels's *Principles of Communism* is such that it invites no other interpretation than that of being a fully joint work (Hunley 1991, 65–79; Carver 1983, 78–95). In fact, it was Engels who suggested dropping the catechism form to call the thing *The Communist Manifesto* (CW 38, 149).

What is perhaps most shocking to first-time readers of the *Manifesto* is its opening hymn of praise to the "most revolutionary part" played by the bourgeoisie. Many commentators tend to register this role somewhat one-sidedly through the lens of Marx and Engels's famous claim about the bourgeoisie increasing society's material wealth: it "has accomplished wonders far surpassing Egyptian pyramids, Roman aqueducts, and Gothic cathedrals; it has conducted expeditions that put in the shade all former Exoduses of nations and crusades." Though the increases in the productivity of labor realized through capitalist social relations are obviously of the first importance to any materialist theory of history, Marx and Engels did not leave matters there. Capitalist development was to be welcomed for its psychological and intellectual as well as material consequences.

> The bourgeoisie, wherever it has got the upper hand, has put an end to all feudal, patriarchal, idyllic relations. It has piti-lessly torn asunder the motley feudal ties that bound man to his "natural superiors," and has left remaining no other nexus between man and man than naked self-interest, than callous "cash payment." It has drowned the most heavenly ecstasies of religious fervour, of chivalrous enthusiasm, of philistine senti-mentalism, in the icy water of egotistical calculation. . . . In one word, for exploitation, veiled by religious and political illusions, it has substituted naked, shameless, direct, brutal exploitation. The bourgeoisie has stripped of its halo every occupation hitherto honoured and looked up to with reverent awe. . . . The bourgeoisie has torn away from the family its sentimental veil. . . . The bourgeoisie cannot exist without constantly revolutionising the instruments of production, and thereby the relations of production, and with them the whole relations of society. . . . Constant revolutionising of production, uninterrupted disturbance of all social conditions, everlasting uncertainty and agitation distinguish the bourgeois epoch from all earlier ones. All fixed, fast-frozen relations, with their train of ancient and venerable prejudices and opinions, are swept away, all new-formed ones become antiquated before they can ossify. All that is solid melts into air, all that is holy is profaned, and man is at last compelled to face with sober senses, his real conditions of life, and his relations with his kind. (CW 6, 487)

To fetter capitalist development was thus to fetter the development of the human spirit—albeit in a dialectical manner: as Marx later put it, progress in this direction "would not drink the nectar but from the skulls of the slain" (CW 12, 222). Perhaps the most important consequence of the emerging "cosmopolitan character to production and consumption" was the expansion of humanity's intellectual and psychological horizons:

In place of the old wants, satisfied by the productions of the country, we find new wants, requiring for their satisfaction the products of distant lands and climes. In place of the old local and national seclusion and self-sufficiency, we have intercourse in every direction, universal inter-dependence of nations. And as in material, so also in intellectual production. The intellectual creations of individual nations become common property. National one-sidedness and narrow-mindedness become more and more impossible, and from the numerous national and local literatures, there arises a world literature. (CW 6, 488)

If, as the *Manifesto* continued, the new material, psychological and intellectual riches brought about by the development of capitalism, were being threatened by a similarly capitalist form of crisis—"the epidemic of overproduction"—the proletariat, which had grown in parallel with the growth of capitalism, was both the first victim of this tendency toward crisis and the potential agent for ending these crises by overthrowing capitalism. However, proletarian struggles were not of a uniform kind. And just as Engels had traced the evolution of working-class struggles in *The Condition of the Working Class in England*, so the *Manifesto* outlined a historical account of the workers' movement. "The proletariat goes through various stages of development. With its birth begins its struggle with the bourgeoisie." However,

[a]t this stage the labourers still form an incoherent mass scattered over the whole country, and broken up by their mutual competition. If anywhere they unite to form more compact bodies, this is not yet the consequence of their own active union, but of the union of the bourgeoisie, which class, in order to attain its own political ends, is compelled to set the whole proletariat in motion, and is moreover yet, for a time, able to do so. At this stage, therefore, the proletarians do not fight their enemies, but the enemies of their enemies, the remnants of absolute monarchy, the landowners, the non-industrial bourgeois, the petty bourgeoisie. Thus the whole historical movement is concentrated in the hands of the bourgeoisie; every victory so obtained is a victory for the bourgeoisie. But with the development of industry the proletariat not only increases in

number; it becomes concentrated in greater masses, its strength
grows, and it feels that strength more. The various interests and
conditions of life within the ranks of the proletariat are more
and more equalised, in proportion as machinery obliterates all
distinctions of labour, and nearly everywhere reduces wages
to the same low level. . . . [T]he collisions between individual
workmen and individual bourgeois take more and more the
character of collisions between two classes. Thereupon the
workers begin to form combinations (Trades' Unions) against
the bourgeois. . . . Here and there the contest breaks out into
riots. Now and then the workers are victorious, but only for a
time. The real fruit of their battles lies, not in the immediate
result, but in the ever-expanding union of the workers. This
union is helped on by the improved means of communication
that are created by modern industry and that place the workers
of different localities in contact with one another. It was just
this contact that was needed to centralise the numerous local
struggles, all of the same character, into one national struggle
between classes. But every class struggle is a political struggle.
And that union, to attain which the burghers of the Middle
Ages, with their miserable highways, required centuries, the
modern proletarians, thanks to railways, achieve in a few years.
This organisation of the proletarians into a class, and consequently into a political party, is continually being upset again
by the competition between the workers themselves. But it
ever rises up again, stronger, firmer, mightier. (CW 6, 492–493)

The modern proletariat exists through an ongoing struggle with capital,
but the uneven and emergent nature of this struggle is such that it can
at a certain early stage of development take the form of an alliance with
the bourgeoisie against feudal and absolutist relations. This was a particularly important point to make in 1848, because some parts of Europe
were clearly in earlier stages of this process than were others. Among the
practical political difficulties associated with this approach is the importance
Marx and Engels attached to navigating between the Scylla of liquidating
the workers' movement into a revolutionary movement dominated by the
bourgeoisie and the Charybdis of sectarian indifference to this movement
in the name of some abstract future goal. They were more than aware
of this problem and insisted that though "[t]he Communists fight for the

attainment of the immediate aims, for the enforcement of the momentary interests of the working class; . . . in the movement of the present, they also represent and take care of the future of that movement" (CW 6, 518). The practical difficulties associated with being a communist "on the eve of a bourgeois revolution" informed the *Manifesto*'s deepening of Engels's critique of other forms of socialism, while simultaneously underpinning its insistence that

> Communists do not form a separate party opposed to other working-class parties [and] are distinguished from the other working-class parties by this only: 1. In the national struggles of the proletarians of the different countries, they point out and bring to the front the common interests of the entire proletariat, independently of all nationality. 2. In the various stages of development which the struggle of the working class against the bourgeoisie has to pass through, they always and everywhere represent the interests of the movement as a whole. (CW 6, 497)

This internationalist and dialectical perspective framed all of Marx and Engels's subsequent political work. The *Manifesto* declared that "[t]hough not in substance, yet in form, the struggle of the proletariat with the bourgeoisie is at first a national struggle. The proletariat of each country must, of course, first of all settle matters with its own bourgeoisie" (CW 6, 495). So, though the essence of the workers' movement is international, its immediate form is national. Specifically, in Germany, communists

> fight with the bourgeoisie whenever it acts in a revolutionary way, against the absolute monarchy, the feudal squirearchy, and the petty bourgeoisie. But they never cease, for a single instant, to instil into the working class the clearest possible recognition of the hostile antagonism between bourgeoisie and proletariat" because they recognised that after the fall of the reactionary classes in Germany, the fight against the bourgeoisie itself may immediately begin. (CW 6, 519)

5

1848

War, Revolution, and the National Question

The project of a German (bourgeois) revolution immediately posed a second complicating factor for Marx and Engels: a unified German state would challenge interests in all the various states and nations around it. The demand for German unity therefore compelled Marx and in particular Engels, who wrote on these matters as part of their division of labor to incorporate national and military questions within their theory of revolution. If the national tensions that Engels had to address were most obvious in Austria's multiethnic empire, they were also much in evidence elsewhere, including the borders with France, Italy, and Denmark, and most especially in Poland, which had been divided between Prussia, Austria, and Russia since 1772.

Revolution in 1848 consequently meant for Germany what it had meant for France half a century earlier: war. Just as "[t]he whole of the French Revolution is dominated by the war with the coalition" (CW 48, 414), so the social revolution of 1848 took the form of a military conflict against the forces of counterrevolution—backed ultimately by Russia. As Engels wrote four decades later in his unfinished study of Bismarck's Blood and Iron policy, *The Role of Force in History* (1887–1888), "Germany's unity . . . had to be won in struggle not only against the princes and other internal enemies, but also against foreign countries" (CW 26, 460). Engels's engagement with these issues has not been well received by his interlocutors—in a typically superficial comment Tristram Hunt compares these "deeply chilling" writings to the language of twentieth-century dictators (Hunt 2009, 167). However, beneath the somewhat confused and confusing Hegelian rhetoric about "nonhistoric nations," the starting point of Engels's approach to these questions was resolutely democratic and internationalist.

The democratic core of Engels's approach to the national question was signaled in a speech he gave at a meeting in London in November 1847. Commenting on the "disgrace" that was Germany's control over part of Poland, he famously announced: "A nation cannot become free and at the same time continue to oppress other nations." Further, and prefiguring what he would later say about the relationship between English imperialism and the struggle for Irish independence, he insisted that support for Polish national liberation was in the interests of "German democrats." Indeed, the liberation of Germany was impossible "without the liberation of Poland from German oppression" (CW 6, 389; CW 43, 363). He viewed Germany's relationship with Poland as essentially one piece of a larger jigsaw of the European state system. This system, which was forged by the victors over Napoleon and institutionalized at the Congress of Vienna in 1815, aimed to subordinate "dynastic conflicts and national interests to the common need to defend traditional, and not so traditional, privileges against the republicanism and egalitarian demons wakened by the French Revolution" (Draper 2005, 19–20). Subsequently, a "Holy Alliance" was formed between Russia, Prussia, and Austria (Britain and France were briefly members) with the aim of extending the reactionary project embedded in the Congress of Vienna by formalizing the mutual exploitation and oppression of Poland by these three states. According to Engels, "the partition of Poland" consequently was not merely the material link that cemented the "Holy Alliance," it also embedded reactionary and counterrevolutionary policies across Germany by making her "dependent on Russia" (CW 7, 350).

This relationship meant that the victory of the forces of freedom and democracy could only be realized by breaking Prussia's and Austria's relationships with Russia. "So long . . . as we help to subjugate Poland . . . we shall remain fettered to Russia and to the Russian policy, and shall be unable to eradicate patriarchal feudal absolutism in Germany." So, for Engels, support for the right of Polish independence was no abstract moral ideal. Rather, it flowed directly from the needs of the German revolution itself: "The creation of a democratic Poland is a primary condition for the creation of a democratic Germany" (CW 7, 351; Benner 1995, 147). This perspective had terrible implications. Because Polish and German freedom could only be won at the expense of Russia, the struggle for freedom in Germany would necessarily take the form of a war against Russia. Indeed, war with Russia was "the only possible means of upholding Germany's honour and Germany's interest." War was the necessary means through which Germany might realize "a complete, open and effective break with the whole of our disgraceful past . . . real liberation and unification . . . and the establishment of democracy on the ruins of feudalism and on the wreckage of the short-lived bourgeois dream of power" (CW 7, 352).

Given Engels's not unrealistic assumptions, this democratic and internationalist perspective is difficult to dispute. Neither, unfortunately, is the rider that he added to the essay:

> [T]he restoration of Poland and the settlement of her frontiers with Germany is not only necessary, it is the most easily solvable of all the political problems which have arisen in Eastern Europe since the revolution. The struggle for independence of the diverse nationalities jumbled together south of the Carpathians is much more complicated and will lead to far more bloodshed, confusion and civil wars than the Polish struggle for independence and the establishment of the border line between Germany and Poland. (CW 7, 352)

Engels addressed the problem of these states through his exploration of the tensions between Slavs, Magyars, and Germans within the Austrian Empire. If his analysis of the position of Poland within his broader revolutionary perspective is obviously democratic, his writings on the Southern Slavs have proved to be much more controversial.

Initially at least, his analysis of Austria's relationship to the (non-Polish) Slav nations in her empire was very similar to that of the relation between Austria and Prussia on the one side and Poland on the other. He argued that

> [t]he fall of Austria has a special significance for us Germans. It is Austria which is responsible for our reputation of being the oppressors of foreign nations, the hirelings of reaction in all countries. Under the Austrian flag Germans have held Poland, Bohemia, Italy in bondage. . . . We have every reason to hope that it will be Germans who will overthrow Austria and clear away the obstacles in the way of freedom for the Slavs and Italians. (CW 6, 535–536)

Engels's analyses of these conflicts followed from the logic of his analysis of the Polish Question. If the aim of the revolution was a unified, democratic Germany, the main impediment to this goal was essentially the same in Austria as it was in Prussia. The reactionary nature of both regimes was reproduced through their relationship with Russia, which had a strategic interest in their survival and so, at the end of the day, propped up their despotic rulers. Revolution was thus likely to take the form of war either with Russia or with one or other of its proxies. This is indeed what happened in 1848–1849. Specifically, an initially successful Magyar (Hungarian) revolt against Austrian rule was defeated through the intervention of Russian arms. Thus, as it turned out, was reactionary Austria saved and the German revolution essentially ended.

Engels's interventions in this conflict have been criticized as contradictory and even racist (Cummins 1980, 40), but though Engels's supposed German nationalism has been widely accepted as a fact—recently by Kevin Anderson who writes that Engels "had a particular animus toward the southern Slavs" and Mike Davis who claims that Engels had a "'Great German' attitude toward the rights of smaller Slav nationalisms, often shockingly expressed" (Anderson 2010, 44; Davis 2018, 261)—this interpretation of his work is superficial and misleading. Unfortunately, the critique of Engels's supposed "violent prejudice" against "non-historical peoples" (Harris 1990, 42) has not been helped by weaknesses with his analysis of the European theater in 1848. His work combined insightful historical accounts of the confusing national configuration across Europe alongside powerful empirical descriptions of contemporary political and military events, but it synthesized these through the analytically useless conceptual architecture that distinguished between so-called historic and nonhistoric nations.

The Ukrainian Marxist Roman Rosdolsky has penned the most comprehensive critique of Engels's analysis of the national question. Rosdolsky argued that the concept of nonhistoric peoples was a piece of idealistic nonsense Engels inherited from Hegel that informed a number of profound strategic errors in 1848. Specifically, the nationalistic frame of reference of Engels's analysis—he wrote of revolutionary and counterrevolutionary peoples—led him (and Marx) to overlook the problematic nature of some of their allies—specifically, the way that the supposedly revolutionary Polish and Hungarian nobilities exploited the allegedly counterrevolutionary Southern Slav peasants (in addition to peasants of their own nationality). This error was purportedly compounded by their belief that the imminent transformation of the bourgeois revolution into a proletarian revolution would lead to the transcendence of class divisions between these landlords and peasants under socialism (Rosdolsky 1987, 4). So, whereas the method outlined in *The German Ideology* should have informed a class analysis of the revolution, what Engels in particular actually produced was an intellectually worthless and politically debilitating account of the revolution in idealistic language directly inherited from Hegel.

There is more than a grain of truth to this argument; the concept of nonhistoric peoples is idealistic and intellectually worthless and it did originate with Hegel. However, Rosdolsky overstates his case because he tends to put the cart before the horse. It is not so much that the concepts of historic and nonhistoric peoples led Engels to impose a false meaning on reality. Rather, he deployed these concepts to explain a very real problem facing revolutionaries in 1848—the Southern Slav movements did tend to side with the counterrevolution. The very real analytical and political problems that characterize Engels's writings on the national question at this time stemmed less from contradictions in the conceptual architecture of his work than from this contradiction in reality itself. He neither ignored the class differences among the national movements he supported (Germans, Poles, and Magyars [Hungarians]), nor did he overlook the progressive movements among the supposed nonhistoric peoples. What he did take from the idea of historic and nonhistoric peoples was a (false) solution to a problem that would not adequately be addressed within the Marxist movement until Lenin differentiated between the right to and the desirability of self-determination some six decades later: how to resolve conflicts between national groups with equally valid claims to specific territories (and where one side can only realize its desires through an alliance with a reactionary power) in the context of interstate military competition (Draper 2005, 51–77, 189–213).

As we have seen, Engels's initial analysis of oppression of the Czechs by the Austrians had much in common with his analysis of the oppression of the Poles. In July 1848 he and Marx commented, "Despite the patriotic shouting and beating of the drums of almost the entire German press, the *Neue Rheinische Zeitung* from the very first moment has sided with the Poles in Posen, the Italians in Italy, and the Czechs in Bohemia." They argued that the intervention by the Austrian military against Prague was an attempt to redirect the energies of the revolution in a reactionary direction: "Gripped by revolutionary ferment, Germany seeks relief in a *war of restoration*, in a campaign *for* the consolidation of the old authority *against* which she has just revolted." By contrast with this reactionary project, Marx and Engels insisted that "[o]nly a *war against Russia* would be a war of *revolutionary Germany*, a war by which she could cleanse herself of her past sins, could take courage, defeat her own autocrats, spread civilisation by the sacrifice of her own sons as becomes a people that is shaking off the chains of long, indolent slavery and make herself free within her borders by bringing liberation to those outside" (CW 7, 212). However, before these lines were written, Engels bemoaned the fate of the Czechs. In the wake of an Austrian suppression of the Prague uprising in June 1848 he suggested that the Czechs would either be defeated by Austrian absolutism or align themselves with Russian absolutism, in which case they would come into conflict with the democratic revolution across Germany:

> Whether they win or are defeated, their doom is sealed. They have been driven into the arms of the Russians by 400 years of German oppression, which is being continued now in the street-fighting waged in Prague. In the great struggle between Western and Eastern Europe, which may begin very soon, perhaps in a few weeks, the Czechs are placed by an unhappy fate on the side of the Russians, the side of despotism opposed to the revolution. The revolution will triumph and the Czechs will be the first to be crushed by it. (CW 7, 93)

Written in June 1848, this analysis elided over an alternative possible outcome of the June events: a revolutionary unity between Czechs and Germans in Bohemia. This gap in Engels's argument is particularly odd as, by contrast with other German periodicals that attempted to frame the conflict in Prague as one between Czechs and Germans in a way to "incite Germans against Bohemians," a German-speaking revolutionary present in Prague at the time of the military suppression of the revolutionary movement wrote in *Neue Rheinische Zeitung* (albeit a month later) to insist that "not the smallest trace of a rivalry between nationalities could be observed during the fighting on the barricades." Indeed, far from protecting the Germans from the Czechs, the Austrian forces rained down shot on German and Czech inhabitants of Prague alike. Against this bombardment "Germans and Czechs stood side by side ready for defence" (CW 7, 213–214).

This moment of radical internationalist possibility was not unique. Austrian repression had at various moments driven diverse communities to unity with revolutionary forces. For instance, a year later Engels commented on "peasants and Jews" being "driven into the arms of the Magyar" revolutionaries by counterrevolutionary Austrian forces, while Draper notes dozens of articles from the *Neue Rheinische Zeitung* that document the dissatisfaction of South Slav peasants with the Hapsburgs and support for the revolutionary movements (CW 9, 351; Draper 2005, 62–63). Unfortunately, these episodes were often momentary and tended to be lost as the dynamic of the revolutionary process pushed these groups apart. Engels signaled the consequences of this most infamously in his essay *The Magyar Struggle* published in January 1849. In many ways this is a powerful essay that outlines the emergence of the German (Austria) and Magyar (Hungary) states bisecting South Slav lands before explaining the unification of these states in opposition to the threat from the Ottomans after the defeat of Byzantium. With the decline of the Ottomans, the external threat that guaranteed Hapsburg power over the empire greatly diminished. Against this background, the Hapsburgs responded to the rise of German-speaking burghers across the empire by attempting to fix the power of the nobility, including the Slav nobility. This movement helped tie the Slavs to the Austrian state. However, the burghers continued to grow, while the progress of agriculture alongside industry changed the position of the peasantry vis-à-vis the nobility in a way that helped foster nationalistic peasant movements. According to Engels, the response of the Austrian chancellor (Metternich) to this situation was to deprive all but the most powerful feudal barons of influence over the state while similarly dividing the bourgeoisie between a diminished lower strata and more powerful financial barons whom he incorporated into the state:

> Supported . . . by the top feudal and financial aristocracy, as well as by the bureaucracy and the army, he far more than all his rivals attained the ideal of an absolute monarchy. Furthermore, he kept the burghers and the peasantry of each nation under control by means of the aristocracy of that nation and the peasantry of every other nation, and he kept the aristocracy of each nation under control by its fear of that nation's burghers and peasantry. The different class interests, the national features of narrow-mindedness, and local prejudices, despite their complexity, were completely held in check by their mutual counteraction and allowed the old scoundrel Metternich the utmost freedom to manoeuvre. (CW 8, 229)

The year 1848 was the moment when this carefully constructed game of divide and rule blew up in Metternich's face, forcing him to flee the country: "The year 1848 first of all brought with it the most terrible chaos for Austria by setting free for a short time all these different nationalities which, owing to Metternich, had hitherto been enslaving one another" (CW 8, 230).

Engels then described the consequences of this social explosion: "The combatants divided into two large camps: the Germans, Poles and Magyars took the side of revolution; the remainder, all the Slavs, except for the Poles, the Rumanians and Transylvanian Saxons, took the side of counter-revolution" (CW 8, 230). Unfortunately, this was an accurate analysis of the configuration of forces in 1848. Even Rosdolsky agrees that Engels was right about the counterrevolutionary role played by the Southern Slavs after June 1848 (Rosdolsky 1987, 98). Engels was also right about pan-Slavism being a reactionary ideology that looked back nostalgically to a moment around the eighth or ninth centuries when the Slavs controlled all of what was to become Austria and Hungary, and that any attempt to recreate this long-past moment was doomed either to failure or at best to produce a Russian vassal state. The problem is not with Engels's description of events—he was an excellent historian (Anderson 1974, 23, 236–237)—but with his explanation for this configuration of forces. The Southern Slavs were destined to act in this way because, or so he wrote, they were "relics of a nation mercilessly trampled underfoot in the course of history, [and] as Hegel says, these *residual fragments of peoples* always become fanatical standard-bearers of counter-revolution and remain so until their complete extirpation or loss of their national character" (CW 8, 234–235). The problem with the Hegelian language that underpins this argument is that, as against Engels's rich descriptions of the various eddy waves against this tendency, it essentializes what are in reality temporary and contingent national characteristics. But though, as Erica Benner argues, the unfortunate Hegelian language has come to be considered the dominant motif of Engels's writings on nationalism around 1848, in fact there is a tension between this language and the social analysis of the dynamic relationship between nationalism and social revolution that Engels had already offered (Benner 1995, 165–166).

Regrettably, Engels's deployment of the concept of nonhistoric nations was no momentary aberration. Alongside the Southern Slavs, Engels discussed the Gaels, the Bretons, and the Basques in similar terms, while his comments on the Irish noted earlier and Mexicans elsewhere

(CW 8, 365) suggest a more general (pre-Marxist) tendency to essential-ize national characteristics as "instinctive"—at least until the 1880s when he first outlined a serious materialist analysis of the emergence of "new nationalities" in the context of capitalist development (CW 6, 3; CW 26, 559; Harman 1992, 19). Nonetheless, despite this theoretical weakness, Engels pointed to a real problem for the left that would have existed with or without the concept of nonhistoric peoples. Contra Rosdolsky, the concept of nonhistoric peoples functions less as a foundational theoretical error that undermined Engels's (and Marx's) practice in 1848 and more as an embarrassing bolt-on to their descriptive discussions of these events. Unfortunately, as Engels wrote, after the bombing of Prague by Austrian forces in June 1848 "all the South-Slav races, following the example of the Croats, put themselves at the disposal of Austrian reaction" (CW 8, 235).

Engels came closest to suggesting a solution to this problem a few months later in his critique of "our friend" Bakunin's idea of "demo-cratic pan-Slavism" (CW 8, 363). He opened his essay by insisting on the reactionary nature of this slogan—which, as he pointed out, could only be realized through support from the most reactionary power in Europe, Russia. However, he somewhat incoherently extended his argument by claiming, on the one hand, an essential distinction between "revolutionary" and "counter-revolutionary peoples," while on the other hand suggesting that alliances between national groupings "come into being not on *paper*, but only on the *battlefield*" (CW 8, 363). The problem with this argument is that whereas the idea that alliances are forged on the battlefield implies a political *process*, the concepts of revolutionary and counterrevolutionary peoples negates this insight through its appeal to sterile static identities.

Interestingly, Engels's justification for this conclusion is open to immanent critique. For instance, he wrote that the Slavs "would have proved their viability . . . if at any epoch while they were oppressed [they] had begun a *new revolutionary history*" (CW 8, 371). But the German commentator writing from Prague in July 1848 for the *Neue Rheinische Zeitung* had suggested precisely that this was the course taken by events. And even if this writer was overemphasizing the internationalism of the June days in Prague, the fact remains that this ideology was part of the mix at this juncture. The problem with Engels's deployment of the con-cept of nonhistoric peoples is that it led him to conflate the fact that this moment ended in the marginalization of these revolutionary and internationalist voices among both Germans and Czechs in Prague with the claim that this was a necessary consequence of the history of these peoples. Consequently, Engels debarred himself from grasping a (Leninist) solution to the political problems in Austria (Draper 2005, 201). This weakness with his analysis is most apparent when he posed the rhetorical question: Should the Germans have guaranteed the Austrian Slavs their independence? His answer was swift and to the point. He had no intention of allowing "hotbeds of counter-revolution at our very door" (CW 8, 377). The problem with this answer is that, unlike Lenin who placed politics at the center of his account of the relationship between nationalism and socialism (Löwy 1993, 71), Engels seems unaware that by denying the Slavs the right to independence the German revolutionaries might have acted to push them away from the revolution. Neither did he grasp, as we noted earlier, the fundamental distinction between the right to independence and the desirability of independence: one can easily defend the former while denying the latter.

If the conceptual infrastructure of Engels's account of the national movements in 1848 meant that his analyses of these events did not rise to the level of Lenin's later approach to the national question, Lenin was nonetheless right (and Rosdolsky wrong) when he wrote that Engels's whole approach in 1848 was imbued with a spirit of internationalism (Lenin 1963c, 340). Indeed, contra Rosdolsky's belief that the concepts of historic and nonhistoric peoples led Marx and especially Engels to underestimate divisions within the "revolutionary" side of the war, far from ignoring the class divisions within the Polish national movement, Marx and Engels thought them so important that they were mentioned in *The Communist Manifesto*. As Draper points out, the *Manifesto* contains the line: "In Poland they [communists—PB] support the party that insists on an agrarian revolution as the prime condition for national emancipation, that party which fomented the insurrection of Cracow in 1846" (CW 6, 518). The English translation of this sentence somewhat weakens the message of the original German, which reads not "in Poland" but "Among the Poles." Now the Poles had been divided along class lines in 1846, and by defending the agrarian revolutionaries of 1846, Marx and Engels were making a very real intervention within the Polish movement of 1848: these lines from the *Manifesto* represent, in Draper's words, a declaration of war on old aristocratic Poland in the name of new plebeian Poland (Draper 2005, 33–39).

There were important weaknesses with Engels's analysis of the national question in 1848, but Rosdolsky misunderstands their nature. Engels was addressing a real issue: how to accommodate within a single political project peoples with equally valid claims to specific territories, and how to do this in an "imperialist" context. When, a decade later, he wrote about the "remnants of peoples that can still be found here and there and that are no longer capable of national existence," he was addressing a real issue. And his comment that these peoples tend to "remain incorporated into the larger nations and either merge into them or are conserved as merely ethnographic relics with no political significance" is a truth that, contra Nigel Harris, betrays no "violent prejudice" to the groups concerned (CW 16, 254; Harris 1990, 42). Whatever the limitations of Engels's approach, it was resolutely internationalist and it did amount to an important political intervention into a real social movement.

6

1848

Intervening in the Revolution

In *The Constitutional Question in Germany* Engels claimed that by sum-moning a diet in 1847 the Prussian king had created conditions that would force the various German "parties" (in a broad sense of the term), who thus far were "vague, confused and fragmented through ideological subtleties," to "clarify for themselves what interests they represent" (CW 6, 78). Whatever else might be said about 1848 it certainly compelled the parties involved to do just this. And it eventually led Marx and Engels to conclude that the bourgeoisie had become utterly counterrevolu-tionary because they were more frightened of the workers below them than they were of absolutism above. But at the beginning of 1848 Marx and Engels were adamant both that the bourgeoisie still had some fight in it—albeit with a strong tendency to vacillate—and that because the workers' movement had a direct interest in the victory of the bourgeoisie in the struggle against absolutism it had a duty to support and provide backbone to this struggle.

This strategic point was of the first importance precisely because Marx and Engels were "above all else revolutionists." The whole thrust of the theoretical perspective they thrashed out in *The German Ideology* cried out against a merely contemplative relationship to reality. They aimed to be actors on the stage of history for whom interpreting and changing reality were two sides of the same coin. Thus, *Neue Rheinische Zeitung*, the newspaper they produced over the course of the revolutionary year, was aimed, as they subsequently insisted, at *intervening* organically within the movement rather than merely documenting it (CW 10, 5). Their "practical materialism" meant that from the start they attempted to engage in the political process with a view to influencing its progress. It was for this reason that they had set up the Communist Correspondence Committee in 1846, through which they helped reshape the League of the Just into the Communist League the following year, and through which in turn they hoped to shape the revolutionary wave of 1848–1849.

In any event, the revolutionary wave opened in Sicily in January 1848 before coming to a head in Paris a month later. Banned by the government from demonstrating for reforms, the Parisians took to the barricades and within days forced the abdication of their king, Louis Philippe. Marx famously called this moment the "nice revolution" because it appeared to unify all of France against the king—it took the form not so much of a conflict between social classes as one between the people as a whole and the monarchy (CW 7, 147). If subsequent events were to reveal the class antagonisms beneath this apparent unity, in the short term events in Paris inspired democrats across Europe to fight for similar ends. In Germany, radicals across the Confederation demonstrated for democracy, and fearing for their own positions the princes responded to this movement with appeasement rather than the usual repression. Most importantly, Friedrich Wilhelm IV, the Prussian king, acceded to the demand for constitutional reforms and then, after a bloody encounter between his troops and a celebrating crowd of democrats, felt compelled to cede further reforms, including granting both a Prussian Constitutional Assembly to sit in Berlin and supporting the call for an all-German Assembly to sit in Frankfurt as a step toward a unified constitutional state.

Meanwhile, fearing revolutionary contagion in their own country, the Belgian authorities responded to the February Revolution in Paris by arresting Marx and other known radicals. After a night in the cells, Marx traveled to France at the invitation of a member of the Provisional Government (CW 6, 649). By this point he had become the key leader of the Communist League, which had responded to the revolution by relocating its center from London to Brussels. Immediately thereafter it conferred upon Marx "full discretionary power for the temporary central direction of all league activities" in Paris (CW 6, 651). Engels followed Marx to Paris a few days later just as the revolutionary wave spread to Germany. He and Marx immediately penned a leaflet that took the general perspectives for Germany outlined in *The Communist Manifesto* and made them concrete. The ensuing *Demands of the Communist Party in Germany* was signed by the two of them alongside four other members of the Communist League's Central Committee. The leaflet opened with its key demand: "Germany shall be declared a single and indivisible republic." Beyond this, it called for the vote for "every German," payment of elected representatives, "universal arming of the people," freeing of legal services, removal of all feudal obligations, the nationalization both of feudal estates and the means of transport, the creation of a state bank, equal salaries for civil servants, the separation of the Church and State, curtailment of inheritance, steeply progressive taxes on income and the abolition of regressive taxes on consumption, and, finally, universal free education (CW 7, 3–7). This program was intended to frame the political intervention of the hundreds of members of the Communist League returning to Germany alongside Marx and Engels. Against adventurers who were trying to organize small armies of émigré revolutionaries to return to Germany as liberators literally from without, Marx and Engels envisaged Communist League members returning home to intervene within the real movement from below (Hammen 1969, 201, 214). As part of this movement, Marx headed for Cologne—the center of German industry and home to a strong communist movement—while Engels went home to Barmen in the hope of raising money to support their venture.

Very quickly thereafter it became apparent that the revolutionary movement was not evolving quite as they had expected. On the one hand, as Engels explained in a letter to Marx, the bourgeoisie in Barmen was showing signs of fearing the workers below them more than they desired to overthrow the princes above: "The fact is, after all, that even these radical bourgeois here see us as their future main enemies and have no intention of putting into our hands weapons which we would very shortly turn against themselves" (CW 38, 172). The conclusions Engels drew from this was to suggest watering down the political stance outlined in the *Demands of the Communist Party in Germany* to avoid isolating themselves from the real movement from below: "If even a single copy of our 17 points were to circulate here, all would be lost for us. The mood of the bourgeoisie is really ugly" (CW 38, 173). Conversely, though workers were struggling for reforms, these struggles tended to be for local, sectional interests rather than oriented toward an alliance with the bourgeoisie against absolutism. As Engels subsequently recalled: "strikes, trade unions and producers' co-operatives were set going [by Communist League members—PB] and it was forgotten that above all it was a question of first conquering, by means of political victories, the field in which alone such things could be realised on a lasting basis" (CW 26, 325).

This political weakness was true in Cologne, home to perhaps the strongest workers' movement in Germany, where, according to Hammen, the leadership of the more than five-thousand-strong local Workers' Society, formed prior to Marx's arrival in the city by Communist League members, was skeptical about the hopes for a bourgeois democratic revolution. Rather than join the political struggle against absolutism, they focused their efforts on maintaining the workers' standard of living against the local bourgeoisie. And where they did engage with political issues, they tended to place themselves to the right not merely of Marx and Engels but also of a good deal of the middle classes—by demanding, for instance, a constitutional monarchy rather than a democratic republic.

In April, Marx and Engels took up the cudgels against this abstentionist position and won the league to a position of supporting the petty bourgeois Democratic Association in the forthcoming elections to the Berlin and Frankfurt assemblies—and if this position meant sitting on the seventeen demands for the time being, then so be it (Hammen 1969, 218–219). Within weeks, they went one step further and replaced the local leadership of the Communist League. However, very quickly thereafter the two of them seemed to have concluded that the workers' movement was simply too weak, too fragmented, and too possessed of the old True Socialist mentality of indifference to the conflicts between the bourgeoisie and the nobility to be able to play an active part in mobilizing for the bourgeois revolution. Their response to this situation was to dissolve the Communist League, or at least to suggest its dissolution (the evidence is unclear), to allow its members to merge as individuals within the broader movement (McLellan 2006, 183). In place of the league they hoped that their new daily newspaper, the *Neue Rheinische Zeitung* launched on June 1, 1848, would pick up where the *Rheinische Zeitung* had left off a few years earlier by acting as an organizing focus for the democratic movement from below (Nimtz 2000, 67–72).

Years later Engels remembered the *Neue Rheinische Zeitung*'s project thus: its goal was "[a] single indivisible democratic German Republic, and war with Russia, including the restoration of Poland" (CW 26, 124). Its daily message was equally straightforward. It said to the masses who had made the revolution in March to not trust the middle-class representatives in either the Berlin or Frankfurt assemblies to win the revolution for you: the revolution had been made by the movement from below and it was only the movement from below that could guarantee its final victory. As Engels put it in the first edition of the *Neue Rheinische Zeitung*, the problem with the Frankfurt Assembly was that from the beginning it had failed to *act*. The German people had "won its sovereign status by fighting in the streets of almost all cities and towns of the country, and especially on the barricades of Vienna and Berlin." This movement was where their strength lay. Unfortunately, the "Professors' Parliament" (so-called because of the preponderance of educated men and academics among its members) was replete with the kind of intellectuals who confused fine phrases and constitution mongering with real power, and rather than *leading* the mass movement that had raised them to their existing position they aimed to substitute themselves and their constitution-writing skills for it. So instead of acting to undermine the forces of reaction, they took the princes at their word and assumed the good faith of a class whose parochialism and ruthlessness in defending their petty interests was renowned across Europe (CW 7, 16)!

This is the behavior that Engels famously condemned as "parliamentary cretinism." He did not reject parliamentary activity tout court—indeed, as I noted earlier, he and Marx had clashed with the True Socialist leadership of the Cologne Workers' Society over precisely this issue in April 1848—but rather the reification of this work and in particular the subordination of the mass movement to it. The problem with the approach taken by the assembly members was that it inverted the real relations of power and, in so doing, risked undermining the real movement beyond parliament. Parliamentary cretinism was, or so he argued in his subsequent history of the movement *Germany: Revolution and Counter-Revolution*,

> a disorder which penetrates its unfortunate victims with the solemn conviction that the whole world, its history and future, are governed and determined by a majority of votes in that particular representative body which has the honour to count them among its members, and that all and everything going on outside the walls of their house—wars, revolutions, railway-constructing, colonizing of whole new continents, California gold discoveries, Central American canals, Russian armies, and whatever else may have some little claim to influence upon the destinies of mankind—is nothing compared to the incommensurable events hinging upon the important question, whatever it may be, just at that moment occupying the attention of their honourable House. (CW 11, 79)

Marx and Engels's approach to politics is best understood in sharp contrast to the passivity characteristic of parliamentary cretinism while avoiding the voluntarism of the military adventurers. Their orientation was toward the real movement from below, which they aimed to help become aware both of its own interests and of what it needed to do to realize those interests. In 1848–1849 they did this through the *Neue Rheinische Zeitung*: in the English edition of their *Collected Works*, three volumes (7–9, about two thousand pages) are devoted to their contributions to this newspaper over the year from its launch on June 1, 1848, until its final edition after its suppression the following May.

Beyond consistently challenging the passivity of the Frankfurt and Berlin assemblies, the content of their criticisms evolved over the year. If the launch of the *Neue Rheinische Zeitung* coincided with the decision to dissolve the Communist League into the democratic movement, within a relatively short space of time Marx and Engels began to shift back toward a more proletarian orientation. A pivotal moment in this process came in the late summer and early autumn of 1848 when, first, Prussia was humiliated in a war with Denmark over Schleswig-Holstein, before, second, a full-blooded counterrevolution broke out in Vienna. But first, in June, France's "nice" revolution turned "nasty" (CW 7, 147).

Among the reforms achieved by the February Revolution, the Parisian working class had won the right to work—"national workshops" had been formed to create jobs for all the unemployed. This policy drove a wedge between the workers and the bourgeoisie, and the newly elected parliament almost immediately began to look to how it could be rescinded. The turning point came on May 15 when workers descended on the assembly, demanding war on Prussia and Russia to free Poland. Right-wing elements in the assembly grew in confidence after the demonstrators were dissipated relatively peacefully. The assembly subsequently began to flex its muscles in a process that initially culminated in the decision, made on June 20, to dissolve the national workshops with the instruction that the workers either be drafted into the army or sent to drain marshes in Sologne. On June 23 barricades were once again raised in Paris to defend the workshops. The assembly responded by giving General Cavaignac dictatorial powers. He used methods that the military had learned in Algiers to suppress forty to fifty thousand revolutionaries fighting for "liberty or death." After four days of bitter conflict, fifteen hundred revolutionaries lay dead, with thousands more wounded and twelve thousand taken prisoner—of whom almost five hundred were eventually deported to Algiers (Rapport 2008, 187–211).

Engels's initial response to these events was to declare that they pointed to the question of state power: "with grape-shot . . . *rebellion ceases and revolution begins*" (CW 7, 127). He was also clear which side of the barricades he was on. By contrast with those German liberals who dismissed the revolutionaries as "rogues" at war with "respectable people," he recorded the "heroic courage" of the Parisian workers against the brutality and overwhelming strength of the "barbaric" bourgeoisie—or rather against the "lumpenproletarian" military hired hands who did the bidding of the individually "cowardly" bourgeoisie (CW 7, 152, 164, 161, 142, 140). He also suggested that this revolution replaced romantic "illusions" characteristic of earlier epochs in the class struggle with a more mundane realization that this new struggle "for their existence" forced a cool realism on the Parisian workers who fought under a banner borrowed from the workers of Lyons in 1834: live working or die fighting (CW 7, 130).

Though the bourgeoisie inflicted a brutal counterrevolution on the Parisian workers in June 1848, Marx continued to insist that the form of the state—bourgeois or absolutist—was not a matter of indifference to the working class: "The best form of state is that [bourgeois state—PB] in which the social contradictions are not blurred, not arbitrarily . . . kept down. The best form of state is that in which these contradictions reach a stage of open struggle in the course of which they are resolved" (CW 7, 149). The truth of this claim became increasingly apparent over subsequent months as the defeat of the French workers gave confidence to counterrevolutionaries (including bourgeois counterrevolutionaries) across Germany. This movement came to a head in September over the issue of Schleswig-Holstein: two dukedoms on the border between Germany and Denmark.

Both Schleswig and Holstein were subject to the personal rule of the Danish king, but neither was part of Denmark proper: Holstein was one of the thirty-nine members of the German Confederation with an almost wholly German population, while Schleswig was not a member of the Confederation and had a population that was around a third Danish-speaking. This relationship, which had not been a problem in the old feudal structures, became profoundly problematic with the rise of democratic movements. And as Denmark moved toward a constitutional government the problem came to a head. By liberalizing Schleswig-Holstein from without, the Danes effectively began to integrate these states into the Danish state while simultaneously providing the population with the voice by which they could deny this right. In February 1848 Engels had much fun ridiculing the German "Schleswig-Holsteiners" for "begging" forty million Germans to help them against Danish attempts to forge a draft constitution through which the Danes made "every possible concession to the Germans" whose response was "absurd national obstinacy" (CW 6, 544–545).

Needless to say, Schleswig and Holstein did ask for admission into the German Empire after their own March revolution, and the Frankfurt Assembly granted their wish. Denmark, reckoning on British and Russian support, intervened to maintain its right. The Frankfurt Assembly, with no troops of its own, was forced to ask Prussia to protect Schleswig and Holstein from the Danes. This the Prussians did, though with an obvious lack of enthusiasm. Friedrich Wilhelm IV was not overly keen on acting as the instrument of democracy against a brother king. The war quickly ground to a halt with an armistice signed by Denmark and Prussia at the end of August. Frankfurt was furious and responded on September 5 by refusing to ratify this decision. There then followed a standoff between absolutist Prussia and the bourgeois assembly at the end of which the assembly capitulated—effectively accepting that Prussia's army made it the real decision-making power in the north of Germany.

Marx and Engels, alongside the bulk of German opinion, were furious at this decision. In the few months since the publication of Engels's previous essay on the subject the political context had changed dramatically. Now, as Engels insisted, the war with Denmark was "the first revolutionary war waged by Germany"—though it was a "ridiculous" shamble, a "comedy" war (CW 7, 42–44, 421). What made Engels change his mind about the significance of Schleswig-Holstein? Oscar Hammen's claim that Marx and Engels became at this point "rabidly and belligerently nationalistic" betrays a profound ignorance of their method (Hammen 1969, 289). Yes, Marx and Engels supported war against Denmark, but their reason for doing so was resolutely internationalist. As Engels explained, the events in Schleswig and Holstein could best be understood in relation to the international state system of the day. Denmark was, for the moment, the front line of the counterrevolution—supported by Russian, English, and *German* counterrevolutionaries:

> [W]ho, from the outset, supported Denmark? The three most counter-revolutionary powers in Europe—*Russia*, *England* and the *Prussian Government*. As long as it was possible the Prussian Government merely *pretended* to be waging a *war* . . . Prussia, England and Russia are the three powers which have greater

reason than anyone else to fear the German revolution and its first result—German unity: Prussia because she would thereby cease to exist, England because it would deprive her of the possibility of exploiting the German market, and Russia because it would spell the advance of democracy not only to the Vistula but even as far as the Dvina and the Dnieper. Prussia, England and Russia have conspired against Schleswig-Holstein, against Germany and against the revolution. (CW 7, 424–425)

The call for war was therefore a defense of the project of a unified German republic as a challenge to Prussian militarism specifically and the Europe-wide forces of counterrevolution more generally. Unfortunately, the assembly was unprepared to unleash the one force capable of challenging the Prussian army: the movement from below that had shaken the power of the princes in March.

In the brief period between Frankfurt's refusal to ratify the armistice and its eventual capitulation to Prussian hegemony, the *Neue Rheinische Zeitung* threw its weight behind the assembly—though without fostering any illusions in this group of "cowardly bourgeois" as Engels called them (CW 7, 414). Engels was encouraged that the assembly had at last "passed an energetic resolution" but warned that it would not have the courage to take up the fight against Denmark. Assembly members would rather, he suggested, "place themselves under Prussian servitude than risk a European revolutionary war" (CW 7, 414). Whatever the merits of the assembly members, the tension between Berlin and Frankfurt dramatically raised the revolutionary temperature in September 1848. Marx made the call to arms: "we are facing a decisive struggle . . . if it thus provokes a civil war between Prussia and Germany . . . democrats know what they have to do" (CW 7, 427–428). As it happens, skirmishes between the local population in Cologne and Prussian soldiers led, on September 13, to a mass meeting at which a Committee of Public Safety was created. Both Marx and Engels served on the committee, which was announced the following day by the *Neue Rheinische Zeitung* in an article that reproduced a letter from Engels to the Berlin Assembly in which he wrote that if there was an attempt to dissolve the Frankfurt Assembly, the committee—itself directly elected to represent "the part of the population not represented in the legally instituted authorities"—would call on members "to do their duty and defend their seats even against the force of bayonets" (CW 7, 585, 583). This was fighting talk, though immediately after the creation of the committee, Engels and Marx sensed that in the wake of the mass meeting of the thirteenth there had been an ebb in the movement in Cologne. This meant that committee members became increasingly isolated, and so, while on September 19 *Neue Rheinische Zeitung* reported Engels's letter to the Frankfurt Assembly in which he declared that "[t]he German citizens here assembled hereby declare that if as a result of the resistance of the Prussian Government to the decisions of the National Assembly and the Central Authority a conflict should arise between Prussia and Germany, they will be ready to sacrifice their lives and property on the side of Germany" (CW 7, 587), by the twenty-third Marx and Engels penned a much less combative statement: "the Committee of Public Safety has notified the authorities here that it has undertaken 1) to co-operate in the preservation of peace and 2) to watch over the gains of the revolution" (CW 7, 450).

News that the Frankfurt Assembly had capitulated to Prussia had by this point reached Cologne, as had the reports of the suppression of a revolutionary movement in Frankfurt against this decision. Confronted by crowds who had once again taken to the barricades, the assembly did what reformist politicians have done on innumerable occasions since. To defend their capitulation in the face of ruling-class interest, they called in the ruling-class (Prussian) troops to suppress the popular movement. Unfortunately, by suppressing the movement, they undermined their own social base and the only force capable of resisting the counterrevolution— Prussia was now one step closer to disposing of the assembly itself (CW 11, 53). Similar events across Germany served to confirm the fact that the counterrevolution was on the offensive. Cologne was placed under martial law at the end of September with arrest warrants out for Engels and the editorial board of *Neue Rheinische Zeitung*.

Engels was now on the run: first to Brussels and then to counterrevolutionary Paris from whence, somewhat bizarrely, he decided to walk to Switzerland. Though this decision was probably informed by lack of money, Engels made the best of it and effectively took time out of the revolution to enjoy a walking holiday—detailed in his diary (CW 7, 507–529). He seemed unaware that martial law was quickly lifted in Cologne, and that the *Neue Rheinische Zeitung* had reappeared celebrating the fresh revolutionary advances in Vienna before having to come to terms with yet another defeat: this time very much along lines previously trod in Paris in June. Marx's explanation for the defeat of the revolution in Vienna was clear and to the point: six times he repeated that blame lay at the feet of "the bourgeoisie." But whereas the French bourgeoisie had waited until it had broken down all feudal barriers to its rule before acting as a counterrevolutionary force,

> [t]he bourgeoisie in *Germany* meekly joins the *retinue* of the absolute monarchy and of feudalism before securing even the first conditions of existence necessary for its own civic freedom and its rule. In France it played the part of a tyrant and made its own counter-revolution. In Germany it acts like a slave and carries out the counter-revolution for its own tyrants. In France it won its victory in order to humble the people. In Germany it humbled itself to prevent the victory of the people. History presents no more *shameful and pitiful spectacle* than that of the *German bourgeoisie.* (CW 7, 504)

The counterrevolution in Vienna, coming as it did in the wake of the capitulation of the Frankfurt Assembly to Prussian hegemony, informed an important shift in the attitude of the *Neue Rheinische Zeitung.* Despairing of the role of the bourgeoisie and the petty bourgeoisie in Germany's bourgeois revolution, Marx and Engels reassessed their earlier decision to dissolve the Communist League.

Engels had returned to the fold in January—and in terms that prefigured Orson Welles's famous comment on cuckoo clocks in *The Third Man* he complained to Marx that his "several weeks of sinful living" was catching up with him: "This lazing about in foreign parts, where you can't really do anything and are completely outside the movement, is truly unbearable. I am rapidly coming to the conclusion that detention for questioning in Cologne is better than life in free Switzerland" (CW 38, 185). The immediate context of his return was rampant counterrevolution across Germany led by Prussia and Austria. First revolutionary Vienna had been subdued, then Berlin had given up without a fight—her assembly quickly dismissed by the Prussian king. The most significant counterweight to this counterrevolutionary charge was the Frankfurt Assembly. In March, Austria essentially declared war on the assembly by asserting the old Austrian Empire was an indivisible monarchy. The assembly's response was bizarre. At the end of March, after a year debating, it agreed on a new constitution in which the Prussian king was offered Germany (minus Austria) as his constitutional empire. Not liking the constitutional side of the offer, the king turned it down. The assembly then (April 12) resolved that the new constitution was indeed the law of the land—with or without the king's approval. The die was cast and war quickly declared between Prussia and the assembly that was offering it the throne! It would have been easy for the left to dismiss this conflict as a shambles. But to have done so would have been to confuse form and content: Friedrich Wilhelm IV attacked the farcical constitution from a position that was substantially less democratic. In this context Marx and Engels threw themselves into the struggle to defend the constitutional monarchy against the reality of resurgent absolutism.

Throughout Germany, towns, cities, and regional governments rose to defend the new constitution against Prussian military might. Marx and Engels engaged with this struggle from a revised standpoint. Such was their disillusion with the bourgeoisie and petty bourgeoisie that on April 15 Marx split from the petty bourgeois Democratic Association. Meanwhile Engels joined (May 11–13) the local militia in his home district. Though he was initially appointed inspector of the barricades, he quickly thereafter had his cynicism about the middle classes confirmed when he was politely asked to leave by the local Committee of Public Safety who feared he was too radical—the local petty bourgeoisie was apparently afraid that he "would proclaim a red republic" (CW 9, 448). He returned to Marx in Cologne, where within days the Prussian authorities decided the time was ripe to suppress *Neue Rheinische Zeitung*—its final issue was printed in defiant red on May 18.

Importantly, the *Neue Rheinische Zeitung*'s parting shot combined a radical defense of the idea of the "emancipation of the working class" with a brief comment cautioning the workers of Cologne against allowing themselves to be provoked into revolutionary adventures when the time was not yet ripe: "Finally we warn you against any putsch in Cologne. In the military situation obtaining in Cologne you would be irretrievably lost" (CW 9, 467; cf. Draper 1986, 158, 383–384). Marx and Engels then left Cologne to trek through Germany looking to involve themselves wherever possible in the struggle against Prussian absolutism: first to Frankfurt, followed by Baden and the Palatinate, before being arrested on their way to Bingen. After their release, Marx made his way to Paris where he hoped a new revolution was brewing—though by July he had been expelled from France, from whence he traveled to London and exile.

In the meantime, Engels made his way to Baden where he joined the military resistance to the Prussian onslaught. Engels was appointed adjutant in a force led by Communist League member August Willich (who, after challenging Marx to a duel because of an argument over political perspectives in 1850, subsequently played a role as a well-respected general in the Union army during the American Civil War). Engels explained his role in a letter to Jenny Marx:

> Willich being the only officer who was any good, I joined him and became his adjutant. I was in four engagements, two of them fairly important, particularly the one at Rastatt, and discovered that the much-vaunted bravery under fire is quite the most ordinary quality one can possess. The whistle of bullets is really quite a trivial matter, and though, throughout the campaign, a great deal of cowardice was in evidence, I did not see as many as a dozen men whose conduct was cowardly *in battle*. (CW 38, 203)

7

Learning Lessons from Defeat

Engels wrote his analysis of *The Campaign for the German Imperial Constitution* in the immediate wake of its defeat as he and thousands of
other defeated fighters found their way into exile. He arrived in London
in November 1849 and published his analysis the following year (CW 10,
149–239). In it he argued that the military campaign illuminated German
social reality just as events of June 1848 had done in France. The leadership
of the social movement had been provided by the petty bourgeoisie who,
unfortunately, could not be counted on in times of crisis:

> this class is invariably full of bluster and loud protestations, at
> times even extreme as far as talking goes, as long as it perceives
> no danger; faint-hearted, cautious and calculating as soon as
> the slightest danger approaches; aghast, alarmed and wavering as
> soon as the movement it provoked is seized upon and taken up
> seriously by other classes; treacherous to the whole movement
> for the sake of its petty-bourgeois existence as soon as there
> is any question of a struggle with weapons in hand.

Behind the petty bourgeoisie stood the proletariat and peasantry who
gave the movement "a more defined and energetic character," while the
bourgeoisie proper was even more "irresolute than its English and French
counterparts" (CW 10, 149–151).

Engels argued that the campaign was defeated because of "its own
half-heartedness and its wretched internal state." More to the point, this
halfheartedness revealed the bourgeoisie to be "incapable of ruling."

Consequently, since 1848 the choice for "the civilised part of the European continent has stood thus: either the rule of the revolutionary proletariat or the rule of the classes who ruled before February" (CW 10, 237). Unfortunately, the proletariat, lacking their own independent political voice, responded to the cowardice and vacillations of the local petty bourgeois leadership of the movement with a growing sense of apathy (CW 10, 209). Ironically, the potential power of a more resolute approach was nowhere more evident than in the tactics of the Prussians. On each occasion when the Prussians engaged the troops with whom Engels served, despite having overwhelming numerical superiority and a history of military ruthlessness, they fought a "lukewarm" campaign. Engels explained this anomaly by reference to the Prussians' lack of certainty about the loyalty of their own men (CW 10, 209). Unfortunately, the kind of decisive action with a clear ideological call to the working-class soldiery that could potentially have undermined the Prussian military machine was beyond the comprehension of the middle-class leadership of the revolutionary movement. Such an approach required the kind of action that the *Neue Rheinische Zeitung* was demanding, but which the middle-class leadership of the movement was unable to deliver. Consequently, though the tactics needed to win the campaign were relatively straightforward, there was no organized voice calling for them. So, Engels's criticism became self-criticism (at least implicitly): "Thanks to the dilapidated organisation of the democratic and workers' party, thanks to the indecision and shrewd cautiousness of most of the local leaders who had come from the petty bourgeoisie, and finally thanks to the lack of time," the revolutionaries failed to do the elementary things necessary to win (CW 10, 163). The first point on this list suggests Marx and Engels had been wrong, despite the many limitations of the Communist League at the opening of the revolutionary wave, to dissolve it in the spring of 1848.

This argument was made most forcefully in a statement jointly written with Marx in March 1850: *Address of the Central Authority to the League*, more commonly known as the *March Address*. After celebrating the role played by league members in 1848–1849, the address bemoaned the way they had "allowed their connections with the Central Authority to become loose and gradually dormant." If this was a somewhat disingenuous statement given that the Central Authority had (probably) suggested dissolving the league into the mass movement, the movement was young, the error had at least been recognized, and a solution was suggested: "An end must be put to this state of affairs, the independence of the workers must be restored." This shift was imperative because "a new revolution is impending, when the workers' party, therefore, must act in the most organised, most unanimous and most independent fashion possible if it is not again to be exploited and taken in tow by the bourgeoisie as in 1848." Indeed, Marx and Engels insisted that any attempt at unity with the democratic petty bourgeoisie must inevitably end in "disadvantage" to the proletariat. The stress throughout the document was clear. Marx and Engels expected a revival of the revolutionary movement and insisted that the workers must have their own independent organization, through which they must participate in all forms of political agitation—including elections on the one hand and military conflict on the other. Independent working-class action with ballots and bullets was their message with an orientation to realizing their own class interests through a "Revolution in Permanence"—the struggle against absolutism would "through a lengthy revolutionary development" morph into a struggle against capitalism (CW 10, 277–287). A few months later, in the *June Address*, Marx and Engels once again reiterated the gap between "the need for a strong secret organisation of the revolutionary party throughout Germany" and the fact that "the defeats of the revolutionary party last summer brought for a moment the League to the point of almost total disorganisation" (CW 10, 371).

This argument should not be interpreted as implying that Marx and Engels had flip-flopped from dissolving the party into the social movement to embracing a form of Blanquism. For just a couple of months earlier they clearly argued that "a true revolution is the exact opposite of the ideas of a *mouchard* [police spy—PB] who like the 'men of action' sees in every revolution the work of a small coterie." Against the "alchemists of revolution" who confused revolutions with insurrectionary putsches by minorities, Marx and Engels insisted that, "[t]o the extent that the Paris proletariat came to the fore itself as a party, these conspirators lost some of their dominant influence, they were dispersed and they encountered dangerous competition in proletarian secret societies, whose purpose was not immediate insurrection but the organisation and development of the proletariat" (CW 10, 311–325; cf. Draper 1986, 158, 383–384). This last point suggests a fundamentally important distinction between (Marxist) revolutionary conspiracies *of* the working class and a Blanquist (or similar) conspiracy *for* the working class. Because Marx and Engels's proposal in the *June Address* was clearly in favor of the former rather than the latter, their model of revolution cannot be reduced to a form of insurrectionary putschism (Draper 1986).

The revolutionary optimism underpinning the urgency of these demands to rebuild the league was evident as late as July of that year (CW 10, 395). However, very quickly thereafter Marx and Engels made a fundamental revision of their perspective. In a joint review written sometime between May and October 1850 but not published until 1895, when Engels integrated it into a revised version of Marx's *The Class Struggles in France*, they argued that economic expansion meant that the revolutionary wave was, for the time being, over. Consequently, the work necessary for the revolution would have a different character. The party needed to be intellectually rearmed and this long-term project would include a critical evaluation of the events of the previous two years:

> With this general prosperity, in which the productive forces of bourgeois society develop as luxuriantly as is at all possible within bourgeois relationships, there can be no talk of a real revolution. Such a revolution is only possible in the periods when *both these factors*, the *modern* productive *forces* and the *bourgeois forms of production*, come *in collision* with each other. . . . *A new revolution is possible only in consequence of a new crisis. It is, however, just as certain as this crisis.* (CW 10, 510, 135)

This new perspective placed Marx and Engels at odds with other members of the Communist League. In so doing it helps make sense of the urgency with which they penned detailed analyses of the 1848 and 1525 revolutions over the next few months. The leadership of the Communist League met in London in September 1850 with a view to reorienting the movement in the wake of its defeat. The meeting occasioned a split and Marx and Engels's effective retreat from active politics for the next decade or so. Peter Röser, a Communist League member in Cologne writing while serving a prison sentence for his part in the revolution, noted of the September conference that Willich and others including Karl Schapper had violently disagreed with Marx's assessment of the new conjuncture, insisting that "come the next revolution, he and his brave men from the Palatinate would introduce communism on their own and against the will of everyone in Germany" (CW 38, 551). It was against this kind of political voluntarism, which substituted the actions of a few brave men for the real movement of the proletariat, that Marx and Engels bent the stick in the direction of insisting on the objective material basis for revolution:

The materialist standpoint of the *Manifesto* has given way to idealism. The revolution is seen not as the product of realities of the situation but as the result of an effort of *will*. Whereas we say to the workers: You have 15, 20, 50 years of civil war to go through in order to alter the situation and to train yourselves for the exercise of power, it is said: We must take power *at once*, or else we may as well take to our beds. Just as the democrats abused the word "people" so now the word "proletariat" has been used as a mere phrase. (CW 10, 626)

Marx and Engels deployed the framework developed in *The German Ideology* and outlined in *The Communist Manifesto* to militate against pseudo-revolutionary posturing. Similarly, the historical studies they went on to write were intended to illuminate the deep material roots of revolutionary movements. To this end, while Engels's *The Peasant War in Germany* nominally functioned as an inspirational study of Thomas Müntzer and the struggle of the Anabaptists in Germany in 1525—he wanted to show that Germany had its own revolutionary heroes—it was also the first application of his and Marx's new approach to the study of history. And whereas the architect of supposedly objective history Leopold von Ranke had explained the peasant rising of 1525 mystically as a "convulsion of nature," Engels treated all the principal characters as rational agents whose behavior could best be understood through an in-depth analysis of contradictory material interests rooted in contemporary social relations (Wolf 1987, 83–85; Perry 2002, 53).

Engels did not apologize that this book was not an original study—he borrowed the detail of the historical narrative from Wilhelm Zimmerman's *The History of the Great Peasant War* (1841–1843). What he did add, as he wrote in the 1870 preface, was a method for bringing the disparate elements of the narrative together into a unified whole:

My presentation, while sketching the historical course of the struggle only in its bare outlines, attempted to explain the origin of the Peasant War, the position of the various parties that played a part in it, the political and religious theories by which those parties sought to clarify their position in their own minds, and finally the result of the struggle itself as following logically from the historically established social conditions of life of these classes; that is to say, it attempted to demonstrate the political structure of Germany at that time, the revolts against it, and the contemporary political and religious theories not as causes but as results of the stage of development of agriculture, industry, roads and waterways, commerce in commodities and money then obtaining in Germany. (CW 21, 94)

Or as he put it in 1850:

> Even the so-called religious wars of the sixteenth century mainly concerned very positive material class interests; those wars were class wars, too, just as the later internal collisions in England and France. Although the class struggles of those days were clothed in religious shibboleths, and though the interests, requirements, and demands of the various classes were concealed behind a religious screen, this changed nothing at all and is easily explained by the conditions of the times. (CW 10, 412)

Engels's intention therefore was to grasp the underlying essence of the revolutionary movement beneath its surface appearance.

In *The Peasant War in Germany* Engels powerfully expressed his and Marx's critique of political voluntarism. The best that the revolutionaries could have achieved in 1525 was to take power at a moment when social development was not yet ripe enough to realize their goals. The consequences would have been tragic:

> The worst thing that can befall the leader of an extreme party is to be compelled to assume power at a time when the movement is not yet ripe for the domination of the class he represents and for the measures this domination implies. What he *can* do depends not on his will but on the degree of antagonism between the various classes, and on the level of development of the material means of existence, of the conditions of production and commerce upon which the degree of intensity of the class contradictions always reposes. What he *ought* to do, what his party demands of him, again depends not on him, but also not on the degree of development of the class struggle and its conditions. He is bound to the doctrines and demands hitherto propounded which, again, do not follow

from the class relations of the moment, or from the more or less accidental level of production and commerce, but from his more or less penetrating insight into the general result of the social and political movement. Thus, he necessarily finds himself in an unsolvable dilemma. What he *can* do contradicts all his previous actions and principles and the immediate interests of his party, and what he *ought* to do cannot be done. In a word, he is compelled to represent not his party or his class, but the class for whose domination the movement is then ripe. In the interests of the movement he is compelled to advance the interests of an alien class, and to feed his own class with talk and promises, and with the asseveration that the interests of that alien class are their own interests. He who is put into this awkward position is irrevocably lost. (CW 10, 469–470; CW 39, 308–309; cf. Marx's similar comments CW 10, 629)

This is Engels's explanation of the social basis for historical tragedy. Caught in an insoluble contradiction between means and ends, such an agent would be doomed to failure. Clearly, this materialist argument was no mere academic point about Müntzer's place in history: it was intended to underpin his and Marx's parallel political critique of putschism.

Engels's approach to the study of history at this moment has been read in diametrically opposed ways. Stephen Rigby has suggested, citing a letter to Marx dated February 13, 1851, in which Engels argued that revolutions should be understood as "a purely natural phenomenon" (CW 38, 290), that Engels presented "history as a process apart from human agency." Conversely, Tristram Hunt has insisted that the hymn of praise to Müntzer recorded in *The Peasant War in Germany* is evidence of a retreat from Marxism toward a "Carlylean great man" approach to history (Rigby 1992, 82; Hunt 2009, 215). The reality of Engels's approach escapes both these interpretations, or rather they each reflect one side of his dialectical method to understanding the relationship between structure and agency in history. As Engels wrote some four decades later, recalling the words of Marx's *Eighteenth Brumaire*, in 1894: "men make their own history, but in a given environment by which they are conditioned, and on the basis of extant and actual relations of which economic relations, no matter how much they may be influenced by others of a political and ideological nature, are ultimately the determining factor and represent the unbroken clue which alone can lead to comprehension" (CW 50, 266). To stress that revolutions have deep causes is not an alternative to exploring the role of agency within them but rather is the necessary prerequisite to such an investigation (CW 10, 357). For instance, his own study of the events of 1848, *Germany: Revolution and Counter-Revolution* (1851)—initially published under Marx's name—opened with an attempt to frame his and Marx's political activity against the background of deeper causes:

> If, then, we have been beaten, we have nothing else to do but to begin again from the beginning. And, fortunately, the probably very short interval of rest which is allowed us between the close of the first and the beginning of the second act of the movement, gives us time for a very necessary piece of work: the study of the causes that necessitated both the late outbreak, and its defeat; causes that are not to be sought for in the accidental efforts, talents, faults, errors or treacheries of some of the leaders, but in the general social state and conditions of existence of each of the convulsed nations. (CW 11, 6)

Engels's comment about revolutions being purely natural phenomena was written in an exchange with Marx in which they vented about the men Marx called "les petits grands hommes" of the émigré milieu in London whose voluntaristic plotting had become "tiresome" (CW 38, 285). Far from embracing a form of political fatalism, Engels went on to suggest that by shifting the emphasis of their work from interventionist journalism to writing more substantial theoretical works, they would, in the period of prosperity, help position themselves to better influence the coming revolution once the present period of prosperity came to an end (Nimtz 2000, 151–155). Contra Rigby, Engels in this passage was not dismissing human agency but rather repositioning his and Marx's role in radically changed circumstances.

This activist interpretation of Engels's argument is much better able than Rigby's charge of fatalism to explain Engels's near simultaneous analysis of the role of human agency in insurrections as a pivotal moment in the revolutionary process. Though he stressed the material basis for the revolution, he was equally clear that insurrections were won and lost by real historical actors:

> Now, insurrection is an art quite as much as war or any other, and subject to certain rules of proceeding, which, when

neglected, will produce the ruin of the party neglecting them. Those rules, logical deductions from the nature of the parties and the circumstances one has to deal with in such a case, are so plain and simple that the short experience of 1848 had made the Germans pretty well acquainted with them. Firstly, never play with insurrection unless you are fully prepared to face the consequences of your play. Insurrection is a calculus with very indefinite magnitudes, the value of which may change every day; the forces opposed to you have all the advantage of organization, discipline and habitual authority; unless you bring strong odds against them, you are defeated and ruined. Secondly, the insurrectionary career once entered upon, act with the greatest determination, and on the offensive. The defensive is the death of every armed rising; it is lost before it measures itself with its enemies . . . in the words of Danton, the greatest master of revolutionary policy yet known: *de l'audace, de l'audace, encore de l'audace!* (CW 11, 85–86)

These lines, which famously influenced Lenin (Lenin 1964, 180), were written in his history of the 1848–1849 revolution in Germany and intended both as a warning against trusting the petty bourgeoisie who showed no evidence of the audacity needed to win and as a general suggestion of what was required of a workers' party in such a situation, are clear evidence of Engels's continued allegiance to the "practical materialism" outlined in *The German Ideology*.

The practical focus of Engels's theoretical work is evident even at the moment of extreme isolation. Within months of the break with the Schapper-Willich tendency, he and Marx had the exchange of letters in which he made the claim, noted earlier, about revolutions being purely natural phenomena. The context of this claim is worth revisiting because it illuminates the coordinates of the important shift in his and Marx's political orientation in the wake of the defeat of the revolutions of 1848. The actual outcome of the September 1850 Communist League meeting at which they had clashed with Schapper and Willich was a compromise. Marx suggested relocating the leadership of the league from London to Cologne (where he rightly guessed that his opponents' fanciful schemes would be ignored by activists on the ground) while splitting the London branch in two to allow his and their groups to coexist separately but together.

By February Marx discovered that it was his opponents who were making headway within the movement—Louis Blanc and George Harney were working with the Schapper-Willich faction at a meeting to which he and Engels had not been invited. Beneath the surface of his sulky response to news of this event, Marx pointed to the future orientation of his work: "I am greatly pleased by the public, authentic isolation in which we two, you and I, now find ourselves. It is wholly in accord with our attitude and our principles. The system of mutual concessions, half-measures tolerated for decency's sake, and the obligation to bear one's share of public ridicule in the party along with all these jackasses, all this is now over" (CW 38, 286). Engels's reply, in which he made the comment about revolutions being natural phenomena, was equally illuminating. As I previously suggested, he looked for the silver lining behind every cloud:

> At long last we again have the opportunity to show that we need neither popularity, nor the SUPPORT of any party in any country, and that our position is completely independent of such ludicrous trifles. . . . We can always, in the nature of things, be more revolutionary than the phrase-mongers because we have learnt our lesson and they have not. . . . The main thing at the moment is to find some way of getting our things published. . . . What price all the tittle-tattle the entire émigré crowd can muster against you, when you answer it with your political economy? (CW 38, 289–291)

This was a period for learning lessons from the struggle, and for deepening and extending their own perspective. Among the lessons they had learned over the previous few years, the key ones were the counterrevolutionary nature of the bourgeoisie, the spinelessness of the petty bourgeois democrats, and the consequent necessity of maintaining the political independence of the workers' party. Beyond this, they never wavered in their belief that the form of the state was important. Against True Socialist disdain for the bourgeois revolution, Marx and Engels always insisted that in the struggle for socialism it was important to register, fight for, and defend more progressive political forms against absolutism and the like. To struggle thus required, in the first instance, recognizing the difference in these forms. If the theory of history they articulated in *The German Ideology* provided them with the tools to make sense of these differences, it also framed their critique of the voluntarism of their opponents within the Communist League in 1850 through an understanding of the role of underlying causal factors in history.

Beyond these general points, they required a more specific account of the underlying tendencies toward revolution characteristic of capitalism. If Marx's forthcoming study of capitalism was, as Engels hoped in 1851, to provide the key to illuminating this process, Engels also played a part in excavating these dynamics through his studies, for instance, of the historical specificity of the state, women's oppression, and the housing question, among others. These insights all assumed the method of inquiry outlined in *The German Ideology*. Unfortunately, this book arguably "had never really existed" and certainly did not exist as a published text in the nineteenth century (Kellerhoff qtd. in Carver and Blank 2014, 1). Marx did once suggest to Engels that he "should very much like to write 2 or 3 sheets making accessible to the common reader the rational aspect of the method which Hegel not only discovered but also mystified" but famously failed to deliver on this promise (CW 40, 249). In lieu of Marx's essay, generations of socialists learned Marx's method through the lens of Engels's polemic against the momentarily influential Eugen Dühring: *Anti-Dühring*. As we shall see, this book became simultaneously both one of the most influential and most controversial texts in the history of the socialist movement.

Anti-Dühring was a long way in the future in 1851. At that moment, the key problem faced by the left was to make sense of the defeat not as a momentary ebb in the revolutionary wave but an important turning point in the class struggle predicated upon the shift toward economic prosperity. Beyond these changed circumstances, the most obvious problem pressing on Engels's mind—other than accepting the soul-destroying requirement that he would have to work for the family firm in Manchester (Engels insisted on having his salary paid from Germany rather than Manchester so as to allow him the free time to research and write [Mayer 1936, 131])—was of how, if at all, it might have been possible for the forces of revolution to defeat Austria and Prussia in 1849. As Engels recognized, it was going to take a lot more than revolutionary enthusiasm to overcome a modern, disciplined military machine.

8

Military Critic

Confronting the Prospect of War

Engels's critics have been inclined to skirt over his military writings. If this tendency has its roots, in part, in a slight embarrassment about the subject matter among the kind of antiwar leftists who overwhelmingly engaged with his work in the twentieth century, this reticence has been reinforced by a sense of the seeming lack of "Marxist" theoretical architecture to these writings. Whether that be the Hegelian concept of nonhistoric peoples noted earlier, or his more mundane technical essays on military history, Trotsky's interest in these works put him very much in a minority (Trotsky 1971, 134–147). This reticence about engaging with Engels as a military critic has been complemented by a tendency to assume that he and Marx held politically dubious positions on numerous nineteenth-century wars. These criticisms are unfounded. Engels's engagement with military literature emerged as a political response to the fundamental unity of war and revolution in the nineteenth century. If his analysis of the relationship between these two processes subsequently evolved as he and Marx became cognizant of a changing social reality, these changes made the problem of the relationship between war and revolution, if anything, all the more pressing.

Engels's interest in military matters can be traced back to a childhood predilection, but the substance of his studies became much more serious and much more urgent as he attempted, first, to intervene in the events of 1848 and, second, to assess this intervention in the immediate aftermath of defeat. As Trotsky wrote, "Engels regarded the question of the conquest of power by the proletariat as a purely practical question, whose solution depended not least of all upon war problems" (Trotsky 1971, 147; Haupt 1986, 136–137). In *Germany: Revolution and Counter-Revolution* (1851–1852) he wrote that events in Paris confirmed that "the invincibility of a popular insurrection in a large town had been proved to be a delusion. . . . The army again was the decisive power in the State" (CW 11, 51–52). This situation demanded serious consideration. In June 1851 he wrote to Joseph Weydemeyer (an ex-officer in the Prussian army who had become a "Marxist" in 1845–1846, led the Communist League in Frankfurt in 1848, and subsequently served as a lieutenant colonel in the Union army during the American Civil War), asking for a systematic reading list on military theory so he might avoid the problems of autodidacticism:

> Since arriving in Manchester I have been swotting up mil-
> itary affairs . . . I was prompted to do this by the immense
> importance which must attach to the *partie militaire* in the next
> movement, combined with a long-standing inclination on my
> part, my articles on the Hungarian campaign in the days of
> the newspaper and finally my glorious exploits in Baden, and
> I would like to take it at least far enough to be able to join
> in theoretical discussion without making too much of a fool
> of myself. (CW 38, 370; cf. Berger 1977, 39)

Needless to say, Engels did avoid making a fool of himself. Indeed, nothing could be further from the truth than Edmund Silberner's comments that Marx and Engels's military writings lacked theoretical depth (Silberner 1946, 250). W. B. Gallie's assessment of Engels's prowess as a military thinker is much more apt. Gallie writes that Engels "turned himself into probably the most perceptive military critic of the nineteenth century" (Gallie 1978, 68). Similarly, Sigmund Neumann writes that what was once said of Clausewitz could easily be repeated of Engels: "He is a genius in criticism. His judgements are as clear and weighty as gold. He shows how greatness in strategic thought consists in simplicity" (Neumann and von Hagen 1986, 265). For his part, Martin Berger waggishly comments that "in a history of the nineteenth century compiled by a truly single-minded military buff, Marx would figure only as Engels's research assistant" (Berger 1977, 50). More to the point, Engels's writings on military issues are no mere idiosyncrasy. As Martin Kitchen writes, Engels's contribution to the field marks "a serious and often illuminating attempt by a dedicated socialist to grapple with a major problem which has yet to be answered" (Kitchen 1977, 123).

The problem Engels confronted in his military writings was how human liberation might be won against capitalism as a concrete totality fixed through ideological, legal, and most importantly military power. This problem cannot be understood, contra Raphael Cohen-Almagor, in terms of Engels's opinions, for or against, violence as an abstract "sacred" category but rather demands a theoretically informed confrontation with the practicalities of revolutionary politics (Cohen-Almagor 1991, 3). And if the practical bent of Engels's work in this field lent itself to journalistic presentation of his ideas, it is simply untrue, contra George Neimanis, that his works do not "seem to rise above the level of very competent journalism" (Neimanis 1980, 31). In fact, there is a clear unity between his theoretical and journalistic studies relating to revolution as a concrete historical problem. Unfortunately, this unified theory has seldom been effectively interrogated by Engels's interlocutors. In fact, while Engels's work continues to command attention in textbook histories of military strategy (Freedman 2013, 247–264), Gallie's complaint that the implications of his military writings have not adequately been integrated into a Marxist theory of revolution remains as true today as it was when he first made this point in the 1970s (Gallie 1978, 67).

Martin Berger has penned the most detailed attempt to remedy this gap in the literature on Engels. Regrettably, his study somewhat misses its target. He argues that the tendency among twentieth-century Marxists to disregard the military dimension of Marx's and Engels's work can be explained by the fact that "the solutions [they] devised lacked continuity, intellectual symmetry, and success" (Berger 1978, 12). As we shall see, the evidence does not support this claim. It is far more reasonable to suppose that the main reason why subsequent Marxists have been reluctant to engage with this aspect of his oeuvre is their belief that with the rise of what Bukharin, Hilferding, Lenin, and Luxemburg called imperialism at the turn of the last century there had been a radical transformation of the European and world theaters after Engels's death. Consequently, twentieth-century Marxists came to view the geopolitical conflicts about which Engels and Marx had written to be of purely historical interest. It is easy to see how this belief, when read alongside a tendency toward embarrassment felt by many subsequent Marxists about his and Marx's seeming support for German militarism and their deployment of the language of "nonhistoric peoples," informed an uneasy reticence to engage with his military writings.

Though understandable, this tendency to skirt over Engels's military writings lends itself to a one-sided account of Marxist political theory. For Marx and Engels, revolution could not be reduced to a simple clash of social classes but operated at numerous levels, including the military: as Engels famously wrote, the class struggle had to be fought at "the theoretical, the political and the economico-practical" levels (CW 23, 631). And the defeat of the revolutionary-military struggle against Prussian absolutism in 1848–1849 informed their strong conviction that the future success of the workers' movement demanded socialists develop a workable strategy for confronting and overcoming the military power of the state. Seen in this light, Engels's military writings form an integral part of his (and Marx's) broader social and political theory (Draper 2005; Achcar 2002; Semmel 1981; Berger 1978; Freedman 2013; Neuman and von Hagen 1986).

The tendency to downplay the military dimension of Engels's work is doubly unfortunate because Engels's military writings indicate an acute understanding of the relationship between the class struggle and contemporary geopolitics while simultaneously evidencing a deep command of military history and theory. His keen awareness of the international dimension of the social revolution meant that he was the first to provide an "astonishingly acute" prediction of the general contours of the First World War (Kitchen 1977, 122) and to frame socialist politics as a necessary bulwark against the drift to this oncoming barbarism. Although Engels ultimately failed to provide an adequate answer to the question of what the left should do about the oncoming war, his discussion of this problem remains a rich source of insight on the relationship between class politics and nationalism in the nineteenth century, and his contribution to Marxist revolutionary strategy repays rereading because of the way he framed social issues within a geopolitical context.

While it was the Magyar struggles against Austria that originally pushed Engels to seriously engage with the literature on the relationship between war and revolution (Semmel 1981, 6), his researches into military matters soon put him in a position where what he wrote was read at the highest level. Among his earliest forays into military matters in the postrevolutionary period were his writings on the Crimean War. Here he evidenced a keen awareness not merely of the detail of military affairs and their geopolitical context but also of the relationship between geopolitical conflicts and the class struggle. While assessing the war in relation to Europe's five powers, he insisted that

> there is a sixth power in Europe, which at given moments asserts its supremacy over the whole of the five so-called "Great" Powers and makes them tremble, every one of them. That power is the Revolution. Long silent and retired. . . . Manifold are the symptoms of its returning life. . . . A signal only is wanted. . . . This signal the impending European war will give, and then all calculations as to the balance of power will be upset by the addition of a new element. (CW 12, 557)

If Engels believed that the class struggle could thus upset even the best-laid military plans, he also insisted on the importance of the political and moral dimensions within war. Though Wellington had died prior to the outbreak of the Crimean War, Engels laid blame for the British army's incompetence squarely at his feet. Wellington's "narrow minded . . . mediocrity" throughout the previous four decades of his command ensured the utter unpreparedness of the British forces for the war (CW 13, 208–214).

Engels's keen eye on the importance of leadership was similarly evidenced in his letters on the American Civil War. Against claims that he embraced a mechanically materialistic and politically fatalistic conception of history, these letters show that he was much more alert than Marx (perhaps too alert) to the importance of the political dimension of history (Maguire 1978, 123). Whereas Marx believed that the North's victory in the Civil War was largely assured by its superior economic strength, Engels initially insisted that the superior leadership and greater determination shown by the Southern forces in the early period of the war might well lead to their eventual triumph (CW 41, 386–388; Hunley 1991, 21, 142; Freedman 2013, 262; Henderson 1976, 2: 435; Blackburn 2011, 38, 194–198). It was only in the wake of, first, the Emancipation Proclamation and, second, the increased prominence given to General Grant in the Union army that he allowed himself to become more optimistic about a Northern victory (Blackburn 2011, 194–198; Mayer 1936, 167; Henderson 1976, 2: 435).

Perhaps more interesting than these letters are his published comments on the sociopolitical limitations of the contending forces in the Franco-Prussian War. While covering the conflict as a military correspondent for the *Pall Mall Gazette* (a forerunner of today's *Evening Standard*), Engels argued that the limitations of the French forces could best be understood not in terms of the level of development of the French economy but rather against the backdrop of the politics of the Second Empire. After declaring war, the French failed to act decisively. Though this decision was inexplicable in purely military terms, especially as the conflict had long been expected and prepared for, Engels suggested that the delay was rooted in the corrupt nature of French politics: "It will be said, we fear, that so far the army of the Second Empire has been beaten by the Second Empire itself. Under a régime which has to yield bounties to its supporters by all the old regular established means of jobbery, it cannot be expected that the system will stop at the intendance of the army" (CW 22, 23, 28, 158–159). Interestingly, Engels claimed that at the time of the Italian War in 1859 the French had proved themselves the best military force in Europe. However, by

> 1870 the French army was no longer that of 1859. The pec-
> ulation, jobbery, and general misuse of public duty for private
> interest which formed the essential base of the system of the
> Second Empire, had seized the army . . . then the demoraliza-
> tion spread to the regimental officers. We are far from saying
> that peculation at the public expense became common among
> them; but contempt for their superiors, neglect of duty, and
> decay of discipline were the necessary consequences. . . . The
> whole thing had become rotten; the atmosphere of corruption
> in which the Second Empire lived had at last taken effect
> upon the main prop of that Empire, the army. (CW 22, 98–99,
> 116, 156)

Engels went on to argue that the French military was undermined not merely by a rotten political system but also by the polarization of domestic class relations. He explained General Trochu's poor leadership in a way that reverberates with accounts of the French actions in 1940: he was a conservative who was more afraid of the Parisian working class than he was of Prussian victory (CW 22, 240–241).

Conversely, though the Prussians were much better organized and led than the French, their forces too suffered from class-based limitations. If the strengths of the Prussian military system stemmed from its desire to train the whole male population for military service in an ongoing process that would maintain a relatively small regular force with massive reserves, this aim was severely undermined by the nature of Prussian absolutism. To maintain class rule at home, a much larger regular force was needed while fewer than the full potential of young men were brought into the Landwehr. The resulting military structure was a compromise that though weaker than the country's potential was nonetheless stronger than its French counterpart (CW 22, 104–105).

Not that Engels held to the reductive claim that a comparative sociological analysis of the material balance of forces could predict success or failure in advance of military engagement. Martin Kitchen is right to point out that, notwithstanding his materialist method and the care with which he applied it, Engels refused to reduce the theory of war "to abstract 'objective' principles" (Kitchen 1977, 119). Indeed, Engels insisted that the efficacy of particular tactics could only be judged on the basis of "practical experience," and in any event the morale of the contending forces could be decisive (CW 22, 172, 242).

If these arguments illuminate the profound problems associated with attempts to reduce Engels's Marxism to a variant of mechanical materialism and political fatalism, they also highlight the importance of an understanding of military power to his and Marx's theory of revolution. From the outset, as Neumann and von Hagen point out, Marx and Engels "raised the question of social change in their time beyond the insurrectionary stage of the isolated Putsch to the plane of world politics. War and Revolution . . . were at that early period seen in their fundamental and continuous interrelationship by these still obscure theorists of world revolution" (Neumann and von Hagen 1986, 264).

Among the most important of Engels's military writings is his seminal pamphlet: *Po and Rhine*. Occasioned by the threat of war between Austria and France over Austria's Italian possessions in 1859, Engels's work was peculiar in that it was aimed neither at a working-class nor a socialist audience. It is also the source of a myth, repeated even by Perry Anderson, among others, that he "virtually sid[ed] with Austrian reaction in the Peninsula" (Anderson 1992, 106). Engels did no such thing. In fact, the pamphlet was written with Marx's agreement, and Marx praised him for the intelligence with which he introduced political matters into technical military discussion. He wrote that the pamphlet was "EXCEEDINGLY CLEVER," including "the political side," which was "splendidly done and that was damned difficult" (CW 17, 114, 40, 400). Marx also agreed that the pamphlet "must first appear *anonymously* so that the public believes the author to be an eminent general. In the *second* edition . . . you will reveal your identity . . . and then it will be a triumph for our party" (CW 40, 393). Visiting Germany two years later, Marx reported to Engels that his pamphlet had been read in the highest military circles both in Berlin and Vienna where it was widely assumed to have been the work of a Prussian general, probably von Pfuel (CW 41, 280). The positive reception of this pamphlet was doubly important. Though it was framed as a neutral work of military science, Engels's conclusions supported the internationalist critique of contemporary German (and French) foreign policy—as it happens it also predicted the Schlieffen plan of 1914, including dismissing the idea of Belgian neutrality as nothing more than a "sheet of paper," while von Schlieffen himself was still only a teenager (CW 16, 213–255)!

At its core, Engels's pamphlet operated as a critique of the widespread assumption within the German military that the Rhine should be defended on the Po. That is, Germany's (meaning greater Germany's, including Austria's) western flank on the River Rhine should be defended across its "natural" southern flank on the River Po in northern Italy. Challenging this argument on its own terms, Engels showed not merely that it made no sense but also that, if generalized, it implied that France had an equally "natural" right to all the lands west of the Rhine. So, far from guaranteeing German security, this argument served to justify French aggression. And it did so by reproducing the oppression of Italy by Austria and thus Italian hatred of Germans. Even in its own terms, this made no sense from a military point of view because, whereas a free Italy could become an ally against France for whom an independent Italy was anathema, Italy oppressed by Austria would become an ally of France. Consequently, defending the Rhine on the Po played into the hands of France without gaining any significant military advantage. The one thing that could help safeguard German interests, by contrast, was national unity—both for Germany and Italy. However, Prussia was against the former for its own parochial reasons—it was for a lesser Germany without Austria in order to guarantee its own hegemony within the new state (Draper 2005, 102)—while Austria was against the latter for equally parochial dynastic reasons—it wanted to maintain its claims in Italy.

The only way that Engels's argument could be mistaken for a piece of pro-Austrian propaganda was on the basis of some version of the George W. Bush doctrine: "Either you are with us, or you are with the terrorists." Interestingly, this is precisely how Ferdinand Lassalle framed his critique of Marx and Engels's position on the war. Lassalle, a participant in the 1848 revolution who had retreated from active politics in the 1850s before forming one of the first German workers' parties in the 1860s, asserted that Marx and Engels must be supporters of Austria because this perspective was the only German alternative to Prussia that he could envision. As Draper points out, academics who would not otherwise take Lassalle's criticisms of Marx and Engels seriously tend blindly to follow his argument on this issue (Draper 2005, 105–109). The reality was very different. Engels was a stern critic of French aggression, and though he and Marx did believe that Napoleon III was a warmonger, they were equally critical of Austria's oppression of Italy and Prussia's desire to create a lesser Germany as its own "barracks." Theirs was an independent working-class perspective, and that is why they were so eager to have it published in the form of an apparently dispassionate essay. They wagered that it would subvert the police state by creating a space for their arguments to move into the mainstream.

As it happens, Austrian policy did push the Italians into the arms of France, though once France defeated the Hapsburg state in the war of 1859 the French immediately annexed Savoy and Nice. Engels engaged with this new situation in *Savoy, Nice and the Rhine*, in which he argued that beneath the largely unfounded rhetoric about the essential French-ness of these regions lay an offensive military strategy that pressed French hegemony against both Italy and Switzerland. Besides, the French policy of occupying land up to its so-called "natural" borders had as its logi-cal conclusion a challenge to Germany on the Rhine. Commenting on Russian support for France during the conflict, he argued that the war risked reproducing the kind of fragmented Germany (and Italy) that had been enshrined in the Treaty of Vienna and against which struggles for national unity had been fought in 1848. The struggle for a unified German republic therefore implied standing up to French (and Russian) aggression toward Germany, Italy, and Switzerland; Austrian oppression of Italy; and Prussia's cynical opposition to Austria (CW 16, 569–610).

Engels navigated this complex terrain admirably. This perspective also set him up as a critic of the forthcoming unification of lesser Germany under Prussian hegemony. If Prussia's tacit support for France against Austria in 1859 was the first step in this process—because Austria was humiliated in this war it was weakened within Germany vis-à-vis Prus-sia—the next step was Bismarck's decision to go to war with Denmark over Schleswig-Holstein. After having France neutralize Britain and Russia, Denmark's erstwhile protectors, he bounced Austria into supporting his campaign against the Danes in 1864. A quick victory for Prussia and Austria produced an unstable outcome in which Prussia controlled Schleswig while Austria controlled Holstein. Quickly thereafter, Bismarck used a dispute over the position of Holstein as a pretext for war with Austria in 1866—which Prussia won, creating the basis for a unified lesser Germany under Prussian domination. The process of unification of non-Austrian Germany (also excluding Luxembourg and Liechtenstein) was ultimately realized through the Franco-Prussian War of 1870.

Engels's response to these developments included engagements with the military, theoretical, and political aspects of the question. His analysis opened with the publication of a powerful strategic document, *The Prussian Military Question and the German Workers' Party* (1865), and included an unfinished theoretical appraisal of Bismarck's Blood and Iron policy: *The Role of Force in History* (1887–1888). These works were intended to frame an independent working-class political perspective on war, an analysis of the social content of the newly unified Germany, and the prospects of a future European (world) war. They also illuminate a moment of transition in Engels's (and Marx's) thinking about war. Specifically, the Franco-Prussian War of 1870 marked a turning point in their appraisal of the threat of war in Europe. Whereas they had previously framed their analyses of the relationship between war and revolution against the backdrop of events in France in 1793 when war and revolution were two sides of the same coin—in 1793 the Committee of Public Safety enacted the *Levée en masse* through which was created a mass revolutionary army that defended the Revolution against Europe's various reactionary powers—after 1870 they came to the conclusion that war had to be avoided at all costs because it was a terrible impending catastrophe, and rather than complementing revolution, war had become a dire threat to the left (Draper 2005, 159). Indeed, Engels, who knew more about these things than almost any of his contemporaries, spent his final decades trying to formulate a viable strategy to deal with the question of militarism and war.

Engels opened *The Prussian Military Question and the German Workers' Party* with the claim that

> until now the debate on the military question has merely been conducted between the government and the feudal party on the one hand, and the liberal and radical bourgeoisie on the other. Now, as the crisis approaches, it is time for the workers' party to make its position known too. . . . The workers' party,

which in all questions at issue between reaction and bourgeoisie stands outside the actual conflict, enjoys the advantage of being able to treat such questions quite cold-bloodedly and impartially. It alone can treat them scientifically, historically, as though they were already in the past, anatomically, as though they were already corpses. (CW 20, 41)

He then outlined an expert survey of the state of the Prussian military followed by an analysis of social relations in Prussia, including returning to the issue of the bourgeoisie in and after 1848: "In 1848 the German workers' party . . . was prepared to do the bourgeoisie's work for it at a very modest price, but the latter was more afraid of the slightest independent stirring of the proletariat than it was of the feudal aristocracy and the bureaucracy" (CW 20, 57). This standpoint was problematic as Prussian military restructuring was, because of its increasing cost and potential political consequences—a strong military created the possibility of a coup—evolving in opposition to the needs of the German bourgeoisie. Would the bourgeoisie seriously resist these developments? Engels thought not.

What then was the attitude of the workers' party to the military question and the divisions between the government and the bourgeoisie? In the first instance, Engels supported universal conscription because it created the potential social basis for real workers' democracy: "The more workers who are trained in the use of weapons the better. Universal conscription is the necessary and natural corollary of universal suffrage; it puts the voters in the position of being able to enforce their decisions gun in hand against any attempt at a *coup d'état*" (CW 20, 67). Furthermore, Engels argued that whereas in fully developed capitalist countries (England) the workers confronted the bourgeoisie in a relatively straightforward opposition, in Germany with its feudal overhang the situation was more socially and thus more politically complex. One potential problem arising from this situation was the risk that workers would one-sidedly focus on their immediate conflicts with the bourgeoisie while disregarding the broader conflict with the reactionary relics of feudalism. Engels claimed that such a perspective would be just as much a mistake in 1865 as it had been in 1848. Capitalist development created the space in which the proletariat was emerging as an independent political force. Consequently, the workers' movement should push the liberal petty bourgeoisie and bourgeoisie from a position of political independence. To do this was important because liberal democratic forms could be used by the workers for their own ends:

To be consistent, [the bourgeoisie—PB] must therefore demand universal, direct suffrage, freedom of the press, association and assembly and the suspension of all special laws directed against individual classes of the population. And there is nothing else that the proletariat needs to demand from it. It cannot require that the bourgeoisie should cease to be a bourgeoisie, but it certainly can require that it practises its own principles consistently. But the proletariat will thereby also acquire all the weapons it needs for its ultimate victory. With freedom of the press and the right of assembly and association it will win universal suffrage, and with universal, direct suffrage, in conjunction with the above tools of agitation, it will win everything else. (CW 20, 77)

This argument includes a fundamental political point. Engels had no truck with ahistorical ideas of inalienable human rights, but he recognized that once these rights and associated liberties were historically constituted they created a framework in which the workers' movement might thrive (Harvey 1996, 331–332). This point was the corollary of his claim that the workers' demands could be met through means of universal direct suffrage.

The Prussian Military Question and the German Workers' Party also included an important exploration of the limits of universal male suffrage in the Prussian context. After suggesting that the workers and bourgeoisie "can only exercise real, organised, political power through parliamentary representation," he pointed out that this claim was dependent on parliament having access to the "purse strings." But, handing over control of finances to parliament was precisely what Bismarck aimed to avoid. Should socialists pour all their hopes into such an institution? "Surely not," was Engels's reply. He suspected that if Bismarck did decree "universal direct suffrage," he, like Napoleon III before him, would so weaken this democracy as to make it essentially worthless:

If the government decreed universal direct suffrage, it would from the outset hedge it about with so many ifs and buts that it would in fact not be universal direct suffrage at all any more . . . one has only to go to France to realise what tame elections it can give rise to, if one has only a large and ignorant rural population, a well-organised bureaucracy, a well-regimented press, associations sufficiently kept down by the police and no political meetings at all. (CW 20, 74)

This important argument was aimed at Ferdinand Lassalle's supporters in the workers' movement. The problem with this group, as previously noted, was that they accepted the parameters of politics as expressed in official discourse: not an independent workers' movement but working-class support for one or the other side within the ruling class in their conflicts—in this case, either for Prussia (which Lassalle championed) or Austria (which Engels insisted was Marx's position). Whereas the Lassalleans' (Lassalle himself had died the year before Engels wrote his pamphlet) uncritically embraced Bismarck's suggestion of universal male suffrage, Engels warned against the way Bismarck was intent on using this particular form of suffrage as Napoleon III had used it before him; not as a means to democracy but rather to bolster his personal power on the one hand and the power of the Prussian Junkers on the other. In a context where the mass of peasants and agricultural workers had not yet been swept up into the independent workers' movement, "universal direct suffrage will not be a weapon for the proletariat but a *snare*" (CW 20, 75). Despite believing that universal direct suffrage could be the means of emancipation, Engels argued that it could equally be used to entrap the proletariat within the parameters of reactionary politics. The utility of universal male suffrage thus depended upon the specific circumstances in which it was introduced. He believed it could help foster the struggle for freedom in the context of a rising workers' movement and universal conscription (Draper 2005, 116).

As to the orientation of the German workers' movement, Engels suggested that the priority was to "preserve the organisation of the work-ers' party as far as present conditions permit." Beyond that, he argued for driving "the Party of Progress on to make *real* progress, as far as possible," and to "let the military question itself go the way that it will, in the knowledge that the workers' party will one day also carry out its own, German 'army-reorganisation'" (CW 20, 79).

This final point illuminates his and Marx's subsequent stance on the Franco-Prussian War of 1870. In a statement written for the First Interna-tional within days of the outbreak of the war, Marx made the point that, for Germany, the war was defensive in nature (CW 22, 5). In a sense this claim was a truism given what was known at the time—though it subse-quently became known, as Engels later noted, that Bismarck intended to entrap Napoleon III into declaring war (and succeeded) so that he could play the victim and pull the southern German states into the conflict and thus into what became the German Empire (CW 26, 487). Despite insisting that this was a defensive war for the Germans, Marx refused to give political support to the Prussian ruling class. The *Address on the Franco-Prussian War* included statements from members of the International both in Germany and France condemning wars, especially "dynastic wars" (CW 22, 3–8). That the statement of the Germans included the phrase "with deep sorrow and grief we are forced to undergo a defensive war as an unavoidable evil" has led many to conclude that Marx and Engels supported the Germans against the French (at least at the outbreak of the war). But this is not the case. As Hal Draper points out, Marx supported Liebknecht's and Bebel's decision to abstain in the vote for war credits in the North German Confederation Reichstag. Indeed, he wrote that members of the International should campaign against the war both in France and Germany (Draper 2005, 129).

Engels, by contrast, did in one letter to Marx suggest that Liebknecht had been wrong to abstain in the vote, but this was because he believed that Liebknecht, by dismissing the war as merely a dynastic form, failed to grasp that it included a progressive dimension: German victory would, in however bastardized a form, lead to the (at least partial) unification of Germany and thus to the creation of a space within which the German proletariat might emerge as an independent political force (CW 44, 45–48). Engels subsequently changed his position on this matter after an exchange with Marx (Draper 2005, 129, 121–157); and Marx was very clear that, as he wrote in a letter to the members of the International who had suggested supporting the war as an unavoidable evil, if Prussia were to annex Alsace and Lorraine (which, of course, it did), "it is the most certain way to convert this war into a *European institution*." This annexation would open a "new world-historical epoch" in which the peace would be converted "into a mere armistice, until France is sufficiently recovered to demand the lost territory back" and until Russia also finds itself "inevitably" at war with Germany (CW 22, 260).

This new context meant that war between the main European powers, far from being a necessary counterpart to revolution had instead become its mortal enemy. To view wars and revolution through the lens of the events of 1793 was therefore no longer adequate or even relevant. Indeed, *The Communist Manifesto*'s demand for a bourgeois revolution in Germany had been realized by the most unlikely force: the Prussian Junkers led by Bismarck. Engels outlined how this had happened in his unfinished essay, *The Role of Force in History* (1887–1888). Here, he suggested that though the German bourgeoisie had shown themselves to be too cowardly to realize the demands of their bourgeois revolution, in the context of heightened international competition Bismarck had unified Germany, and though he had carried out this task for the Junkers, his role was underpinned by the needs of the bourgeoisie:

> [I]t was the desire of the practical merchant and industrialist arising out of immediate business needs to sweep away all the historically inherited small state junk which was obstructing the free development of commerce and industry, to abolish all the unnecessary friction the German businessman first had to overcome at home if he wished to enter the world market, and to which all his competitors were superior. German unity had become an economic necessity. (CW 26, 458–459)

Engels was adamant that in so unifying Germany, Bismarck had realized the tasks of the bourgeois revolution behind the backs of the bourgeoisie: "And then—at long last!—the ugliest abuses of the small state system were abolished, those that, on the one hand, most obstructed capitalist development, and, on the other, the Prussian craving for power" (CW 26, 483, 478, 498). However, once this historic demand had been realized, the negative consequences of Bismarck's Junkerism came to the fore. With the defeat of the French in 1870, Bismarck moved not to stabilize Europe but to "extort" reparations. At this point Bismarck "appeared for the first time as an independent politician, who was no longer implementing in his own way a programme dictated from outside, but translating into action the products of his own brain, thereby committing his first enormous blunder" (CW 26, 491). The rash decision was not so much to demand the French pay the Germans monetary compensation, though this was bad enough; rather, it consisted in Bismarck's seizure of Alsace and Lorraine, which had the effect of pushing France into the arms of Russia, ensuring that, at some point, Europe would once again be plunged into war (CW 26, 495–496).

All of this maneuvering happened in a context of deepening industrialization that had as a corollary a constant revolutionizing of the means of destruction. Engels noted that though these technologies made modern armies ever more efficient killing machines, in the short term they also mediated against war because they made each new type of armaments obsolete almost as soon they were deployed. In *The Foreign Policy of Russian Tsardom* (1889–1890) he wrote that both Russia and France on one side and Germany and its allies on the other were

> preparing for a decisive battle, for a war, such as the world has not yet seen, in which 10 to 15 million armed combatants will stand face to face. Only two circumstances have thus far prevented the outbreak of this fearful war: first, the incredibly rapid improvements in firearms, in consequence of which every newly-invented arm is already superseded by a new invention, before it can be introduced into even *one* army; and, secondly, the absolute impossibility of calculating the chances, the complete uncertainty as to who will finally come out victor from this gigantic struggle. (CW 27, 46)

Unfortunately, this was a highly unstable situation: Alsace-Lorraine acted as a fault line across Europe that made war increasingly inevitable, while new technologies meant that the coming war would make previous conflicts seem like child's play. He insisted that Bismarck had created the conditions not merely for a European war but for a world war. This prospect, as Engels famously and presciently predicted in 1887, was terrifying:

> And, finally, the only war left for Prussia-Germany to wage will be a world war, a world war, moreover, of an extent and violence hitherto unimagined. Eight to ten million soldiers will be at each other's throats and in the process they will strip Europe barer than a swarm of locusts. The depredations of the Thirty Years' War compressed into three to four years and extended over the entire continent; famine, disease, the universal lapse into barbarism, both of the armies and the people, in the wake of acute misery; irretrievable dislocation of our artificial system of trade, industry and credit, ending in universal bankruptcy; collapse of the old states and their conventional political wisdom to the point where crowns will roll into the gutters by the dozen, and no one will be around to pick them up; the absolute impossibility of foreseeing how it will all end and who will emerge as victor from the battle. Only one consequence is absolutely certain: universal exhaustion

and the creation of the conditions for the ultimate victory of the working class. (CW 26, 451)

It was against the backdrop of this perspective that Engels spent the last decades of his life trying to work out how revolution might save humanity from this impending barbarism. In the most comprehensive survey of Engels's military writings, Martin Berger argues that, whereas Engels had previously proselytized for a war against Russia as a stimulus to revolution, in the wake of the Franco-Prussian War he "consistently deplored and feared" it and hoped for "revolution as a means of avoiding war" (Berger 1977, 127, 129). This new context, combined with his long-standing doubts about the *military* utility of barricade fighting—Berger comments that Engels's views on the military effectiveness of barricade fighting ranged from "sober to dismal" (Berger 1977, 59)—informed a profound *private* pessimism about the prospects for war that is evident in his letters to several of his closest comrades. In 1889 he wrote:

> As for war, that is, to my mind, the most terrible of eventualities. Otherwise I shouldn't give a fig for the whims of Mme la France. But a war in which there will be 10 to 15 million combatants, unparalleled devastation simply to keep them fed, universal and forcible suppression of our movement, a recrudescence of chauvinism in all countries and, ultimately, enfeeblement ten times worse than after 1815, a period of reaction based on the inanition of all the peoples by then bled white—and, withal, only a slender hope that that bitter war may result in revolution—it fills me with horror. Especially when I think of our movement in Germany, which would be overwhelmed, crushed, brutally stamped out of existence, whereas peace would almost certainly bring us victory. (CW 48, 283)

Commenting on this letter, Gilbert Achcar writes that Engels developed a twofold strategy in response to this situation (Achcar 2002, 81). On the one hand, he did whatever he could to foster the Peace Party within the various national states—thus many of his military writings of the period were aimed at persuading an elite audience of the ultimate futility and self-defeating costliness of maintaining a standing army (CW 27, 367–393; cf. Kiernan 2001, 34). On the other hand, he began to think through an altogether more radical approach to overcoming the army. In the much (willfully) misunderstood 1895 introduction to Marx's *Class Struggles in France*, he wrote that barricades had only ever been of use as a moral rather than as a military counter to the army: "Even in the classic time of street fighting . . . the barricade produced more of a moral than a material effect. It was a means of shaking the steadfastness of the military" (CW 27, 518). How then to overcome the resistance of the army to revolution? Engels's answer was a strategy aimed at transforming the "bourgeois army from within" (Achcar 2002, 80). In *Anti-Dühring* he wrote:

> Militarism dominates and is swallowing Europe. But this militarism also bears within itself the seed of its own destruction. Competition among the individual states forces them, on the one hand, to spend more money each year on the army and navy, artillery, etc., thus more and more hastening their financial collapse; and, on the other hand, to resort to universal compulsory military service more and more extensively, thus in the long run making the whole people familiar with the use of arms, and therefore enabling them at a given moment to make their will prevail against the warlords in command. And this moment will arrive as soon as the mass of the people—town and country workers and peasants—*will have* a will. At this point the armies of the princes become transformed into armies of the people; the machine refuses to work and militarism collapses by the dialectics of its own evolution. What the bourgeois democracy of 1848 could not accomplish, just because it was *bourgeois* and not proletarian, namely, to give the labouring masses a will whose content would be in accord with their class position—socialism will infallibly secure. And this will mean the bursting asunder *from within* of militarism and with it of all standing armies. (CW 25, 158)

This argument illuminates why Engels attached so much weight to the idea of universal conscription. Though this policy was undertaken for reactionary ends, he believed that by arming the (newly enfranchised) proletariat, conscription could undermine militarism from within—an armed electorate could potentially impose its own will rather than act as mere servants of the will of others. This strategy was clearly revolutionary—though one that was alive to the profound changes in the terrain of struggle since 1793, 1848, and 1870. That Engels's writings from this period could nevertheless be deployed by reformist critics of the revolutionary project in the period after his death can be explained by two facts. First, willful misinterpretation of his latter writings, especially his 1895 *Introduction to Marx's Class Struggles in France*—we shall return to this later; and, second, through a one-sided reading of one of his most important, and easily misunderstood, later public statements on the prospects of war: *Socialism in Germany* (1891).

Socialism in Germany is particularly interesting because its arguments were deployed by the apologists for German Social Democracy's vote for war credits in 1914 (Losurdo 2015, 85). They were able to use it thus because Engels had, by contrast with all of his writings on the subject subsequent to 1870, clearly called for the defense of Germany in the event of a war with France and Russia. His reasoning was thus: despite being a bourgeois republic, France through its alliance with Russia was acting as a tool of absolutist reaction. Against this force, German socialists would have to defend the many hard-fought gains they and their predecessors had won over the previous century:

> In the interest of the European revolution [German socialists— PB] are obliged to defend all the positions that have been won, not to capitulate to the enemy from without any more than to the enemy within; and they cannot accomplish that except by fighting Russia and its allies, whoever they may be, to the bitter end. If the French republic placed itself at the service of His Majesty the Tsar, Autocrat of all the Russias, the German socialists would fight it with regret, but they would fight it all the same. (CW 27, 244)

This argument seems a clear reversion back to the politics of 1848 (though certainly not a justification for Germany's offensive strategy in 1914—and Engels always insisted that even victorious proletarian regimes could not "forcibly confer any boon whatever on another country without undermining its own victory in the process" [CW 46, 322–323]). But why revert to this anachronistic position? Draper suggests that beneath its superficial call to arms for the German left, *Socialism in Germany* was first published in French as an attempt to subvert the prowar arguments among the republican left. To this end, Engels pointedly agreed both that Germany's occupation of Alsace-Lorraine was oppressive and wrong and

that the French Republic was politically progressive vis-à-vis the German
Empire. Notwithstanding these facts, he insisted that an alliance with Russia
would mean the "repudiation of France's revolutionary mission" (CW 49,
270). If both Achcar and Draper are right to argue that Engels's main
concern was to avoid war by warning French socialists against justifying an
alliance with Russia because of Alsace-Lorraine, they both fail to address
the significance of Engels's embrace of revolutionary defensism. Achcar is
right that Engels wrote in a very specific context and Draper is equally
right that he was uneasy about articulating this position (Achcar 2002,
77; Draper 2005, 164–178). But though he was uneasy about expressing
his opinion to the French, he was absolutely serious about the analogy
with 1793. In a letter to Adolph Sorge, he wrote:

> Bebel and I have been corresponding about this and are of
> the opinion that if the Russians start a war against us, German
> socialists should lash out *à outrance* [with all their strength—
> PB] at the Russians and their allies, whoever they may be. If
> Germany is crushed, so shall we be, while at best the struggle
> will be so intense that only revolutionary means will enable
> Germany to hold its own, and hence there is every likelihood
> that we may be forced to take the helm and play at 1793.
> (CW 49, 266–267)

This argument is highly problematic at many levels. On the one hand,
there are profound limitations with the idea of *attaque à outrance*—the
claim developed in the nineteenth century that in the context of the new
overwhelming superiority of defensive technologies of warfare in the late
nineteenth century victory would go to the side with the greatest courage
and élan. It is not merely that this idea was to be decisively falsified in
1914, but more to the point, Engels had been clear as early as 1852 that
a repetition of the success of the enthusiasm of the *levée en masse* would
be nigh on impossible in modern conditions:

> Moreover, our French revolutionaries are known to follow
> tradition and their first cry will be: *Levée en masse! Deux mil-
> lions d'hommes aux frontières!* The two million men would be all
> very well if one could again expect from the Coalition such
> stupidities as those of 1792 and 1793 and if one had time
> for gradually training these two million men. But there is no

question of that. One must be prepared to encounter a million active enemy soldiers on the frontier within two months,
and it is a matter of opposing this million with a chance of
success. (CW 10, 560)

Elsewhere, Engels did suggest a way out of this impasse: the growth in
support for the Social Democratic Party across Germany, especially in
"the rural districts of the six eastern provinces of Prussia," would mean
that "the German army is ours" (CW 49, 229). If he thus hoped for a
transformation of the army from within to give a new form to the *levée
en masse*, this optimism was at best speculative in 1891 and was certainly
innocent of any medium akin to the moral aspect of barricade fighting
noted earlier by which the army might be won over politically. Likewise,
his analysis of the pressures to war in 1891 were relatively trivial: neither
dynastic ambition nor Alsace-Lorraine could bear the weight of explanation of the general war that was brewing in Europe. That Engels died on
the cusp of the modern epoch of imperialism may be enough to explain
this lacuna in his thought, though he should have been more alert to the
tactical error of having a German try to explain why the French should
not bow to chauvinism in relation to Alsace-Lorraine! More importantly,
he needed a clearer conception of how the revolutionary left might
undermine the army from within.

9

Revolutionary Continuity

Whatever its tactical limitations, Engels's defensist position in 1891 did not in the slightest entail support for the German government. His perspective was a form of *revolutionary* defensism predicated upon a creative and undogmatic revolutionary strategy to overcome the army from within. Indeed, the necessity of revolution was the guiding strategic thread of Engels's interventionist political thought from the 1840s onward: his "ultimate revolutionary aims," as Gallie put it, "never varied" (Gallie 1978, 87). To this end, in 1879 he wrote that he and Marx had "combatted this same petty-bourgeois socialism ever since the *Manifesto* (indeed since Marx's anti-Proudhon piece)" (CW 45, 433). This statement should not be interpreted as justifying a sectarian conception of political truth to be handed down from intellectuals to workers. Rather, it is best understood as a reaction against attempts to impose abstract sectarian truths (even the nominally "Marxist" truths of supposedly Marxists sects) on the real workers' movement. Marxism is not a "dogma," he argued in a letter of March 11, 1895, but an aid "to further investigation and the method for such investigation" (CW 50, 461; Draper 1978, 518).

This approach is evident in comments he made about the electoral success of the German left in an illuminating interview with the British *Daily Chronicle* in July 1893. When asked about the Social Democratic Party's program, Engels answered: "Our programme is very nearly identical with that of the Social-Democratic Federation in England, although our policy is very different." Despite having a "Marxist" program, the British SDF, unlike its German counterpart, acted in practice like a sect: "The English Social-Democratic Federation is, and acts, only like a small sect. It is an exclusive body. It has not understood how to take the lead of the working-class movement generally, and to direct it towards socialism. It has turned Marxism into an orthodoxy" (CW 27, 550). For Engels, programmatic certitude was less important than participation within the real movement from below to win influence within that movement. He defended his and Marx's understanding of the prime significance of the real movement from below in a letter to the American Florence Kelley-Wischnewetzky in 1886:

> It is far more important that the movement should spread, proceed harmoniously, take root and embrace as much as possible the whole American proletariat, than that it should start and proceed, from the beginning, on theoretically perfectly correct lines. There is no better road to theoretical clearness of comprehension than to learn by one's own mistakes. . . . And for a whole large class, there is no other road, especially for a nation so eminently practical and so contemptuous of theory as the Americans. The great thing is to get the working-class to move as a class; that once obtained, they will soon find the right direction, and all who resist . . . will be left out in the cold with small sects of their own. (CW 47, 541)

Engels had first elucidated his understanding of the enormous significance of the real workers' movement from below in *The Condition of the Working Class in England*. In a comment on the defeat of the 1844 strike of Durham and Northumberland miners, he wrote: "the fight had not been in vain. First of all, this nineteen weeks' strike had torn the miners of the North of England forever from the intellectual death in which they had hitherto lain; they have left their sleep, are alert to defend their interests, and have entered the movement of civilisation, and especially the movement of the workers" (CW 4, 545). Thus it was that he underpinned his and Marx's unswerving defense of trade unionism. Despite the limitations of trade unionism—in 1891 Engels reminded his audience that while unions could be successful in "periods of average and brisk business; in periods of stagnation and crisis they regularly fail," and that the major weakness of trade unionism was a failure to "remove the main thing that needs abolishing: capitalist relations" (CW 27, 98)—Marx and Engels consistently supported the trade union movement because they understood these struggles to represent an elemental form of working-class self-activity.

Marx and Engels's perspective is best differentiated from other tendencies within the socialist movement by their understanding of how their ideas related to working-class struggles. Their aim was to comprehend such struggles to help them become self-aware so that they could realize their full potential. Consequently, they maintained their political independence from other groups who, in one way or another, inhibited this process of theoretical and political self-realization. Engels's 1873 comment to August Bebel, that "old man Hegel said long ago: A party proves itself victorious by splitting and being able to stand the split" (CW 44, 514), is best understood in this light. Far from contradicting his critique of the sectarianism of, for instance, the SDF, Engels's willingness to countenance splits was the flipside to his and Marx's resistance to sectarianism. They would join coalitions with other groups, as Marx did at the time of the First International, when they judged that this would aid the real movement from below, but would equally be willing to split from other tendencies on the left when they believed that involvement with these groups had begun to act as a barrier to the deepening of the real movement from below. Engels's unsectarian approach to politics was evident in a letter to Kautsky, September 4, 1892, in which he rejected the latter's claim that the Fabians were an unfinished project through the medium of some very sharp criticism of their politics, while simultaneously insisting that while it would be a mistake to "treat these people as enemies . . . they should no more be shielded from criticism than anyone else" (CW 49, 516).

Engels's orientation toward the real movement informed his belief that the best way to build a workers' party was not to attempt to "entice away a few individuals and memberships here and there from one's opponent, but to work on the great mass, which is as yet uninvolved." He suggested that the "cry for unity" often comes from

> either people of limited intelligence who want to stir everything into one nondescript mush, which, the moment it is left to settle, throws up the differences again but in much sharper contrast, because they will then be all in one pot . . . or else they are people who unconsciously . . . or consciously want to adulterate the movement. For this reason the biggest sectarians and the biggest brawlers and rogues shout loudest for unity at certain times. (CW 44, 510–514)

In 1881 Engels returned to the themes of trade unionism in an, as it turned out, unsuccessful, attempt to give shape to the English labor movement through a series of editorials for the newspaper of the English trade union movement, *The Labour Standard* (for a discussion of Engels's relationship to the English labor movement see Kapp 1976, 423–599). While once again pointing to the limitations of trade unionism—Engels noted that they did not so much challenge the wages system as enforce its logic—he was careful not to dismiss socialist work within the trade unions. Rather, he claimed that without the trade unions workers would be pushed below the market rate for the job. This made socialist trade unionism indispensable to the workers' movement: "The great merit of Trades Unions, in their struggle to keep up the rate of wages and to reduce working hours, is that they tend to keep up and to raise the standard of life" (CW 24, 380). But if trade unions were to aspire to become more than the institutions through which the logic of the wages system was enforced, they should replace the motto "a fair day's wages for a fair day's work" with the demand to "abolish the wages system" (CW 24, 376, 384–385). Such a demand, Engels suggested, should not be understood as an abstract imposition from the left but was immanent to trade unionism itself. Because trade unions are an institutional expression of the existence of "the struggle of the labourer against capital," and because this social struggle necessarily tended to "become a political struggle," the unions should aim to extend their implicit struggle for power into an explicit political challenge through the creation of an independent workers' party along the lines of continental socialist parties (CW 24, 386–387, 404–405; Blackledge 2013).

Engels outlined the general architecture of his understanding of the correct socialist "policy" in his 1874 preface to *The Peasant War in Germany*. Commenting on the strengths of the renewed German left, he wrote, "It must be said to the credit of the German workers that they have exploited the advantages of their situation with rare understanding. For the first time since a workers' movement has existed, the struggle is being waged pursuant to its three sides—the theoretical, the political and the economico-practical (resistance to the capitalists)—in harmony and in its interconnections, and in a systematic way" (CW 23, 631). All his mature political writings—and throughout this period he excelled at brief but rich journalistic engagements into contemporary political debates—return one way or another to this theme of developing a fully rounded strategy for socialism. These essays did not merely defend the perspective he and Marx had formulated in the 1840s, but by their engagement with the real movement from below they also acted to deepen it.

Upon returning to London after his twenty-year exile running the family firm in Manchester, Engels threw himself into political work. He was immediately co-opted onto the General Council of the First International at the moment between the outbreak of the Franco-Prussian War and the emergence of the Paris Commune. These were world-shaking events, and though in retrospect the defeat of the Parisian workers sounded the death knell for the International, in the short term "the International was now at the height of its fame" (Collins and Abramsky 1965, 220). Shortly after the fall of the Commune, Marx defended it in arguably the most brilliant of his pamphlets, *The Civil War in France*.

Reaction was on the move everywhere, and Marx's defense of the Commune meant that he and the International became the bête noire of the European bourgeoisie. Marx joked to Kugelmann, "I have the honour to be AT THIS MOMENT THE BEST CALUMNIATED AND THE MOST MENACED MAN OF LONDON. That really does one good after a tedious twenty years' idyll in the backwoods" (CW 44, 158). Though a couple of prominent English trade unionists did resign from the General Council amid all this hullaballoo, it is a myth that the trade unions deserted the International at this moment: none did. In fact, the International's campaign to support refugees from France was well supported—even John Stuart Mill sent a message deploring "the horrors now being perpetuated at Paris" to a public meeting organized by the International. There was pressure from France to ban the International, but after Marx supplied copies of all public statements to the Home Secretary the matter was dropped. In this context, a conference of the International was arranged for September 1871 in London. At Engels's behest it was a private affair—he did not want its existence to become a reason for delegates from the Continent to be picked up by the police.

As it happens the key debates at the conference were with anarchists over the questions of the powers of the General Council and political action. The latter point had been an ongoing concern for Marx and Engels since their engagement with the True Socialists in the 1840s. Having discovered the social question, many of the radicals of the 1840s dismissed political matters out of hand. To the extent that a renewed version of this approach was justified within the International, anarchists around Bakunin argued that as the state was the key enemy of the left, engaging with it would be an unpardonable error. Marx was dismayed and compared this argument to the nonsense claim that because socialists are against the wages system they should refrain from taking an interest in the wages question (Draper 1990, 154).

As it happens Engels took up the argument at the conference. In a speech, *On the Political Action of the Working Class*, he argued that abstaining from political issues was not so much wrong as it was impossible. Politics existed and to abstain from it simply meant leaving it to the left's opponents: "to preach abstention would be to push them [the workers] into the arms of bourgeois politics." And precisely because the International sought "the abolition of classes" it must fight for the "political domination of the proletariat" through "the supreme act of politics": "revolution." It was not simply the revolution that was political. Rather, the "political freedoms, the right to assembly and association and the freedom of press" were, as he and Marx had argued in relation to the benefits of a bourgeois revolution in the 1840s, "our weapons." Consequently, it would be absurd not to defend them when they were under attack from reactionary forces (CW 22, 415–418).

This reiteration of the general line of *The Communist Manifesto* set the scene for all Engels's political work over the next two and a half decades. One early important theoretical intervention within the German workers' movement was his pamphlet *The Housing Question* (1872). In the context of a housing shortage during the economic boom in the wake of the Franco-Prussian War, Engels's pamphlet, whose arguments continue to resonate to this day, was intended to counter the analyses of this crisis by a Proudhonist writer, Mülberger, and a free-market writer, Sax (CW 26, 423; Robbins 2018, 231).

Engels's argument was intended to show not merely that a revolution was the only long-term solution to the housing question, but also that despite their formal differences the Proudhonists and liberals came to similarly moralistic and utopian conclusions. Against Mülberger's Proudhonist account of the housing question, he insisted that there was no golden preindustrial age against which the present could be measured and to which we should aim at returning. This reactionary utopia was rooted in a false understanding of the housing shortage as a uniquely capitalist phenomenon. Engels insisted that housing had been in short supply well before the advent of capitalism, and that though capitalist industrialization had made the situation of workers worse, it had also, by creating the modern working class, created the potential agency to overcome this condition:

That the situation of the workers has on the whole become

materially worse since the introduction of capitalist production on a large scale is doubted only by the bourgeois. But should we therefore look backward longingly to the (likewise very meagre) fleshpots of Egypt, to rural small-scale industry, which produced only servile souls, or to "the savages"? On the contrary. Only the proletariat created by modern large-scale industry, liberated from all inherited fetters including those which chained it to the land, and herded together in the big cities, is in a position to accomplish the great social transformation which will put an end to all class exploitation and all class rule. The old rural hand weavers with hearth and home would never have been able to do it; they would never have been able to conceive such an idea, not to speak of desiring to carry it out. (CW 23, 324)

The specific modern form of the housing shortage was not, contra Mülberger, the primary evil in the modern world. Rather, it was one of many "secondary evils" underpinned by the unequal distribution of resources springing from the wage-labor relationship (CW 23, 318–320). Rather than suggest a utopian solution to this problem, Engels merely pointed out that in the existing world there were "sufficient quantity of houses in the big cities" to overcome the housing shortage. The problem was not a *natural* lack of housing but a *sociopolitical* failure to distribute housing stock rationally, and this failure, he insisted, could not be remedied until "the proletariat has won political power" (CW 23, 330).

Mülberger's reference to Proudhon's idea of "eternal justice" to remedy the housing shortage was inadequate because for each laborer to receive the full value of their labor (the core meaning of Proudhon's concept) then either there must be a reversion to preindustrial barter (though here the idea of the comparable "value" of products of labor would be meaningless) or socially produced values (everything in the modern world) should be possessed socially—something possible only through the proletariat in the wake of industrialization (CW 23, 325–326). To imagine individuals receiving as individuals the full value of their labors outside such a situation is to imagine capitalism without its contradictions: a utopian nonsense.

If the Proudhonist challenged capitalism from the abstract ahistorical perspective of "eternal justice," Sax, writing from the perspective of the philanthropic bourgeoisie, hoped to defend capitalism while overcoming its necessary evils. Rather than explain the housing shortage in relation to capitalism, he insisted that the workers' inability to find houses was a consequence of their lax morals: drinking and smoking rather than saving was the problem. As Engels pointed out, recalling arguments he had first articulated thirty years earlier in *The Condition of the Working Class in England*, "The fact that under the existing circumstances drunkenness among the workers is a necessary product of their living conditions, just as necessary as typhus, crime, vermin, bailiff and other social ills, so necessary in fact that the average figures of those who succumb to inebriety can be calculated in advance, is again something that Herr Sax cannot allow himself to know" (CW 23, 343). In a line that could today be aimed at middle-class wine-drinking condescension to working-class "lager louts," Engels wittily added: "My old primary school teacher used to say, by the way: 'The common people go to the pubs and the people of quality go to the clubs,' and as I have been in both I am in a position to confirm it" (CW 23, 343). The key point was simple: the problem was not drink—almost everyone partook—but capitalism, and the only way to overcome the unequal distribution of resources therein was through "the abolition of the capitalist mode of production" (CW 23, 368).

Engels's critique both of Mülberger's moral condemnation of capitalism and of Sax's moralistic apology for free markets were aimed at helping the working class avoid false solutions to the problems of their existence. In particular, the emergence of a Proudhonist current in Germany was worrisome because if triumphant it would mark an important retreat from the German working-class movement's own traditions (CW 23, 317).

Though often portrayed as "sectarian" by those interlocutors unencumbered by the problems of practical political work, criticisms such as this are of the first importance to "practical materialists." For instance, Marx and Engels's criticisms of the True Socialists in the 1840s had a direct political corollary: engagement with or abstention from the demands of the bourgeois revolution. Similarly, after 1848, Engels was time and again confronted with what he considered to be mistaken strategic perspectives within the left: reformist, anarchist, and insurrectionary. In this context, the critique of True Socialism that he and Marx had articulated in the 1840s set the scene for these subsequent interventions.

For example, in 1850 in a comment on the anarchist call for the abolition of the state, Engels wrote that what differentiated his and Marx's politics from anarchism was Marxism's infinitely greater sense of the concrete. The problem with demanding the abolition of the state is that this idea had a changing social content through history:

In *feudal* countries the abolition of the state means the abolition of feudalism and the creation of an ordinary bourgeois
state. In *Germany* it conceals either a cowardly flight from the
struggles that lie immediately ahead, a spurious inflating of
bourgeois freedom into absolute independence and autonomy
of the *individual*, or, finally, the indifference of the bourgeois
towards all forms of state, provided the development of bourgeois interests is not obstructed. (CW 10, 486)

By contrast with this approach, Engels insisted that the demand for the
abolition of the state be imbued with a historically specific social content
(Blackledge 2012c). Consequently, he differentiated not merely between
bourgeois and feudal states, and thus emphasized the continuing importance
of the concept of a bourgeois revolution for socialists, but also between
differential conceptions of the abolition of the state itself. He made it plain
that socialist antistatism had nothing in common with vacuous anarchistic statements of this type: "The abolition of the state has meaning with
the Communists, only as the necessary consequence of the abolition of
classes, with which the need for the organised might of one class to keep
the others down automatically disappears" (CW 10, 486, cf. 333). If this
concluding caveat illuminates the formal overlap between Marxist and
anarchist conceptions of freedom, the profound difference between these
two traditions was most pointedly articulated in his short, punchy essay
On Authority. Here, he commented that in their discussion of the idea of
autonomy, anarchists tended to deploy an abstract and consequently useless
conception of authority. At this suitably abstract level, as Engels mocked,
the terms authority and subordination "sound bad" and especially "dis-
agreeable to the subordinated." Unfortunately, the demand for the absolute
freedom of the individual in the modern context in which production had
become highly socialized was "tantamount to wanting to abolish industry
itself." Indeed, the concepts of "authority and autonomy are relative things
whose spheres vary with the various phases of the development of society." If this point is obviously pertinent across industry where cooperation
demands some form of authority, it was all the more so in a revolution.
As to this, he wrote, "a revolution is certainly the most authoritarian
thing there is; it is the act whereby one part of the population imposes
its will upon the other part by means of rifles, bayonets and cannon."
Nonetheless, Engels insisted that this fact should not be confused with

the continued existence of the "political state" and "political authority." Though in the immediate aftermath of a revolution some form of the political state would continue to exist until its social basis had withered away, as its base withered this authority would increasingly take a merely administrative form (CW 23, 422–425). As Herbert Marcuse comments, in this essay Engels looked not to the ending of authority but rather to its complete democratization (Marcuse 2008, 87). Engels extended this argument in a letter to Theodore Cuno, January 24, 1872, in which he argued that Bakunin's error was to invert the relationship between state and capital by supposing that the state had created capital and thus that the state was the chief evil. By contrast, Engels insisted that "the abolition of the state is nonsense without a social revolution beforehand; the abolition of capital is the social revolution and involves a change in the whole mode of production" (CW 44, 307; CW 47, 10).

If Blanqui imagined a similar postrevolutionary politics, as noted earlier the fundamental difference between his ideas and those of Marx and Engels is that whereas he envisioned a temporary postrevolutionary dictatorship until the masses were fit to rule, they insisted that workers became fit to rule through participation in the revolution itself. It is because Blanqui never understood this that, as Engels wrote, he was a "socialist only in sentiment" (CW 24, 13). Not that Engels dismissed the Blanquists in toto. Interestingly, in a letter of April 23, 1885, to Vera Zasulich he imagined that the Blanquists might play a positive role of detonating a revolution, but thereafter any revolutionary movement worth its name would overwhelm their elitist organization (CW 47, 280–281). Engels's general critique of Blanquism was made in a survey of the revolutionary left in the immediate aftermath of the Paris Commune of 1871, *Refugee Literature* (1874–1875).

The defeat of 1871, like the defeat of 1848, had spawned a radical but largely impotent milieu of ex-revolutionaries keen to rekindle the revolutionary wave that had left it high and dry in a seemingly impregnable London. Unfortunately, paralleling the situation Marx and Engels had found themselves in after 1848, the postrevolutionary situation escaped the comprehension of most members of this milieu. Engels wrote:

> After every unsuccessful revolution or counter-revolution, fever-
> ish activity develops among the émigrés who escaped abroad.
> Party groups of various shades are formed, which accuse each
> other of having driven the cart into the mud, of treason and of
> all other possible mortal sins. They also maintain close ties with

the homeland, organise, conspire, print leaflets and newspapers, swear that it will start over again within the next twenty-four hours, that victory is certain and, in the wake of this expectation, distribute government posts. Naturally, disappointment follows disappointment, and since this is attributed not to inevitable historical conditions, which they do not wish to understand, but to accidental mistakes by individuals, recriminations accumulate and result in general bickering. (CW 24, 12)

This context spawned competitive radicalisms as each grouping tried to outdo the others in revolutionary fervor. One manifestation of this pseudoradical posing was a tendency, most extreme among Blanquists and Bakuninists, for each faction to represent itself as "the most far-reaching, most extreme trend . . . as regards atheism" (CW 24, 15). Militants within both these groupings regarded religion one-sidedly in its legitimizing role and thus imagined the ideological struggle against it as an essential precondition for liberation.

According to Engels, this form of atheist politics was doubly problematic. It both misunderstood the practical materialism of large sections of the European working class, while simultaneously playing into the hands of the religious right who wanted to roll back this practical materialism. Engels suggested that both German and French workers were to all intents and purposes atheistic in their day-to-day practice: "it can be said that atheism has already outlived its usefulness for them; this pure negation does not apply to them, since they no longer stand in theoretical, but only in practical opposition to all belief in God: they are simply through with God, they live and think in the real world and are, therefore, materialists" (CW 24, 15–16). Conversely, to impose atheism from the top-down by decree would serve only to play into the hands of the religious authorities:

this demand to transform the people *par ordre du mufti* into atheists is signed by two members of the Commune, who surely must have had sufficient opportunity to discover, first, that anything can be decreed on paper but that this does not mean that it will be carried out; second, that persecution is the best way of strengthening undesirable convictions! This much is certain: the only service that can still be rendered to God today is to make atheism a compulsory dogma and to surpass Bismarck's anticlerical Kulturkampf laws by prohibiting religion in general. (CW 24, 16)

These arguments clearly had roots going back to Marx's earlier analysis of religion. Unfortunately, and perhaps in part because of the infamy of Marx's claim that religion is the "opium of the people," the fundamental distinction between the Enlightenment critique of religion and Marx's much more nuanced approach to the issue has often been overlooked by his interlocutors. Even Reinhold Niebuhr, the academic editor of an otherwise excellent selection of Marx and Engels's writings on religion, argued that Engels's study of Thomas Müntzer and the Anabaptists in Germany in 1525 "is not quite in agreement with Marxism's central thesis that religion is a weapon always used by the established social forces" (Niebuhr 1964, viii).

As Paul Siegel points out, this claim betrays a misunderstanding of Marx and Engels's view of religion (Siegel 1986, 26). It is of course true that religion often acts to legitimize the position of those in power, and Marx and Engels were keenly aware both of this fact and the fact that the struggle for freedom in Europe from the late medieval period onward often took the form of an ideological struggle against the Catholic Church. However, though this context underpinned the unity of Enlightenment thinkers' "hostility to traditional Christianity and the Church" (Goldmann 1968, 32), Marx and Engels differentiated themselves from this tradition by insisting upon a social interpretation of religion. As Engels wrote in his review of Marx's *A Contribution to the Critique of Political Economy*, "the materialist conception of history" starts from the proposition that "all social and political relations, all religious and legal systems, all theoretical conceptions which arise in the course of history can only be understood if the material conditions of life obtaining during the relevant epoch have been understood and the former are traced back to these material conditions" (CW 16, 469). This method effectively informed Marx's argument, made three decades earlier, that religion was not mere error but was an expression of a real social need: "religious distress is at the same time the expression of real distress and also the protest against real distress. Religion is the sigh of the oppressed creature, the heart of a heartless world, just as it is the spirit of spiritless conditions. It is the opium of the people" (CW 3, 175). The phrase "opium of the people" has tended to be misunderstood by those who view this drug through the lens of the moralistic discourse that portrayed it as an unmitigated evil from the late nineteenth century onward. However, when Marx wrote half a century earlier, opium was seen as a social good answering a very real need. Indeed, Andrew McKinnon has suggested that Marx's phrase could usefully be updated to read that religion be understood as "the penicillin of the people" (McKinnon 2006, 12).

Religion, from this perspective, served a real social need. In *Anti-Dühring* Engels argued that religion arose as an ideological reflection of, first, the natural and, later, the social forces that dominate human life.

> All religion, however, is nothing but the fantastic reflection in men's minds of those external forces which control their daily life, a reflection in which the terrestrial forces assume the form of supernatural forces. In the beginnings of history it was the forces of nature which were first so reflected, and which in the course of further evolution underwent the most manifold and varied personifications among the various peoples. . . . But it is not long before, side by side with the forces of nature, social forces begin to be active—forces which confront man as equally alien and at first equally inexplicable, dominating him with the same apparent natural necessity as the forces of nature themselves. (CW 25, 300–301)

Consequently, contra Roland Boer's claim that Engels assumed that "material causes and scientific advances would bring about the swift demise of religion" (Boer 2012, 277), he actually insisted that so long as such alien forces dominate people's lives, religious ideas will continue to exist as the elemental relation to our social and natural environment: "religion can continue to exist as the immediate, that is, the sentimental form of men's relation to the alien, natural and social, forces which dominate them, so long as men remain under the control of these forces" (CW 25, 301). And precisely because capitalism is characterized by such alien social relations, it will reproduce the social basis for religion: "in existing bourgeois society men are dominated by the economic conditions created by themselves, by the means of production which they themselves have produced, as if by an alien force. The actual basis of the religious reflective activity therefore continues to exist, and with it the religious reflection itself" (CW 25, 301). Far from Engels predicting the "total secularisation" of society as Alasdair MacIntyre mistakenly claimed, these lines evidence his belief that the social roots of religion will not wither until after the socialist transformation of society (MacIntyre 1967, 10). Commenting on this situation three decades earlier, Marx had written:

To abolish religion as the illusory happiness of the people is to demand their real happiness. The demand to give up illusions about the existing state of affairs is the demand to give up a state of affairs which needs illusions. The criticism of religion is therefore in embryo the criticism of the vale of tears, the halo of which is religion. . . . Thus the criticism of heaven turns into the criticism of the earth, the criticism of religion into the criticism of law and the criticism of theology into the criticism of politics. (CW 3, 176)

In *Anti-Dühring* Engels returned to this theme as part of his critique of crude anti-theism: "Mere knowledge . . . is not enough to bring social forces under the domination of society. What is above all necessary for this, is a social act" (CW 25, 301). The only way to overcome the need for religion would be to overcome the alienated social relations through which it is reproduced. To demand atheism without overcoming capitalism, as do modern writers such as Christopher Hitchens and Richard Dawkins, is at best to tilt at windmills and often lends itself to the tendency to apologize for reactionary alienated, though secular, powers that function to uphold the very system that reproduces the need for religion in the first place (Eagleton 2009).

Beyond the politically dubious conclusions to which latter-day crude atheists tend, approaches that see only error in religion are wont to misunderstand the nature of religious movements. Engels made this point in his *The Peasant War in Germany* where he complained that "the German ideology," that is those theorists who had failed to move beyond the Enlightenment's critique of religion, "still see nothing except violent theological bickering in the struggles that brought the middle ages to an end" (CW 10, 411). By contrast with this jaundiced view, he aimed to unravel the social content of the religious conflicts that dominated Germany in the early sixteenth century. To this end he located three tendencies within this social conflict: the conservative Catholic camp, the moderate reformist Lutheran burghers, and the revolutionary party led by Thomas Müntzer and the Anabaptists (Siegel 1986, 27).

The Peasant War in Germany is thus a concrete example of Engels's claim that religion could not be reduced either to power-legitimizing consciousness or a soporific drug. It could in fact be the medium through which progressive and indeed revolutionary social forces struggled for political supremacy. As Michael Löwy points out, Engels recognized that while religion could function to legitimize the kind of despotic power its Enlightenment critics highlighted, and which he had fought against as part of the Young Hegelian circle in the early 1840s, it could also play a "critical, protesting and even revolutionary role" (Löwy 1996, 8). And if this claim is true, to dismiss the religious form through which revolutionary hopes came to be expressed as mere error would be politically unpardonable.

In stark contrast to those who see in religion only error, Engels had a long-standing interest in unpicking long-lost social realities illuminated by the Bible. If biblical contradiction was the rope that, as Boer puts it, "Engels used to haul himself out of his biblical past" (Boer 2012, 244), he quickly deployed his knowledge of the Bible to illuminate the history of the Holy Lands. Thus, in an 1853 letter to Marx he commented that because "the genealogy given in Genesis" reflected the Bedouin tribes of the time, it followed that the Jews were "themselves nothing more than a small Bedouin tribe" who found themselves in opposition to other Bedouin tribes (CW 39, 326–327).

Three decades later he celebrated the life of Bruno Bauer through a critical survey of his work on religion: *Bruno Bauer and Early Christianity* (1882). Engels opened this essay with a point that is as valid today as it was when he wrote it. The problem posed by any world religion is not primarily an issue of whether its postulates are true or false, but rather why these ideas came to the fore at a particular juncture characterized by a wide variety of competing religious viewpoints.

> A religion that brought the Roman world empire into subjection and that dominated by far the larger part of civilised humanity for 1,800 years cannot be disposed of merely by declaring it to be nonsense gleaned together by deceivers. One cannot dispose of it before one succeeds in explaining its origin and its development from the historical conditions under which it arose and reached its dominating position. This applies especially to Christianity. The question to be solved, then, is how it came about that the masses in the Roman Empire preferred this nonsense—which was preached, into the bargain, by slaves and oppressed—to all other religions so that the ambitious Constantine finally saw in the adoption of this religion of nonsense the best means of exalting himself to the position of autocrat of the Roman world. (CW 24, 428)

Engels claimed that Bauer had shown that Christianity emerged as "a fusion of allegorically and rationalistically conceived Jewish traditions with Greek, particularly stoic, philosophy" (CW 24, 429). With the defeat of the radical sense of liberation evident in the oldest New Testament source, the book of Revelation, this synthesis appealed to a mass of people, particularly slaves, who "despairing of material salvation, sought in its stead a spiritual salvation" (CW 24, 433). Among other things, Christianity offered this class a universal religion that did away with the culturally specific ceremonies that might otherwise have limited its appeal beyond its original local birthplace. And through the doctrine of original sin it addressed the problems of evil in the world by blaming the victims themselves: "thou art to blame, ye are all to blame for the corruption of the world, thine and your own internal corruption" (CW 24, 435).

A year later he returned to these themes in his essay *The Book of Revelation* (1883). Engels agreed with historian Ernest Renan's provocative claim that early Christian communities resembled sections of the International Working Men's Association (First International). Written around 67 or 68 CE, the book of Revelation was innocent of the ideas of original sin and the trinity, Jesus was placed on a par with Moses rather than God, and instead of one Holy Ghost there are seven "spirits of God" (CW 26, 114). Far from the universal spiritual consolidations of later Christian doctrine, the book of Revelation illuminated an apocalyptic faith in imminent redemption on the part of a Jewish sect. The number of the beast is 616 not 666, and this number referred very clearly to John's belief that Nero, "the first great persecutor of the Christians," was to return from death to take back power in Rome at which point, probably around 70 CE, will prevail "a reign of terror under [Nero] which is to last forty-two months, or 1,260 days. After that term God arises, vanquishes Nero, the Antichrist, destroys the great city by fire, and binds the devil for a thousand years. The millennium begins, and so forth." (CW 26, 117).

What interested Engels was less the detail of John's predictions and more the sense conveyed in his book, accurately according to John Pickard, of revolutionary fervor characteristic of the original Christian community (Pickard 2013, 180–181). A decade later Engels reiterated his belief in the parallels between the early Christian church and the modern workers' movement. In *On the History of Early Christianity* (1894), in which he synthesized and deepened his previous thoughts on early Christianity, he insisted that Christianity was originally "a movement of oppressed people: it first appeared as the religion of slaves and freedmen, of poor people deprived of all rights, of peoples subjugated or dispersed by Rome" (CW 27, 447).

If the parallels between Christianity and modern socialism were manifest, so too were the differences. Christianity emerged at a moment when a material solution to the evils of the day were beyond the capabilities of the time: the low level of the development of the forces of production meant that overcoming class inequalities was then impossible. This meant early Christian "socialism" was necessarily utopian and could only be imagined in a religious form as realizable in the hereafter (CW 27, 448).

Strangely, in an otherwise perceptive discussion of Marxist writings on religion, *The War of Gods*, Michael Löwy argues that by contrast with his view of the revolutionary potential of religion in the past, "Engels was convinced that since the French Revolution religion could no longer function as a revolutionary ideology" (Löwy 1996, 10). Though he does not substantiate this claim in this book, elsewhere Löwy makes the same point by reference to Engels's 1892 preface to the English edition of *Socialism: Utopian and Scientific* (Löwy 1998, 84). In this essay Engels traced the roots of modern materialism, often seen in Victorian Britain as a foreign import, to sixteenth- and seventeenth-century Englishmen such as Bacon, Hobbes, and Locke (CW 27, 285). This argument set the scene for his claim that historical materialism is the modern heir of this older materialism, and that historical materialism constitutes the scientific study of society (CW 27, 289). Similarly, Engels argued that Marxism was the heir of a revolutionary tradition that breached the old feudal order in three acts: the Protestant Reformation, the English Revolution, and the French Revolution. And while the first two moments were articulated in the language of religion, the third "entirely cast off the religious cloak" (CW 27, 290–294). If Marxism's scientific status distinguished it from earlier utopian forms of socialism, the religious forms that the Continental bourgeoisie had relearned from their British counterparts to help legitimize their power in the wake of the French Revolution would not be able to withstand "the rising proletarian tide": "religion will be no lasting safeguard to capitalist society" (CW 27, 300).

If this argument seems to confirm Löwy's claim that Engels believed the French Revolution to be a turning point in the history of religion after which it could no longer fulfill its earlier revolutionary role, in actual fact, as Löwy acknowledged (Löwy 1998, 86), Engels made no such assumption. According to Engels, because the English workers' movement would emerge in a fragmentary and uneven manner, it was to be expected that its ideology would include a religious component. The workers' movement "moves, like all things in England, with a slow and measured step, with hesitation here, with more or less unfruitful, tentative attempts there; it moves now and then with an over-cautious mistrust of the name of Socialism, while it gradually absorbs the substance; and the movement spreads and seizes one layer of the workers after another" (CW 27, 301). Coming from a religious standpoint, and in a world dominated by the alien power of capital, it was to be expected that the workers' movement would only gradually shed its religious coloration. Engels suggested that within the existing workers' movement anticapitalism was taking a religious form. Indeed, some aspects of the ideology propagated by revivalists and the Salvation Army harked back to the radicalism of the early Church. The Salvation Army "revives the propaganda of early Christianity, appeals to the poor as the elect, fights capitalism in a religious way, and thus fosters an element of early Christian class antagonism, which one day may become troublesome to the well-to-do people who now find the ready money for it" (CW 27, 297). Any socialist worth his or her salt would have to learn to work with movements of this sort, and though Marxists were atheists, Engels's atheism had nothing in common with the crude atheism of the Blanquists and the Bakuninists. Similarly, when Marx was compelled by French Proudhonists to address the "religious idea" within the First International, he did the least required to keep the French integrated within the International without succumbing to their crude attacks on religion and the Church (Collins and Abramsky 1965, 110–112, 120–121). As Lenin wrote: "Engels blamed the Blanquists for being unable to understand that only the class struggle of the working masses could, by comprehensively drawing the widest strata of the proletariat into conscious and revolutionary social *practice*, really free the oppressed masses from the yoke of religion, whereas to proclaim that war on religion was a political task of the workers' party was just anarchistic phrase-mongering" (Lenin 1963a, 403). The flipside of Blanqui's pseudoradical critique of religion was what Engels called his "obsolete" model of revolution as "dictatorship" through a "coup de main by a small revolutionary minority" (CW 24, 13).

This comment is interesting precisely because Engels described the Paris Commune as an instance of "the dictatorship of the proletariat." What is the distinction between the Blanquist concept of a "revolutionary dictatorship" and the Marxist idea of the "dictatorship of the proletariat"? Marx famously wrote that the "secret" of the Commune "was this. It was essentially a *working-class government*, the product of the struggle of the producing against the appropriating class, the political form at last discovered under which to work out the economical emancipation of Labour" (CW 22, 334). The idea of "the political form at last discovered under which to work out the economical emancipation of Labour" is probably the most important instance of Marxism evolving through the generalization of lessons from the history of the working-class movement. Marx and Engels had long held to a democratic conception of the socialist revolution as the "self-emancipation of the working class"; what the Commune pointed to was the democratic political form through which this goal would be realized—though without votes for women on which scandalously neither Marx nor Engels commented! The Blanquists, by contrast, despite accounting themselves bravely in the Commune—sadly Blanqui himself was arrested the day before the Commune and missed the one great chance he had to realize his life-long hope of leading a revolution—never progressed beyond the elitist vision of a revolution as a "dictatorship on behalf of the general interest and human progress" (Bernstein 1971, 81–83).

Marx's idea of a working-class government was fundamentally different to this. As Engels explained in a critique of the reformism emerging within the German socialist movement, "of late, the Social-Democratic philistine has once more been filled with wholesome terror at the words: Dictatorship of the Proletariat. Well and good, gentlemen, do you want to know what this dictatorship looks like? Look at the Paris Commune. That was the Dictatorship of the Proletariat" (CW 27, 191). Far from being an apology for some kind of proto-Stalinist monstrosity, not only should the idea of the dictatorship of the proletariat not be conflated with a dictatorship by an elite, it should not even be conflated with the more general idea of a state. Engels wrote that the Commune, against the general trend to increase state power, "made use of two infallible means" to militate against this:

> In the first place, it filled all posts—administrative, judicial and educational—by election on the basis of universal suffrage of all concerned, subject to the right of recall at any time by the same electors. And, in the second place, all officials, high or low, were paid only the wages received by other workers. . . . In this way an effective barrier to place-hunting and careerism was set up, even apart from the binding mandates to delegates to representative bodies which were added besides. This shattering

of the former state power and its replacement by a new and truly democratic one is described in detail [by Marx] in the third section of *The Civil War in France*. (CW 27, 190)

He thus reiterated a point he had first made in 1875 at the time of the unification of the Marxist and Lassallean wings of the German workers' movement: the word "state" is misleading when used in connection with the Commune. "All the palaver about the state ought to be dropped, especially after the Commune, which has ceased to be a state in the true sense of the term" (CW 45, 64). It was because workers' states, unlike all previous states, are expressions of the rule of the majority rather than of a minority, that it made little sense to conflate them with existing or historical states. Unlike these earlier forms they were no longer specialized coercive apparatuses maintaining exploitative social relations.

These points were intended as a critique of the proposed new unified party program to be voted on at the Gotha conference. Marx criticized this document in his *Critique of the Gotha Programme* written in May 1875. It is interesting that the core of Marx's criticism had been made two months earlier by Engels in a letter to August Bebel. Marx and Engels had had a semi-detached relationship to the German workers' movement since their exile in England. If this situation was somewhat modified by especially Marx's involvement in the First International after 1864, the fact that the International was based in London meant that Britain had become the focus of their work. The high-water mark of the International was simultaneously its swan song: the Paris Commune. The defeat of the Commune marked, on the one hand, a profound defeat for the International workers' movement generally and the International more specifically, while, on the other hand, it was the moment from which the center of gravity of the European labor movement moved from Paris to Berlin.

The workers' movement in Germany had been on the retreat for more than a decade after 1848. Things began to turn around from the 1860s onward. In 1862 Lassalle formed the General German Workers' Association that aimed at political power, while in 1869 a Social Democratic Workers' Party (or the Eisenachers, after the place of their founding conference) was formed by the rump of Leopold Sonnemann's Assembly of German Worker Associations after its leader had left to form the liberal People's Party. Led by Wilhelm Liebknecht and August Bebel, the Eisenachers were the closest thing to a Marxist party in Germany in the early 1870s. By 1875 the Eisenachers and Lassalleans came together in a unity Congress at Gotha.

The program agreed to by the newly formed German Social Democratic Party (SPD) at the Gotha unity congress in 1875 was in many ways an odd amalgam that brought together some ultra-radical verbiage, the content of which was either meaningless or simply wrong, alongside a series of practically moderate political demands. Both aspects of this "synthesis" were evident in the program's central demand for a "free state." Marx's *Critique of the Gotha Programme* subjected the document as a whole to a brutal interrogation. He pointed to the authoritarian implications of the claim that the SPD would fight for a "free state" and insisted that in the transitional period from capitalism to communism the state could only exist as "the revolutionary dictatorship of the proletariat," and that in avoiding this issue the SPD had opened itself up to a possible evolution toward liberalism (CW 24, 95).

In his earlier critique, Engels had argued, "Our party has *absolutely nothing to learn* from the Lassalleans in the theoretical sphere." Specifically, he stridently denied various Lassallean notions, including: the claims that in relation to the working class all other classes are a reactionary mass, the denial that the workers' movement was international in character, the "outmoded" idea of an "iron law of wages" by which workers receive a minimum for their work, the demand for state aid for workers' cooperatives as the means to liberation, and conversely the dismissal of work in the unions. These comments culminated, first, in his prefiguring of Marx's critique of the demand for a "free state" and, second, in a warning that should the program be adopted "Marx and I could *never* give our allegiance to a *new* party set up on that basis and shall have to consider most seriously what attitude—public as well as private—we should adopt towards it" (CW 45, 60–66). In a letter written later that year after the adoption of the program, Engels explained why neither he nor Marx had found it expedient to break with the new party. He pointed out that the bourgeois press had in fact read into it his and Marx's views. More importantly, the workers had done the same: "it is this circumstance alone which has made it possible for Marx and myself not to disassociate ourselves publicly from a programme such as this" (CW 45, 97–98).

In this context, Marx and Engels wagered that, despite the shortcomings of the party's program, the general superiority of the perspectives of the party's Marxist tendency would lead to its eventual hegemony within the organization. In the medium term this was the turn taken by events. Schorske points out that as Bismarck "unleashed his fury" against the socialist left, in the period between 1878 and 1890 the party "became really receptive to Marxism" (Schorske 1983, 3). Bismarck's authoritarian turn coincided with the publication of Engels's *Anti-Dühring* (1878), which, as we shall see later, won over many of the organization's cadre to Marxism. This process culminated with the revision of the party's program at the Erfurt congress of 1891.

While Engels welcomed the Erfurt Program as an improvement on the Gotha Program, he once again criticized the failure of the Germans to address the question of state power scientifically: "The political demands of the draft have one great fault. It lacks precisely what should have been said." Noting that "opportunism" (reformism) was "gaining ground in large sections of the Social-Democratic press," Engels argued that it was incumbent upon the framers of the program to spell out clearly to the German workers that the transition to socialism could only come "by force." He insisted that if the SPD did not make this clear then, in the long run, the party would go "astray." In this context he reminded his comrades, "[O]ur party and the working class can only come to power under the form of a democratic republic. This is even the specific form of the dictatorship of the proletariat" (CW 27, 217–232).

If opportunism was a problem in Germany, it seemed to dominate in England. In 1881 Engels eventually gave up writing for *The Labour Standard* because, as he wrote to the editor, he saw no evidence that the newspaper was progressing to become the kind of coherent socialist voice within the labor movement that it might be "if there was an undercurrent among the British working class tending towards emancipation from the liberal Capitalists." The problem was not so much with *The Labour Standard* as it was with the British working class itself, which showed no signs of moving to articulate its own independent political perspectives (CW 46, 123). Engels explained this situation by reference to a concept he and Marx had borrowed sporadically from common parlance since the 1850s: sections of the workers had formed a "labour aristocracy" (Draper 1978, 105–108). In 1885, he wrote,

> the great Trades Unions . . . are the organisations of those trades
> in which the labour of grown-up men predominates, or is alone
> applicable. Here the competition neither of women and children
> nor of machinery has so far weakened their organised strength.

The engineers, the carpenters and joiners, the bricklayers, are each of them a power, to that extent that, as in the case of the bricklayers and bricklayers' labourers, they can even successfully resist the introduction of machinery. That their condition has remarkably improved since 1848 there can be no doubt, and the best proof of this is in the fact that for more than fifteen years not only have their employers been with them, but they with their employers, upon exceedingly good terms. They form an aristocracy among the working class; they have succeeded in enforcing for themselves a relatively comfortable position, and they accept it as final. (CW 27, 265–266)

Engels explained this situation by reference to material benefits in Britain's monopoly of trade:

The truth is this: during the period of England's industrial monopoly the English working class have, to a certain extent, shared in the benefits of the monopoly. These benefits were very unequally parcelled out amongst them; the privileged minority pocketed most, but even the great mass had, at least, a temporary share now and then. And that is the reason why, since the dying-out of Owenism, there has been no Socialism in England. With the breakdown of that monopoly, the English working class will lose that privileged position; it will find itself generally—the privileged and leading minority not excepted—on a level with its fellow-workers abroad. And that is the reason why there will be Socialism again in England. (CW 27, 268)

If the rational core of this argument is its tangential reference to Britain's astonishing level of economic expansion after 1848, the concept of a labor aristocracy itself has proved to be far less satisfactory as an explanatory tool to make sense of working-class politics. Gareth Stedman Jones, for instance, comments on the "ambiguous and unsatisfactory" nature of this concept, while Charlie Post suggests that it "was neither theoretically rigorous nor a factually realistic explanation of working-class reformism" (Stedman Jones 1983, 62; Post 2010, 7). Indeed, though the concept of a labor aristocracy obviously had a descriptive resonance in nineteenth-century Britain, it was much less successful as an explanation of the nonrevolutionary nature of the working class at the time. The simple fact is that by creating more and better jobs on the one side and a framework within which workers could embed their own reformist institutions within the fabric of civil society on the other, economic expansion in the wake of the psychological blow to the idea of revolutionary politics that followed the defeat of Chartism provided the material underpinnings to explain why Engels's revolutionary interventions did not resonate with the readers of *The Labour Standard* in 1881 (Kirk 1985, 351; Saville 1988, 9–22; Hinton 1983, 10–13). Hobsbawm argues that industrial growth after the defeat of Chartism meant that "by and large the lives of most Britons improved" from 1850 to 1900, with a marked upswing after 1870. This secular trend toward improvements in workers' standard of living came to an end around 1900, such that by 1914 there had been a "perceptible stagnation or even decline in real wages" which underpinned the "extremely acute and widespread labour unrest" in the years leading up to and during the First World War (Hobsbawm 1999, 137). If improvements in the standard of living (in part won and policed by trade union struggle) rather than a monopoly of trade per se explains the nonrevolutionary character of the English working class long after the psychological reverberations of the defeat of Chartism had died away, the real lacuna in Engels's argument is any sense of the resilience of reformism within the labor movement after the ending of this period of rising living standards.

James Hinton for instance has detailed how supposed "labour aristocrats" in engineering became the vanguard of an increasingly revolutionary workers' movement in the years up to and especially during the First World War, and how this group came into conflict not only with capitalists and the state but also with their own union leaders (Hinton 1973, 57; 99). If some of Engels's comments on the labor aristocracy had hinted at the importance of the distinction between union leaders and their members, it was not until Rosa Luxemburg published *The Mass Strike* a decade after his death that this insight was transformed into a coherent account of the bureaucratic conservatism of the structurally reformist trade union leadership (Luxemburg 1970b).

Without a coherent structural theory of working-class reformism, Marx's and Engels's responses to the thing itself tended to be somewhat ad hoc in nature. Their most important joint statement (written by Engels) against incipient reformist tendencies within the German Social Democratic Party was penned as a *Circular Letter* to the leadership of the party in 1879. Over the previous few years, as we shall detail later, they had taken up the theoretical challenge of reformism through Engels's powerful critique of Eugen Dühring's proto-revisionism. Engels's response to Dühring was published in installments before eventual publication as a book in 1878. At the same time Bismarck introduced his antisocialist laws. By narrowing the space for reformist practice, Bismarck effectively ensured a keen audience for Engels's rich recapitulation of the politics of the *Manifesto*. However, in the short term, moderate elements within the SPD continued as before. Indeed, one social democratic member of the Reichstag with the connivance of the party's leadership but against its stated policy voted for monies for Bismarck. Upon discovering this Marx and Engels called the vote a "disgrace for the party" (CW 24, 260) and insisted that if the party did not change tack they would be forced to make a political break with it:

> For almost 40 years we have emphasised that the class struggle is the immediate motive force of history and, in particular, that the class struggle between bourgeoisie and proletariat is the great lever of modern social revolution; hence we cannot possibly co-operate with men who seek to eliminate that class struggle from the movement. At the founding of the International we expressly formulated the battle cry: the emancipation of the working class must be achieved by the working class itself. Hence we cannot co-operate with men who say openly that the workers are too uneducated to emancipate themselves, and must first be emancipated from above by philanthropic members of the upper and lower middle classes. If the new party organ is to adopt a policy that corresponds to the opinions of these gentlemen, if it is bourgeois and not proletarian, then all we could do—much though we might regret it—would be publicly to declare ourselves opposed to it and abandon the solidarity with which we have hitherto represented the German Party abroad. But we hope it won't come to that. (CW 24, 269)

The *Circular Letter* thus amounted to a powerful critique of the reformist substance of aspects of the party's practice. However, Marx and Engels combined this critique of practical reformism with a weak explanation for the roots of this reformism. They essentially dismissed reformism as a reflection of the malign influence within the party of "representatives of the petty bourgeoisie" (CW 24, 264, 267). Whether or not this was true in this specific instance, it is inadequate as a theory of working-class reformism. And though Marx had previously nuanced this position through his claim that workers too could act as the conduit of bourgeois influence once they "give up working and become *literati by profession* . . . always ready to consort with addleheads of the supposedly 'learned' caste," nowhere in their oeuvre did either he or Engels adequately address the problem of structural working-class reformism in the modern world (CW 45, 283; Fernbach 1974, 63; Johnson 1980). If this lacuna in their thought is remarkable given the power of their social interpretation of religion, it can partially be excused by the fact that the issue of structural reformism only came to a head after Engels's death during the so-called Revisionist Controversy. Nonetheless, as we shall see later, this lacuna in Engels's thought weakened his political radar when it came to dealing with the increasingly moderate leadership of the SPD in the years leading up to his death in 1895.

10

Method and Value

(Mis)Understanding *Capital*

The importance of Engels's contribution to the production, publication, and dissemination of Marx's *Capital* is difficult to overstate. First, his *Umrisse* was the inspiration for Marx's original turn to the critique of political economy. Second, and most famously, he supplied Marx with the financial and moral support without which not even the first volume of *Capital* would have been completed in Marx's lifetime. Third, especially in the early period of Marx's research on the political economists, the two men engaged in theoretical discussions about these ideas. Fourth, after he returned to work for his father's firm in 1850 he used his position at the heart of the Manchester bourgeoisie to supply Marx with crucial information on the details of the capitalist production and circulation processes. Fifth, he pressured Marx to break from the paralysis caused by his perfectionism to at least finish the first volume of *Capital*. Sixth, he did what he could by means of reviews and so forth to publicize Marx's ideas once *A Contribution to the Critique of Political Economy* and *Capital*, volume 1, had been published. Seventh, he carried out the painstaking job of getting Marx's almost unreadable and disorganized manuscripts into print in the dozen years following the death of his friend and comrade. What is more, he executed this final role as an ageing man with failing eyesight and, eventually, cancer, and while playing a key part in rearming a renewed international left through the exchange of innumerable letters and the (re)publication of many of Marx's old texts (Marx and Engels 1983). For all of these acts, the left owes Engels an enormous debt of gratitude.

Nonetheless, in reconstructing Marx's notes for volumes 2 and 3 of *Capital* Engels did, as modern scholars have discovered, tend to present Marx's ideas in a more finished and seamless form than was in fact the case (Vollgraf and Jucknickel 2002). This has led some of Engels's critics to claim that whereas Marx meant *Capital* to operate as a general analysis of all capitalist economies, because Engels included materials in volume 3 that were of a more local significance, he gave the impression that Marx believed that characteristics he viewed as specific to nineteenth-century English capitalism were of a more general import (Heinrich 1996–1997). Commenting on these criticisms, Fred Mosely rightly points out that though Engels can be criticized from the standpoint of modern methods of editorial scholarship, he nonetheless performed the superhuman task of editing Marx's manuscripts to the best of his abilities and to the great benefit of the left. Though he made mistakes, and while the revised edition of Marx's manuscripts should form the basis of future research, "Marx's theory of the distribution of surplus-value is by and large faithfully and accurately presented in Engels's Volume III . . . [and] Engels's Volume III should be considered Marx's Volume III" (Moseley 2016, 44). This is not to suggest that his errors in presenting Marx's ideas are unimportant, some at least are not. Rather, it is to locate these errors in their historical context and to recognize that they pale into insignificance when compared to the good done by Engels in getting volumes 2 and 3 of *Capital* to the publisher (just) before his own death (Moseley 2016).

However, even a charitable interpretation of Engels's role as Marx's editor cannot ignore the fact that he greatly misunderstood Marx's theory of value in a way that had profoundly deleterious theoretical and political implications for twentieth-century Marxism.

Chris Arthur has argued that Engels's misunderstanding of value theory illuminates deeper methodological concerns with Engels's thought (Arthur 1996). In 1859 Marx and Engels published outlines of their basic methodology. According to Arthur, discrepancies between the two essays illuminate deep divergences between the two of them. The first of these essays was Marx's preface to *A Contribution to the Critique of Political Economy*, followed by Engels's two-part review of this book. Both of these works are, for different reasons, somewhat opaque and difficult to interpret. In the first instance, as Arthur Prinz points out, Marx's preface was written with an eye to the censor (Prinz 1968). Secondly, Engels's review is incomplete: it was supposed to run to three parts, but only the first two installments were written because the journal in which it was being serialized, *Das*

Volk (effectively edited by Marx), went bankrupt before Engels had time to complete the final part of the review (CW 16, 673–674).

The central paragraph of Marx's preface is an infamously dense rehash of themes from *The German Ideology* (for a comparison of these texts, see Carver 1983, 72–77).

> In the social production of their existence, men inevitably enter into definite relations, which are independent of their will, namely relations of production appropriate to a given stage in the development of their material forces of production. The totality of these relations of production constitutes the economic structure of society, the real foundation, on which arises a legal and political superstructure and to which correspond definite forms of social consciousness. The mode of production of material life conditions the general process of social, political and intellectual life. It is not the consciousness of men that determines their existence, but their social existence that determines their consciousness. At a certain stage of development, the material productive forces of society come into conflict with the existing relations of production or—this merely expresses the same thing in legal terms—with the property relations within the framework of which they have operated hitherto. From forms of development of the productive forces these relations turn into their fetters. Then begins an era of social revolution. The changes in the economic foundation lead sooner or later to the transformation of the whole immense superstructure. (CW 29, 263)

This condensed summary of Marx's theory of history has been a source of debate since its first publication. Most controversially, it has been suggested that the Marx of the 1859 preface held to a mechanical and fatalistic theory of history (Ferraro 1992, 38). This interpretation is somewhat ironic given that Marx downplayed the active, agential side of his revolutionary politics, as Prinz points out, for the eminently practical reason of bypassing the censor to influence activists on the German left (Prinz 1968; Ste. Croix 1983, 47; Blackledge 2006a, 21, 27). Nonetheless, Marx's theory of history has often been interpreted thus, and this misunderstanding began early. Indeed, in response to a variant of this misunderstanding Engels felt compelled to distance his and Marx's ideas from crude forms of

"Marxism." In a famous letter to Joseph Bloch he argued:

> According to the materialist conception of history, the ulti-
> mately determining element in history is the production and
> reproduction of real life. Other than this neither Marx nor I
> have ever asserted. Hence if somebody twists this into saying
> that the economic element is the only determining one, he
> transforms that proposition into a meaningless, abstract, senseless
> phrase. The economic situation is the basis, but the various
> elements of the superstructure—political forms of the class
> struggle and its results, to wit: constitutions established by the
> victorious class after a successful battle, etc., juridical forms, and
> even the reflexes of all these actual struggles in the brains of
> the participants, political, juristic, philosophical theories, religious
> views and their further development into systems of dogmas—
> also exercise their influence upon the course of the historical
> struggles and in many cases preponderate in determining their
> form. There is an interaction of all these elements in which, amid
> all the endless host of accidents (that is, of things and events
> whose inner interconnection is so remote or so impossible of
> proof that we can regard it as non-existent, as negligible), the
> economic movement finally asserts itself as necessary. Otherwise
> the application of the theory to any period of history would
> be easier than the solution of a simple equation of the first
> degree. (CW 49, 34–35)

More specifically, in a letter to Conrad Schmidt, Engels argued that the
state, in contrast to economic reductionist readings of historical materialism,
would enjoy a degree of "relative independence" from the economic base,
such that "political power can wreak havoc with economic development"
(CW 49, 60). Engels stressed the importance of political, ideological, and
other "factors" within the historical process. However, rather than outline a
detailed map of his and Marx's method, he suggested that if Bloch wanted
to understand historical materialism he should read Marx's *Eighteenth Brumaire* and *Capital* alongside his own *Anti-Dühring* and *Ludwig Feuerbach
and the End of Classical German Philosophy*. In an unduly self-deprecating
comment, Engels wrote:

> Marx and I are ourselves partly to blame for the fact that the

younger people sometimes lay more stress on the economic side than is due to it. We had to emphasise the main principle vis-à-vis our adversaries, who denied it, and we had not always the time, the place or the opportunity to give their due to the other elements involved in the interaction. But when it came to presenting a section of history, that is, to making a practical application, it was a different matter and there no error was permissible. (CW 49, 36)

If the 1859 preface has been misinterpreted as advocating a fatalist theory of history, Marx might have mitigated this misunderstanding had he chosen to publish the much more substantial draft introduction he had written two years earlier. He elected not to do so because he believed the 1857 introduction anticipated results that had yet to be published: "A general introduction, which I had drafted, is omitted, since on further consideration it seems to me confusing to anticipate results which still have to be substantiated, and the reader who really wishes to follow me will have to decide to advance from the particular to the general" (CW 29, 261). This somewhat unfortunate decision meant that one of Marx's more substantial, mature methodological reflections was kept from Engels. First published in 1902–1903, Marx's 1857 introduction is important to anyone hoping to understand his method. In it, Marx famously argued:

> The economists of the seventeenth century, e.g., always begin with the living whole, with population, nation, state, several states, etc.; but they always conclude by discovering through analysis a small number of determinant, abstract, general relations such as division of labour, money, value, etc. As soon as these individual moments had been more or less firmly established and abstracted, there began the economic systems, which ascended from the simple relations, such as labour, division of labour, need, exchange value, to the level of the state, exchange between nations and the world market. The latter is obviously the scientifically correct method. The concrete is concrete because it is the concentration of many determinations, hence unity of the diverse. It appears in the process of thinking, therefore, as a process of concentration, as a result, not as a point of departure, even though it is the point of departure in reality and hence also the point of departure for observation and conception.

Along the first path the full conception was evaporated to yield an abstract determination; along the second, the abstract determinations lead towards a reproduction of the concrete by way of thought. In this way Hegel fell into the illusion of conceiving the real as the product of thought concentrating itself, probing its own depths, and unfolding itself out of itself, by itself, whereas the method of rising from the abstract to the concrete is only the way in which thought appropriates the concrete, reproduces it as the concrete in the mind. (Marx 1973, 101; CW 28, 37–38)

The clearly dialectical but not Hegelian method suggested in this paragraph has been subject to much interrogation, and we shall return to the parallels between it and Engels's conception of dialectics later (Ilyenkov 2013). As it happens Engels's review of Marx's *Contribution to the Critique of Political Economy* was written without sight of the 1857 introduction, and both Arthur and Carver argue that it suffers by comparison (Arthur 1996, 180; Carver 1983, 96–97). In his review, Engels wrote that whereas the Germans had previously lacked a first-rate political economist, Marx had now filled this gap. What is more, his contribution to political economy superseded those of his predecessors because his approach was rooted in a new, scientific approach to the study of history: "The essential foundation of this German political economy is the materialist conception of history, whose principal features are briefly outlined in the Preface to the above-named work" (CW 16, 469). Whereas Smith and Ricardo had proved themselves incapable of grasping the essence of capitalism because they could not see beyond its horizons, Marx's *historical* materialism allowed him to view capitalism in its essence as a transitory rather than a natural form. This was the first time that the phrase "the materialist conception of history" was used, and Carver makes much of it. He claims that this "brief notice represents a turning point in his thought, his career and in the Marx-Engels intellectual relationship." At this moment, according to Carver, Engels began to reduce Marx's thought to a crudely materialist caricature of itself that was subsequently picked up to become the methodological cornerstone of Soviet Marxism: "Marx's work was transmogrified in Engels's 1859 review into the academic philosophy that the self-clarification of *The German Ideology* had triumphantly superseded" (Carver 1983, 116).

Carver's evidence for this claim is flimsy indeed. To begin with, Marx was editing the journal in which Engels's essay was published, had asked Engels for the review, and Engels had offered it with a cover note suggesting, "[I]f you don't like it *in toto*, tear it up and let me have your opinion" (CW 40, 478). More specifically, the phrase "materialist conception of history" may have been new, but it certainly is not an eccentric description of either Marx's 1859 preface or the approach outlined in *The German Ideology*. Indeed, in the first version of *The German Ideology* Marx and Engels had written that "we know only a single science, the science of history" (CW 5, 28).

In his argument to the contrary, Carver suggests that, for Engels, 1859 marked a "turning point" after which he retreated from the insights of *The German Ideology* to embrace a warmed-over interpretation of Hegelianism. Carver writes: "Engels implied that Hegel's work . . . was the model for . . . 'a science in its own inner interconnections,'" and that the goal of such a science would look like Hegel's attempted "encyclopaedic system" of knowledge (Carver 1983, 100–102; cf. CW 16, 472). But Engels, who wrote in his preparatory notebooks for *Anti-Dühring* that "after Hegel" systems were "impossible" (Schäfer 1998, 43), suggested no such thing. Rather he asked a rhetorical question: How was the totality to be appropriated in the mind? He pointed out that Kant and especially Hegel had demolished the "metaphysical method" (of which more later), while Hegel's own method was "in its existing . . . essentially idealist . . . form quite inapplicable" (CW 16, 373). Carver acknowledges Engels's criticism of Hegel but does not adequately explore the substance of Engels's actual relationship to Hegel—other than by ridiculing his claim (repeated by Marx) that Marx had unpacked the rational kernel from the mystical shell of Hegel's philosophy (Carver 1983, 101–103; CW 16, 474–475; Marx 1976, 103; cf. Arthur 1996, 180–181). As we shall see, there are problems with Engels's formulation of his (and Marx's) debt to Hegel. But these problems did not lead him to search for an encyclopedic system of knowledge (Schäfer 1998). His goal was much more prosaic. He aimed to explicate the method underlying "Marx's critique of political economy" (CW 16, 475). In a sense, Carver is right to recognize a shift in the late 1850s, but this shift was inaugurated by Marx and it constituted, as Henri Lefebvre has argued, a deepening of the historical method outlined in *The German Ideology* (Lefebvre 2009, 69–74). Marx famously wrote to Engels in January 1858 stating: "I am, by the way, discovering some nice arguments. E.g. I have completely demolished the theory of profit as hitherto propounded. What was of great use to me as regards method of treatment was Hegel's *Logic* at which I had taken another look BY MERE ACCIDENT,

Freiligrath having found and made me a present of several volumes of Hegel, originally the property of Bakunin" (CW 40, 249). This letter was dated midway through the period in which Marx wrote the *Grundrisse* and clearly evidences that he had found Hegel useful when formulating his theory of value. It was this point that was registered by Engels a year later in his review of *A Contribution to the Critique of Political Economy*. A few months later, upon receiving from Marx a draft outline of the proposed structure of *Capital*, Engels complained that the "study of your ABSTRACT of the first half-instalment has greatly exercised me; IT IS A VERY ABSTRACT ABSTRACT INDEED—inevitably so, in view of its brevity—and I often had to search hard for the dialectical transitions, particularly since ALL ABSTRACT REASONING is now completely foreign to me" (CW 40, 304).

Clearly, Engels's task would have been easier had he had sight of the 1857 introduction, but he had not. Arthur argues that Engels's essay points to a very different conception of dialectic to that outlined in Marx's 1857 introduction. In his introduction, Marx argued that "[i]t would . . . be unfeasible and wrong to let the economic categories follow one another in the same sequence as that in which they were historically decisive. Their sequence is determined, rather, by their relation to one another in modern bourgeois society, which is precisely the opposite of that which seems to be their natural order or which corresponds to historical development" (Marx 1973, 107). For his part, Engels suggested that "the critique of political economy could still be arranged in two ways—historically or logically . . . [But] the logical method . . . is indeed nothing but the historical method, only stripped of the historical form and of interfering contingencies" (CW 16, 475). Arthur comments that whereas Marx had learned from Hegel the necessity of distinguishing "systematic dialectic (a method of exhibiting the inner articulation of a given whole) and historical dialectic (a method of exhibiting the inner connection between stages of development of a temporal process)," Engels "conflated the two" (Arthur 1996, 182–183). As to why Marx, as Engels's editor, had let this comment pass in 1859, Arthur suggests that it may well have been because "he was still undecided about the relevance of his logical arrangement of the categories for historical research" (Arthur 1996, 186).

Arthur claims that Engels's conflation of the logical and historical methods opened the door to his profound misunderstanding of Marx's *Capital*. In his preface to volume 3, Engels famously wrote that "at the beginning of Volume I, where Marx takes simple commodity production as his historical presupposition, only later, proceeding from this basis, to come to capital . . . he proceeds precisely there from the simple commodity and not from a conceptually and historically secondary form, the commodity as already modified by capitalism" (Marx 1981, 103). Elsewhere, in his supplement to the second edition of *Capital*, volume 3, he expanded on the implications of this argument: "the law of value applies universally . . . for the entire period of simple commodity production," which dates back to at least 3,500 BC (Marx 1981, 1037). This statement, as John Weeks points out, "leaps off the page at the reader." Weeks rightly argues that, if true, the implications of Engels's claim are profoundly destructive to Marx's critique of political economy: "To argue that the law of value ruled for five to seven thousand years . . . is to argue that exchange can occur amongst independent, self-employed producers without generating capitalism." Engels's claim amounts to a variant of Proudhon's ideas that Marx had so devastatingly criticized in 1847, and that, as noted earlier, he himself criticized so ably in his essay *The Housing Question*. To assume the truth of Engels's argument consequently strikes at the core of both his and much more substantially Marx's critique of Proudhon's reformist "critique of political economy from the standpoint of political economy." The law of value is not 3,500 years old but operates in a system of generalized commodity production where labor has been separated from the means of production such that the ability to work becomes commodified as labor power. Marx detailed the emergence of this system in his famous discussion of the primitive accumulation of capital (Marx 1976, 873–876). The fact that this argument and Marx's earlier critique of Proudhon built on insights from Engels's *Umrisse*, and that Engels himself insisted on the historical character of economic "laws" (CW 42, 136), makes his misunderstanding of value theory all the more unfortunate. In fact, his error implicitly opened the door to the sort of utopian and reformist politics he had explicitly fought against since the 1840s (Weeks 1981, 45).

Simply put, in his preface and supplement to volume 3 of *Capital*, Engels evidenced that he had "completely misconstrued Marx's value theory"; and he did so because he confused "concrete and abstract labour" (Weeks 1981, 8, 55). In his introduction to Marx's original draft of volume 3, Fred Moseley has lamented that the questions Engels asked of Marx about this volume evidence that "when Engels started this very difficult project, he appears to have had very little knowledge and overall understanding of Marx's Book III" (Moseley 2016, 3). It is difficult to overstate the importance of Engels's misunderstanding of the theoretical architecture of *Capital*. The distinction between the concepts of abstract and concrete labor sits at the core of Marx's mature critique of political economy—indeed, he wrote to Engels that it was one of the "the best points in my book" (CW 42, 407). This distinction is important because it is through the concept of abstract labor that Marx overcomes fundamental problems with the variants of the labor theory of value as conceived by Adam Smith and David Ricardo (Rubin 1979, 248–255; Elson 1979). Whereas neither Smith nor Ricardo fully grasped how distinct types of concrete labor could be compared, Marx solved this problem through the argument that labor has a dual character. It is both "concrete labour"—the specific act of working to produce useful things—and "abstract labour"—the process of value creation through the equalization of concrete acts of labor under the discipline of competition (Saad-Filho 2002, 26–29; Rubin 1973, 131–158; Colletti 1972, 82–92). Whereas Smith's and Ricardo's studies in political economy ultimately failed because they were unable to extricate their accounts of the labor theory of value from the superficial materiality of labor as a multiplicity of distinct concrete acts, Marx's concept of abstract labor allowed him to abstract from these concrete forms to grasp the more general value form. It was through the concept of abstract labor that Marx realized the scientific task of illuminating the essence of capitalism as a distinct mode of production (Meikle 1985, 63–70).

Unfortunately, Engels's misunderstanding of value theory framed the bulk of twentieth-century studies of the subject. One consequence of this theoretical failure was that the conception of the labor theory of value held by Marx's epigones became susceptible to the criticisms that had proved to be so devastating to Ricardo's and Smith's variants of the theory. This is exactly what happened in the 1970s and 1980s when the so-called neo-Ricardian critics of value theory mounted an overwhelming critique of the labor theory of value; or at least a critique that overwhelmed the variant of value theory that had roots in Engels's misunderstanding of Marx (i.e., Steedman 1977). Among the many malign consequences of this critique, capitalism disappeared as a specific object of inquiry— the neo-Ricardians proved themselves unable to distinguish between the exploitation of modern proletarians and the exploitation of other producers in precapitalist societies (Rowthorn 1980, 14–47). Furthermore, the neo-Ricardians reduced exploitation to a moral concept—not getting the rate for the job—with a simple reformist solution: a fair day's pay for a fair day's work. Consequently, by rejecting value theory a generation of left-wing intellectuals rejected Marxist revolutionary politics for a moralistic and reformist alternative (Fine and Harris 1979, 30; Elson 1979).

But if the defense of a scientific analysis of capitalism required that Marxists drop Engels's version of value theory, it is not at all clear that Arthur is right to suggest that Engels's errors on this score were caused by his conflation of the logical and historical methods in his conception of the dialectic. Diane Elson points out that the historical aspect of Engels's gloss on the dialectical method functions to evidence the historical character of determinate abstractions (Elson 1979, 140; cf. Zelený 1980, 70). Bertell Ollman has suggested that there is no clear-cut division between historical and logical methods: "by uncovering the connections between these and other social factors Marx is also displaying a moment in their unfolding historical relations" (Ollman 2003, 131). Similarly, Ben Fine, Costas Lapavitsas, and Dimitris Milonakis insist that the link between systematic and historical dialectic should be maintained because otherwise systematic dialectic risks becoming unhinged from the material world: "it grants unlimited degrees of freedom to the theorist when it comes to explaining particular historical phenomena" (Fine et al. 2000, 136). Meanwhile Alfredo Saad-Filho agrees that "purely conceptual reasoning is limited because it is impossible to explain why relations that hold in the analyst's head must also hold in the real world. . . . The concrete can be analysed theoretically only if historical analysis belongs within the method of exposition" (Saad-Filho 2002, 19–20; cf. Ilyenkov 2013, 202–208). More specifically, Jacques Bidet has shown that Marx deploys systematic dialectical analyses at various points within *Capital*, some of which have a clearly historical character while others do not (Bidet 2007, 170–174).

These arguments suggest that the fundamental problem with Engels's comments on simple commodity production relate not to his understanding of dialectics generally but to the narrower matter of his misunderstanding of value theory. As has been suggested, this weakness is important because it implies that Marx was wrong to believe, first, that value theory was the key to understanding modern capitalism as a historically specific mode of production and, second, that there was an intrinsic link between his critique of political economy and revolutionary politics (Colletti 1972, 91; Weeks 1981, 45). Nonetheless, because the error in respect to value theory contradicted the general trajectory of his politics, to correct it is a relatively simple matter within the theoretical framework he outlined most comprehensively in *Anti-Dühring*. It is thus a much less destructive weakness than is the claim that Engels's understanding of dialectics and method was fundamentally flawed.

Engels's interlocutors tend to agree with Arthur that the negative aspects of his contribution to value theory reflect broader weaknesses with his version of the dialectical method. But whereas Arthur is careful to distance himself from the more extreme claims of what he calls the "anti-Engels faction"—for instance, he does not allow his awareness of the errors marring Engels's presentation of *Capital* to detract from an appreciation of the fundamental importance of his role in the monumental task of preparing volumes 2 and 3 published in the decade after Marx's death (Arthur 1996, 175–179; Moseley 2016, 4)—commentary on Engels does tend to suffer from what he calls "Engels phobia" (Arthur 1996, 175–176). This is unfortunate not only because Engels's correspondence with Marx, especially in relation to his own role as a capitalist in Manchester, deeply influenced *Capital* (Harvey 2010, 214), but also because it is highly unlikely that Marx would have completed even volume 1 of *Capital* had it not been for Engels's encouragement. For instance, in this letter to Marx of January 31, 1860:

> The early appearance of [*Capital*] is obviously of paramount importance in this connection. . . . Do try for once to be a little less conscientious with regard to your own stuff; it is, in any case, far too good for the wretched public. The main thing is that it should be written and published; the short-comings that catch your eye certainly won't be apparent to the jackasses; and, when times become turbulent, what will it avail you to have broken off the whole thing before you have even finished the section on capital in general? I am very well aware of all the other interruptions that crop up, but I also know that the delay is due mainly to your own scruples. Come to that, it's surely better that the thing should appear, rather than that doubts like these should prevent its appearing at all. (CW 41, 14)

Engels's deep sense of the political importance of Marx's work, alongside his refusal to worry about what the "jackasses" might say about his own work, informed the production of his unjustly maligned defense of Marx's thought: *Anti-Dühring*.

11

Philosophy and Revolution

Anti-Dühring

A s I noted in the introduction to this book, Engels's ironically titled *Herr Eugen Dühring's Revolution in Science* proved to be his most influential and consequently his most controversial work. *Anti-Dühring* was written in response to the growing influence of Eugen Dühring's moralistic reformism within the German socialist movement at around the time of the Gotha Unity Congress of 1875, and as such it proved to be the most important theoretical response to the emerging reformist tendencies within European socialism prior to the publication of Rosa Luxemburg's *The Mass Strike* and Lenin's *The State and Revolution*.

Interestingly, because Dühring's book offered a global vision of social-ism through the medium of a critique of Marx's ideas, by following the order of Dühring's argument Engels's reply turned into a global defense of "Marxism." This approach informs the charge that Engels transformed Marx's ideas into an abstract "system" (Carver 1981, 85; 1989, 244; Thomas 2008, 12). But Engels explicitly rejected the claim that he was a system builder and rebuked other socialists for falling into the trap of system building. For instance, he wrote to Kautsky, February 20, 1889:

> Altogether you generalise far too much and this often makes you absolute where the utmost relativity is called for. . . . I would say a great deal less about the modern mode of production. In every case a yawning gap divides it from the facts you adduce and, thus out of context, it appears as a pure abstraction which,

far from throwing light on the subject, renders it still more obscure. (CW 48, 267–268; Schäfer 1998, 40)

The "Marxism" he defended was anything but a closed dogmatic system. Nonetheless, precisely because *Anti-Dühring* is "the only more or less systematic presentation of Marxism" written by either Marx or Engels, anyone wanting to reinterpret Marx's ideas has found it necessary to first detach this book from his seal of approval (Draper 1977, 24). Consequently, *Anti-Dühring* has become, alongside Lenin's *What Is to Be Done?*, one of the two most caricatured texts within the classical Marxist tradition. And just as Lenin's actual politics was very different from mythical versions of "Leninism" constructed from a misreading of *What Is to Be Done?* (Lih 2006; Blackledge 2006b; 2010a), the actual interpretation of Marxism presented in *Anti-Dühring* is very different from the way it is typically caricatured within the anti-Engels literature. In fact, because *Anti-Dühring* was and remains a superb introduction to Marx's ideas, critics of so-called "Engelsism" as a supposed distortion of "Marx's thought" tend inevitably to the conclusion that "many of Marx's own statements" were "too 'Engelsian'" (Timpanaro 1975, 77).

Engels's response to Dühring's criticism of Marx's dialectical method included a clear recapitulation of (his and) Marx's revolution in philosophy. Whereas, Dühring claimed that Marx's use of Hegelian terminology marked him out as a mystic, Engels defended Marx's method for its revolutionary transcendence of older forms of materialism and idealism into a new materialism through which social change could for the first time be adequately understood as revolutionary practice:

The old materialism was . . . negated by idealism. But in the course of the further development of philosophy, idealism, too, became untenable and was negated by modern materialism. This modern materialism . . . is not the mere re-establishment of the old, but adds to the permanent foundations of this old materialism the whole thought-content of two thousand years of development of philosophy and natural science. It is no longer a philosophy at all, but simply a world outlook which has to establish its validity and be applied not in a science of sciences standing apart, but in the real sciences. Philosophy is therefore "sublated" here, that is, "both overcome and preserved"; overcome as regards its form, and preserved as regards its real content. (CW 25, 128–129)

Because Marx's revolution in philosophy involved a synthesis of materialism and idealism, his new materialism incorporated the active side of philosophy that the old idealism had stressed, but which it had not been able fully to comprehend. Similarly, *Anti-Dühring* amounted to an important moment in what Steven Rose calls Engels's "long-running attempt to transcend mechanical materialism by formulating the principles of a materialist but non-reductionist account of the world and humanity's place within it: dialectical materialism" (Rose 1987, 25; cf. Benton 1979, 136).

Eugen Dühring was himself an academic convert to socialism who was also apparently something of an iconoclastic and charismatic lecturer at the University of Berlin. A radical when the academy was decidedly conservative, he was disliked by the university establishment almost as much as he was loved by a layer of young left-wing students. He was also blind, and this helped foster his reputation as the isolated academic champion of the oppressed. Unfortunately, Dühring's iconoclasm had more style than substance, and it underpinned what, in effect, amounted to a project for ridding German socialism of any orientation to class-based revolutionary politics. To this end, Dühring was dismissive of the rest of the left: the utopian socialists were fools, Fourier was "crazy" while Owen "had feeble and paltry ideas," Lassalle was "pedantic" and Marx's work was "without any permanent significance" (CW 25, 31). Conversely, Dühring portrayed his own work as the solution to all that was lacking in contemporary socialist theory.

In and of itself Dühring's extreme self-belief is a relatively unin-teresting characteristic: a charismatic egomaniac in the academy is hardly front-page news. Nonetheless, though he is only remembered today as the object of Engels's polemic, in the 1870s Dühring challenged the influence of Marxism on the German left. Indeed, both August Bebel and Eduard Bernstein were briefly drawn into his orbit. For this reason, in 1875, Wilhelm Liebknecht requested that Marx and Engels rise to the challenge of Dühring's growing ascendancy within the party. After a brief exchange of letters between the two old friends, Engels was tasked with writing a reply (CW 45, 118–124). When he eventually got around to writing *Anti-Dühring* a year later, he commented to Marx that, despite its profound limitations, the strength of Dühring's work lay in its appeal to a certain layer of would-be intellectuals: it was "arrant rubbish. Windy platitudes—nothing more, interspaced with utter drivel, but the whole thing is dressed up, not without skill, for a public with which the author is thoroughly familiar—a public that wants by means of a beggar's soup and little effort to lay down the law about everything." Consequently,

Engels's engagement with Dühring had nothing to do with the intrinsic merits of his work—there were few—but was rather intended to counter Dühring's damaging influence on the party (CW 45, 131). Commenting on this influence, Marx wrote to Sorge:

> In Germany a corrupt spirit is asserting itself in our party, not so much among the masses as among the leaders (upper class and "workers"). The compromise with the Lassalleans has led to further compromise with other waverers; in Berlin (via *Most*) with Dühring and his "admirers," not to mention a whole swarm of immature undergraduates and over-wise graduates who want to give socialism a "higher, idealistic" orientation, i.e. substitute for the materialist basis (which calls for serious, objective study if one is to operate thereon) a modern mythology with its goddesses of Justice, Liberty, Equality and *Fraternité*. (CW 45, 283)

This was a political problem of the first importance, and Carver's account, noted in the introduction to this volume, of Marx's tolerance toward Engels's apparently wrongheaded response to Dühring is highly implausible. Apart from anything else, while no evidence exists that Marx disagreed with Engels, there is plenty of evidence to the contrary. In the first instance, *Anti-Dühring* was written between five and seven years prior to Marx's death and while he was, if not at his peak, nonetheless intellectually active. Second, Engels claimed that he had read drafts of each chapter to Marx before sending them off for publication (CW 45, 119–120; CW 25, 9). And though it is conceivable, as Carver suggests, that Engels may have lied about this, the fact that Marx read at least the published version of the book is the most obvious interpretation of his criticisms to Wilhelm Bracke for the fragmentary way it was being serialized in *Vorwärts*, his grumblings about the quality of other materials published alongside it in the newspaper, and his decision to send a copy of the book to Moritz Kaufmann with a note suggesting that it was "very important for a true appreciation of German Socialism" (CW 45, 218, 285, 333–334).

    That Marx also wrote a foreword to the 1880 French edition of *Socialism: Utopian and Scientific*, which is made up of chapters from *Anti-Dühring*, should really silence critics who insist that he disagreed with the general thrust of its arguments. And though this claim is complicated by the fact that this foreword was initially published under Paul Lafargue's name, this decision is easily explicable. Lafargue had asked for a French edition of the most important sections from *Anti-Dühring* to help him in his struggle against opportunism on the French left; he had translated it, he had some influence in the revolutionary wing of French socialism, and he had a hand in revising Marx's text: Marx asked him to "polish the phrases, leaving the gist intact" (CW 45, 15). Against Carver's rather forced attempt to suggest that Marx had little or no knowledge of its content, Stephen Rigby is surely right to argue that it is almost inconceivable that Marx would either have left it unread or, having read it, left it uncriticized if he disagreed with it in important ways (Rigby 1992, 154–155). This conclusion is easier to accept once we recognize the misguided nature of Carver's and Thomas's interpretations of the substance of Engels's mature thought.

    Anti-Dühring was written in installments for the SPD newspaper *Vorwärts* before republication as a book in 1878. After an attempt by Dühring's supporters to prevent its publication in the party's press (McLellan 2006, 407), it was almost immediately banned under Bismarck's newly introduced antisocialist laws—though by effectively closing the door to reform, Bismarck helped confirm Engels's case for revolution. Substantively, Engels's response to Dühring involved, like Marx's 1859 preface and Engels's review of the same, a return to the themes of *The German Ideology*. And like its predecessor, *Anti-Dühring* was intended as a defense of revolutionary politics against what he believed were the sterile abstractions of moralistic reformism. But whereas *The German Ideology* was a creative work of self-clarification, *Anti-Dühring* interrupted Engels's creative engagement with natural science; albeit, it was enriched by themes from his unfinished *Dialectics of Nature*.

    The relationship of *Dialectics of Nature* to *Anti-Dühring* is another bone of contention among proponents of the divergence thesis. Carver suggests that Engels kept *Dialectics of Nature* from Marx because he was "canny enough to avoid creating disagreements with" him. This claim is highly dubious. Marx actually wrote to Liebknecht saying that Engels's engagement with Dühring "entails considerable sacrifice on his part, as he had to break off an incomparably more important piece of work [*Dialectics of Nature*—PB] to that end," while Gareth Stedman Jones has pointed out that the manuscript of Engels's *Dialectics of Nature* includes "comments in Marx's handwriting" (Carver 1983, 131; CW 45, 154; Stedman Jones 1977, 84; 1982, 295). More to the point, despite the often-dismissive tone of Engels's critics—of which Tristram Hunt's is merely the most ill-informed

(Hunt 2009, 283–289)—the arguments presented in *Dialectics of Nature* exhibit a direct continuity with the claim made in *The German Ideology* that "[w]e know only a single science, the science of history. One can look at history from two sides and divide it into the history of nature and the history of men. The two sides are, however, inseparable; the history of nature and the history of men are dependent on each other so long as men exist" (CW 5, 28–29). It is also likely, despite Terry Eagleton's suggestion to the contrary (Eagleton 2016, 61–62), that Marx shared Engels's views about the relationship between the social and natural sciences. Indeed, Marx described the theoretical sections from *Anti-Dühring* published in *Socialism: Utopian and Scientific* as "*an introduction to scientific socialism*" (Foster et al. 2010, 226; Rigby 1992, 150–153; CW 24, 339). And he was keenly aware that Engels was, by contrast with recent attempts to denigrate his understanding of science (for an anti-critique of some of these criticisms, see Foster and Burkett 2017, 165–203), as Hilary Putnam notes, "one of the most scientifically learned men of his century" (Putnam 1978, 237; cf. Cohen 1985, 351). Indeed, no less an authority than J. D. Bernal could write of Engels that if he were to be compared with other major figures from the philosophy of science writing in the nineteenth century such as "Haeckel, Lange and Spencer," he would be judged "not only their equal" but in many cases he would "far outstrip these figures" (Bernal qtd. in Roberts 1997, 167).

    Anti-Dühring's key argument was set forth in its opening paragraph. Whereas Dühring claimed that socialism was "the natural system of society" underpinned by a "universal principle of justice" (CW 25, 271), Engels insisted that as a concrete historical movement "[m]odern socialism" was inconceivable prior to the emergence of modern capitalist social relations: "[it] is, in its essence, the direct product of the recognition, on the one hand, of the class antagonisms existing in the society of today between proprietors and non-proprietors, between capitalists and wage-workers; on the other hand, of the anarchy existing in production" (CW 25, 16). Despite sitting uneasily with his (mis)understanding of value theory, this perspective helped frame Engels's famous critique of utopian socialism. Far from articulating a disparaging denunciation of the intellectual failings of his predecessors—this was Dühring's dismissive attitude—Engels recognized that the contemporary left owed a great debt to the utopians, and he believed that their weaknesses, as we noted earlier in relation to Fourier, were a consequence not of their folly but of the limited cultural parameters of the historical period in which they lived (Levitas 1990, 51).

The utopians were able to recognize the evils of the world, but, prior to the emergence of the modern working class, they could conceive of no mechanism inherent to the world in which they lived through which these evils might be addressed (CW 25, 246).

So, contra Dühring, Engels suggested that "to a make a science of socialism, it had first to be placed upon a real basis" (CW 25, 21). Engels claimed that the emergence of the modern working class meant that socialism had been transformed from an abstract and empty ideal into a concrete historical possibility. His socialism was consequently a novel, emergent force with a corresponding emergent value system. So, whereas Dühring claimed that morality stands as a "special . . . absolutely immu table . . . truth . . . above history" (CW 25, 79), Engels countered that though some eternal truths did exist, these were few and far between and usually took the form of platitudes. He distinguished between three levels of scientific enterprise: the study of inanimate objects, the study of living organisms, and the study of human history. If exact, universal truths are most likely to occur in the first group; in reality, because the sciences relating to these areas are replete with competing hypotheses, such truths are "remarkably rare." The situation with regard to the second group is even less certain, while, in the third group where "repetition of condition is the exception and not the rule," knowledge becomes "essentially relative." Consequently, it is close to impossible to talk of "immutable truths" in respect to human societies (CW 25, 81–85). And the contested nature of the human sciences was magnified when applied to the study of ethics:

> If, then, we have not made much progress with truth and error, we can make even less with good and evil. This opposition manifests itself exclusively in the domain of morals, that is, a domain belonging to the history of mankind, and it is precisely in this field that final and ultimate truths are most sparsely sown. The conceptions of good and evil have varied so much from nation to nation and from age to age that they have often been in direct contradiction to each other. (CW 25, 86)

Though Engels believed that the profound historical variation of morality should consign the idea of transhistorical moral truths to the dustbin of history, this belief did not entail that he embraced a form of nihilism (Blackledge 2010b). In fact, the opposite is the case. This insight actually underpinned his value system. His rejection of the idea of timeless moral precepts informed the questions he posed of contemporary morality. Which moral standpoint at the present juncture, he asked, "contains the maximum elements promising permanence which, in the present, represents the overthrow of the present, represents the future"? His answer was "proletarian morality," or the system of values congruent with the struggle of the modern working class for freedom against alienation (CW 25, 87).

Clearly, proletarian morality is rooted in sectional concerns that emerged as a historical phenomenon alongside and in opposition to modern capitalism. Nevertheless, it is not a *mere* sectional interest: by creating a world system of universal interconnection, capitalism created for the first time the basis for a universal interest. Meanwhile workers' struggles against alienation had emerged as the practical means to realize this universal human interest. Engels provides a useful historical sketch of the roots of this conflict. In medieval society both production and appropriation were individualized and local. This was a parochial world in which the idea of a concrete universal human interest was simply meaningless. With the development of capitalism, however, production became ever more interconnected and concentrated. But if capitalism had thus transformed production from an individual to a social system, appropriation remained privatized. The structural antagonism between capitalists and workers was underpinned by this antagonism between social production and individual appropriation (CW 25, 258). The intertwining of these contradictions suggested that the coming "proletarian revolution" simultaneously represented a sectional class conflict against capital and a struggle for the general interest against capitalist alienation: "this act of universal emancipation is the historical mission of the modern proletariat" (CW 25, 269–270).

Proletarian morality is therefore an emergent property within history intimately linked to a specific group that, nevertheless, represents, for the first time in history, a real movement for the general human interest. Engels defended this proposition through a concrete application of what he called the "dialectical method used by Marx" (CW 25, 114). *Anti-Dühring* is, among many other things, a powerful defense of this method. Engels felt he had to make such a defense to counter the seeming power of Dühring's analytical argument from first principles to transhistorical conclusions (CW 25, 88, 33). Leaving to one side the unwitting biases smuggled into Dühring's axioms, a more fundamental problem with his approach was of how he treated these abstractions.

Engels argued that although modern science from the middle of the fifteenth century onward marked a profound breakthrough in knowledge, it did so at a cost. The analytical method of dissecting problems into their constituent parts informed a strong tendency for modern science to study these parts in isolation. This assumption is problematic because it is impossible to comprehend real movement except at the level of conceptual wholes—evolution by natural selection, for instance, is only conceivable through the dynamic interaction between individuals, species, and environment across time (Levins and Lewontin 1985, 134). Conversely, the study of isolated parts, even when brought into relation with each other, lends itself to a "narrow, metaphysical mode of thought" (CW 25, 22). Engels borrowed the term "metaphysical" from Hegel, and like him and Marx, he used it in a disparaging way to describe the one-sidedly abstract and static conceptions of reality associated especially with classical empiricism:

> To the metaphysician, things and their mental reflexes, ideas, are isolated, are to be considered one after the other and apart from each other, are objects of investigation fixed, rigid, given once for all. He thinks in absolutely irreconcilable antitheses. . . . For him a thing either exists or does not exist; a thing cannot at the same time be itself and something else. Positive and negative absolutely exclude one another; cause and effect stand in a rigid antithesis one to the other. (CW 25, 22; cf. CW 4, 125; Sayers 1980a, 1–7; Wood 2004, 167–168)

Whatever the undoubted strengths of their works, the metaphysicians tended to squeeze real motion and qualitative change out of their image of reality. And by recombining constituent parts as externally related monads, they remained trapped in a narrow empiricist conception of causality. If this approach more-or-less fitted with the cutting edge of scientific progress in the seventeenth and eighteenth centuries, its limits became increasingly apparent in light of further scientific advances in the nineteenth century.

Darwin's theory of evolution by natural selection was merely the most important of a series of scientific discoveries that pointed in the direction of dialectical thinking. According to Engels, Darwin "dealt the metaphysical conception of nature the heaviest blow" because he showed in practice, though he did not always grasp the deeper theoretical implications of his own approach, that a real scientific understanding of nature is impossible without a conception of the mediated and contradictory essence of wholes. Engels thus suggested that "nature," especially as it was understood through the most advanced parts of science in the nineteenth century—alongside

Darwinism he notes the discovery of the cell and the transformation of energy (CW 26, 385)—"is the proof of dialectics" (CW 25, 23). This is because modern science has shown, contra the metaphysicians, that "*[m]otion is the mode of existence of matter*" (CW 25, 55).

Engels was adamant that the empiricist approach was unable to fully grasp the dynamic essence of what we might now call the ecological whole. On the one hand, because facts could not be understood except through the lens of theory, to suppose an empiricist contempt for theory leads to mysticism: "However great one's contempt for all theoretical thought, nevertheless one cannot bring two natural facts into relation with each other, or understand the connection existing between them, without theoretical thought. The only question is whether one's thinking is correct or not, and contempt of theory is evidently the most certain way to think naturalistically, and therefore incorrectly" (CW 25, 354; CW 27, 287). Galvano Della Volpe comments: "the correctly anti-empiricist and anti-positivist Engels . . . noted that it was impossible to prove the evolution of the species through induction alone" and that concepts like species, genus, and class had been "rendered *fluid*" by Darwin, becoming "*relative* or *dialectical* concepts" (Della Volpe 1980, 174–175). On the other hand and more generally, Engels clearly distanced his realist method from the surface realism of positivism and empiricism—"anyone who merely considered the surface of things would say that all was confusion" (CW 48, 487)—while insisting on the provisional character of knowledge: "The history of science is the history of the gradual elimination of that rubbish and/or its replacement by new, if progressively less ridiculous, rubbish" (CW 49, 62). Indeed, despite admitting in a letter to Ferdinand Tönnies of January 24, 1895, that Auguste Comte had a brilliant mind, he complained that his insights were ruined by his "narrow philistine outlook" (CW 50, 430). For Engels science or *Wissenschaft* refers to a method rather than to positivist results (Green 2008, 319). This is why John O'Neill is right to argue, against claims to the contrary (Thomas 2008, 5, 15–22), that Engels was not a positivist (O'Neill 1996; cf. Benton 1979; Creaven 2000).

If Darwinism was the high-water mark of the scientific revolution that underpinned the movement from a metaphysical to a dialectic viewpoint in the study of the natural world, this process was complemented within classical German philosophy through the work of Hegel. In *Ludwig Feuerbach and the End of Classical German Philosophy*, Engels argued that "the true significance and the revolutionary character of Hegelian philosophy" lay in its recognition that truth was no longer a collection of ready-made dogmatic statements, which, once discovered, had merely to be learned by heart. Truth now lay in the process of cognition itself, in the long historical development of science, which ascends from lower to ever higher levels of knowledge without ever reaching, by discovering so-called absolute truth, a point at which it can proceed no further, where it has nothing more to do than to sit back and gaze in wonder at the absolute truth to which it had attained. (CW 26, 359)

Unfortunately, or so Engels claimed, in his mature writings Hegel incoherently combined this insight with the suggestion of the "absolute truth" of his system (CW 26, 360). After Hegel's death, the contradiction between these two aspects of his thought became manifest as a division between those of his followers who embraced his conservative system and their left-wing "Young Hegelian" critics who extended his revolutionary method (CW 26, 363). This conflict took the form of a struggle over the nature of religion, specifically the Prussian state's embrace of a literal interpretation of the gospels, while the Young Hegelians gravitated toward the powerful criticisms of religion outlined by the eighteenth-century French materialists. This process initially culminated with the publication of Feuerbach's *Essence of Christianity*.

Feuerbach argued that religious ideas were mental reflections of real human powers: by worshipping god(s), people were kneeling before an alienated image of their own powers. Similarly, because Hegel conceived the real world as an emanation of absolute spirit, his system was but a variant of religious alienation. The simple and profound point caught the imagination of the German philosophical left in the 1840s, and for a moment, or so Engels claimed, "everyone" was a Feuerbachian. But Hegelianism had suffered a strange defeat. Unlike Marx, who moved to work through the contradictions of Hegel's system, the Feuerbachians merely discarded Hegel's philosophy (CW 26, 365; cf. CW 1, 84; Arthur 1986, 108).

By contrast with this approach, as I noted earlier, in *The German Ideology* Marx and Engels answered Stirner's critique of the True Socialist implications of Feuerbach's humanism by working through the contradictions of Hegelianism. Commenting on this process, Engels wrote that while Feuerbach and the materialists were right in respect to "the great basic question of all . . . concerning the relation of thinking and being," mechanical materialism failed to recognize that though being determines consciousness, this is not a mechanical process. Whereas in nature "laws assert themselves unconsciously," because in the social world "everything which motivates men must pass through the brains," which play an active part in the process of cognition, these determinations are applied "consciously" (CW 26, 365, 373, 383). By this route Marx and Engels placed the Hegelian dialectic "upon its head." Consciousness was, as Hegel had argued, an active and never-ending process of cognition, but, contra Hegel, consciousness was best understood as an aspect of nature making sense of, and acting upon, its material determinants to meet its consciously desired ends (CW 26, 383). This is the philosophical underpinning of the claim that people make history but not in circumstances of their own choosing, and it is the reason why Engels insisted that "[t]he German working-class movement is the heir to German classical philosophy" (CW 26, 398). So, while Engels argued that the "epoch-making" power of the Hegelian method lay in its recognition of the fact that "for the first time the whole world, natural, historical, intellectual, is represented as a process" (CW 25, 24), he simultaneously insisted that this insight was undermined by Hegel's idealism. By inverting the relationship between consciousness and reality, Hegel was unable to grasp real historical change. His system was consequently a "colossal miscarriage." This criticism suggests that it would be wrong to assume that Engels imposed Hegelian categories on nature. As he wrote in the *Dialectics of Nature*, "to me there could be no question of building the laws of dialectics into nature, but of discovering them in it and evolving them from it" (CW 25, 12–13; cf. Levins and Lewontin 1985, 279). So while Engels drew on Hegel, his understanding of natural evolution involved an explicit break with his mentor's system (Sayers 1996, 168–169). Specifically, he argued that to escape both the contradictions of Hegel's system and the limitations of Feuerbach's materialism, he and Marx (though he downplayed his own role) had, in the 1840s, gravitated toward a new dialectical materialist method of analysis (CW 25, 27).

By deploying both materialist and dialectical terminology in their work—on Hegel Marx wrote, "I therefore openly avowed myself the pupil of that mighty thinker, and even, here and there in the chapter on the theory of value, coquetted with the modes of expression peculiar to him" (Marx 1976, 103)—Marx and Engels opened themselves up to a century-long tendency for their critics to dismiss them as either mechanical materialists or dialectical obscurantists. If, as we have seen earlier, the charge that their "practical materialism" was but a rehash of eighteenth-century mechanical materialism does not hold water, the actual relationship between their dialectical method and Hegel's approach is much more complex than is implied by superficial similarities. Indeed, to coquette with Hegelian categories may well mark a homage paid, but it certainly does not imply agreement (Ilyenkov 2013, 149–167).

Unfortunately, there is a problem with Engels's claim that while Marx rejected the political conclusions of Hegel's conservative system he embraced his dialectical method. As many scholars have pointed out, Hegel's system cannot be separated from his method. Fortunately, this claim is less problematic for Engels than critics such as Rosen suggest (Rosen 1982, 28), for beneath his superficial comments about the distinction between Hegel's method and his system, Engels did in fact recognize that the Hegelian method was as flawed as was its system. He wrote: "according to Hegel, dialectics is the self-development of the concept . . . in its Hegelian form this method was no use" (CW 26, 383; cf. CW 42, 138; CW 49, 287). He consequently ridiculed Dühring for committing "the blunder of identifying Marxian dialectics with the Hegelian" (CW 25, 114). In fact, when Engels wrote that Marx had taken up Hegel's method but not his system, he is best understood as making the more limited claim that, for Marx, as for Hegel at his best, the process of searching for truth would never be "final and complete." But whereas the Hegelian concept developed deductively, for Marx conceptual deepening emerged through the successive introduction of more complex determinations as he sought to raise theory to the concrete level of practice. From this perspective, as Allen Wood points out, Engels's comments on the method/system distinction is "not necessarily wrong, but it is superficial and possibly misleading" (Wood 2004, 215).

But if Engels could have avoided much misunderstanding had he detailed the differences between his (and as he claimed Marx's) method on the one side and Hegel's on the other, he did not do this because the main thrust of his argument was to counter Dühring's claim that his system was "final and complete." Commenting on Dühring's assertion that the idea that contradictions existed in reality was "absurd," Engels accepted that the logical criticism of internal contradictions was true enough, but only within the narrow parameters and when viewing things in isolation and at rest. An adequate understanding of change demanded that theory move beyond these parameters. According to Engels, to grasp the reality of motion it was important to recognize the existence of contradictions in reality (CW 25, 110–111). Dühring seemed to confirm this claim when he suggested that "up to the present there is 'no bridge' whatever 'in rational mechanics from the strictly static to the dynamic' " (CW 25, 111). Engels had much fun pointing out that by this statement Dühring effectively granted the existence of contradictions in reality because motion so obviously was a constituent part of reality; Dühring's denial of this suggested his method of analysis was moribund (CW 25, 111–112).

Far from evidencing the absurdity of his thought, Marx's coquetting with the Hegelian concept of contradiction was his way of trying to cognize movement in history. He wrote of "the correctness of the law discovered by Hegel in his *Logic*, that at a certain point merely quantitative differences pass over by a dialectical inversion into qualitative distinctions" (CW 25, 116; Marx 1976, 423). In relation to this claim, Scott Meikle notes that the key to Marx's critique of Ricardo was not his criticism of the latter's ahistorical conception of capitalism—though important, this argument merely proved the negative point that markets were not natural. It was much more significant that Ricardo had failed to conceptualize value as a specifically capitalist form. This conceptual critique had profound political implications. Marx insisted that only on the basis of a proper appreciation of the contradictory unity of the use and exchange values of commodities could capitalism adequately be understood in its dynamic, antagonistic, and historically transient essence. So, to move beyond the negative claim that capitalism was not natural to the positive claim that it was pregnant with its alternative demanded that it be conceptualized as a contradictory unity of diverse elements (Meikle 1985, 65).

From this perspective, Marx's conceptual architecture deepens and changes as more and more diverse elements are integrated into the concept of the concrete totality as a "concentration of many determinations." And though Engels may have misunderstood the value form, he clearly understood, as he wrote in the preface to the third volume of *Capital*, that where "things and their mutual relations are conceived not as fixed but rather as changing, their mental images too, i.e. concepts, are also subject to change and reformulation" (Marx 1981, 103; Saad-Filho 2002, 14). As Dill Hunley writes: "Engels did not speak of 'rising from the abstract to the concrete.' . . . But a careful reading of his comments shows his little-appreciated understanding of the overall role theoretical paradigms played in the thought process. In the introduction to *Anti-Dühring* and his comments to Conrad Schmidt, Engels once again expressed views very close to those of Marx without using his precise wording" (Hunley 1991, 92). This conception of reality illuminates the key difference between the dialectical and nondialectical approaches: the former unlike the latter points to the possibility of qualitative change because of the way it views relations as internal to things rather than as expressions of external interactions between them. Bertell Ollman insists that Marx and Engels agreed on this methodological issue: "Marx's ontology declares the world an internally related whole; his epistemology breaks down the whole into relational units whose structural interdependence is reflected in the meanings of his concepts; his inquiry, by tracing the links between these units, fills in the details of this whole" (Ollman 2003, 147; cf. 1976, 52).

In *Anti-Dühring* and more so in *Dialectics of Nature*, Engels explored those characteristics of dialectical thought that facilitated an understanding of the real in its fully dynamic essence: the way in which, as Marx put it, "the ideal is nothing but the material world reflected in the minds of man, and translated into forms of thought" (Marx 1976, 102). Engels's exposition of this method includes his infamous three "laws of dialectics": "The law of the transformation of quantity into quality and vice versa; The law of the interpenetration of opposites; The law of the negation of the negation" (CW 25, 356). A sea of ink has been spilled debating these "laws," and most of it generates more heat than light. Part of the problem is that Engels, drawing from Hegel, gave very problematic illustrative examples of the laws. Besides, the laws as stated—and it should be remembered that they were stated most explicitly in the incomplete and unpublished manuscript of *Dialectics of Nature* (where they are mentioned in *Anti-Dühring*, by contrast, Engels merely gave examples of two of the laws as concrete counters to Dühring's criticisms of Marx)—are general almost to the point of banality. Nonetheless, they do illuminate important characteristics of reality that Dühring and contemporary analytical philosophers miss (Sayers 1980a, 1–7).

Engels was right that both nature and society are in a constant process of flux, and that if we are to escape the need for some external stimulus for change—God setting the planets in motion in Newton's system, for instance—we need an account of immanent tendencies to change. To follow formal logic in demanding a law of noncontradiction—that A be equal to A while not being equal to not A—is all well and good, but in and of itself it does not get us very far. Humans are humans and not chimps, but not very long ago we shared a common ancestor, suggesting that this distinction is not quite so clear-cut as it first appears. To understand the process of evolution, for instance, requires some account of a dynamic internal to nature. Engels's concept of the transformation from quantity to quality allows us to conceptualize speciation as a process. Small quantitative changes over generations lead eventually to qualitative leaps as new species are born (and old ones die out). This model is dependent on an account of things not as isolated and fixed entities but rather as processes constituted through their internal relations.

It was to these internal relations that Engels referred when he deployed the Hegelian concept of the interpenetration of opposites. He insisted that if we are to conceive real concrete wholes in movement, they need to be understood in all their contradictory richness. Conversely, attempts to make sense of these wholes by using the category of identity tend to an impoverished conception of change (Sayers 1980b, 67–143). For Marx, dialectics is consequently a higher form of method not a higher form of logic (Meikle 1979, 14). By striving to break down wholes into noncontradictory parts, analytical philosophers willfully blind themselves to essential characteristics of reality. It may be true, for instance, that commodities can be understood as mere utilities, but this approach tells us nothing about capitalism as a historically specific, antagonistic and crisis-prone system. Theory should aim at articulating concepts adequate to the task of illuminating reality in all its complexity. By contrast with the reduction of commodities to utilities, Marx's view that they are constituted, in the first instance, simultaneously and essentially as exchange and use values has the great merit of underpinning his account of capitalism not only as a historically specific mode of production, but also one that is dynamic and replete with the immanent potential for change.

This conceptual innovation was the essential first step in *Capital*'s movement to grasp capitalism as "a rich totality of many determinations and relations" (Marx 1973, 100). *Capital* is thus the most detailed instance of the dialectical method at work. Its aim is to grasp the totality as a rich interplay between these determinations and relations in a way that "comprehends things and their representations, ideas, in their essential connection, concatenation, motion, origin, and ending" (CW 25, 23).

As to the notion of the "negation of the negation," which Dühring criticized as a "dialectical crutch," that added nothing to Marx's otherwise useful sketch of the primitive accumulation of capital. Engels's reply was effectively a rehearsal of the power of the obstetric metaphor by which existing society is viewed as being pregnant with its alternative (Blackledge 2015). He suggested that as capitalism evolved there developed a concentration of wealth on the one side and misery on the other—a process that creates the potential for revolutionary transformation of capitalism into a new social formation within capitalism itself (CW 25, 124). Far from imposing Hegelian categories on reality, Engels insisted that Marx generalized the concept of the negation of the negation from his concrete analysis of capitalism. He deployed this concept to make sense of the way that capitalism not only dehumanizes people (the negation) but also of how, in rebelling against this condition, these dehumanized people create networks of solidarity that point toward a *positive* alternative to capitalism (the negation of the negation) (Marx 1976, 929; CW 25, 124). This was a specific example of Engels's more general claim that his dialectical laws, far from being imposed on reality, were generalized from the study of reality. "It is . . . from the history of nature and human society that the laws of dialectics are abstracted" (CW 25, 356).

If the new materialism insisted that nature could best be understood as a dynamic unity of its myriad parts, it also recognized that humanity itself had a history. Clearly, it is impossible to deny human history as a trivial succession of events—one damn thing after another, as Toynbee complained. The new materialism departed from the old by starting from a recognition of the profundity of Hegel's claim that the Greeks were different from the moderns: social evolution was a reality. By recognizing this insight, the new materialism was historical as well as dialectical. Whereas the "old materialism looked upon all previous history as a crude heap of irrationality and violence; modern materialism sees in it the process of evolution of humanity, and aims at discovering the laws thereof" (CW 24, 303). Only from this perspective could the reality of modern socialism be grasped as a truly novel phenomenon congruent with the emergence of capitalist society. According to Engels, Marx's greatness lay in the fact that he had pierced beneath the surface appearance of reality to reveal the historical novelty of the *inner essence* of the new capitalist system.

So, whereas truth and morality were for Dühring absolutes, Engels insisted that truth was better understood as a process of becoming. Marx and Engels had made precisely this point in *The German Ideology*. By contrast with modern liberal political theory's axiomatic assumption of a transhistorical "man," the starting point of their analysis was real concrete historical men and women as they emerged at a specific historical juncture. As biological beings these people were products of natural selection, but as social beings they were also products of cultural evolution. This insight, alongside his keen sense of history, underpinned Engels's attempt to put meat on the bones of the obstetric metaphor. Borrowing from Marx, he argued that with the emergence of the modern working class, society becomes pregnant with the possibility of socialism (CW 25, 171; Marx

1976, 92, 916; CW 42, 494, 498; CW 20, 224). If this metaphor illuminates both the dynamic nature of social relations and the concrete nature of Marx and Engels's ideals (Bloch 1986; Blackledge 2012a, 132–134), like any metaphor it tends to absurdity if pushed too far; societies are not pregnant women and social change does not occur with a biological inevitability. But deployed sensibly, it is the methodological basis of Lukács's claim that the Marxist dialectic underpinned Marx and Engels's recognition of "the present as a historical problem" (Lukács 1971, 157).

Despite some clumsy formulations, Engels's deployment of the concept of the interpenetration of opposites does suggest that socialism is a historical *potentiality* rather than an inevitability. Indeed, Rosa Luxemburg's interpretation of *Anti-Dühring* as a call to arms is rooted in his claim that society is a contradictory whole capable of moving toward "ruin, or revolution" (CW 25, 153). As noted earlier, Luxemburg's proclamation that the alternatives for humanity were "socialism or a regression into barbarism" was drawn from Engels's suggestion that "if the whole of modern society is not to perish, a revolution in the mode of production and distribution must take place, a revolution which will put an end to class distinctions" (Luxemburg 1970c, 269; CW 25, 146). If this interventionist reading of Engels seems odd to those who assume he embraced a mechanical and empiricist conception of science, once we recognize that the whole thrust of his argument in *Anti-Dühring* is that mechanical models of science are inadequate, the interventionist implications of his "practical materialism" shine through. He may well have argued that human history remains part of natural history, but he was equally explicit that the former should not be subsumed within the latter. He insisted, as previously noted in the discussion of his writings on religion, that to move beyond capitalist alienation required political intervention: "mere knowledge . . . is not enough . . . what is above all necessary . . . is a social *act*" (CW 25, 301).

This demand for political intervention illuminates both the continuities between *The German Ideology* and *Anti-Dühring* and the nature of Engels's materialism. By contrast with critics such as Meikle who suggest he had reverted back to a form of mechanical materialism (Meikle 1999), Engels was adamant that his conception of materialism is nonreductive (Sayers 1996, 153). Indeed, with respect to the natural sciences he insisted that

> the transition from one form of motion to another always remains a leap, a decisive change. This is true of the transition from the mechanics of celestial bodies to that of smaller

masses on a particular celestial body; it is equally true of the transition from the mechanics of masses to the mechanics of molecules—including the forms of motion investigated in physics proper: heat, light, electricity, magnetism. In the same way, the transition from the physics of molecules to the physics of atoms—chemistry—in turn involves a decided leap; and this is even more clearly the case in the transition from ordinary chemical action to the chemism of albumen which we call life. Then within the sphere of life the leaps become ever more infrequent and imperceptible. (CW 25, 61–62)

Beyond the emergent properties of distinct aspects of nature—physics, chemistry, biology, and so forth—Engels also insisted that human agency was a further emergent property that could not be mechanically reduced to our nature (Benton 1979, 122; Creaven 2000, 34). In *Ludwig Feuerbach and the End of Classical German Philosophy* he suggested:

In nature—in so far as we ignore man's reverse action upon nature—there are only blind, unconscious agencies acting upon one another, out of whose interplay the general law comes into operation. Of all that happens—whether in the innumerable apparent accidents observable upon the surface, or in the ultimate results which confirm the regularity inherent in these accidents—nothing happens as a consciously desired aim. In the history of society, on the contrary, the actors are all endowed with consciousness, are men acting with deliberation or passion, working towards definite goals; nothing happens without a deliberate intention, without a desired aim. (CW 26, 387; cf. CW 25, 492)

If these lines point to the nonreductive core of Engels's social theory, his analysis of the relationship between freedom and necessity shows how he simultaneously avoided the opposite error of reifying "free will" (Timpanaro 1975, 103). Again, he found Hegel useful here. By contrast with the sterile opposition between autonomy and heteronomy, he returned to Hegel's famous definition of freedom as the appreciation of necessity: "Necessity is blind only in so far as it is not understood" (CW 25, 105). Commenting on this line, Engels wrote, "Freedom does not consist in any dreamt-of independence from natural laws, but in the knowledge of these laws, and in the possibility this gives of systematically making them work towards definite ends" (CW 25, 106). Andrew Collier observes that, conceived thus, freedom's understanding of necessity does not imply the nominal freedom of the prisoner who bows before necessity by agreeing to "come quietly," but rather it is more analogous to the freedom of the yachtswoman who uses her skill and knowledge of the sea to sail near to the wind rather than to be merely buffeted, and possibly sunk, by it (Collier 1994, 193). From the invention of fire through the industrial revolution and beyond, humanity's powers of understanding and concomitant level of control over nature tended to increase through history. And the development of humanity's productive powers underpinned the development of human freedom: "Freedom therefore consists in the control over ourselves and over external nature, a control founded on knowledge of natural necessity; it is therefore necessarily a product of historical development. The first men who separated themselves from the animal kingdom were in all essentials as unfree as the animals themselves, but each step forward in the field of culture was a step towards freedom" (CW 25, 106). And while Engels's use of the language of "control" to describe humanity's relationship with nature might suggest a promethean tendency in his thought, he simulta-neously insisted that humanity's relationship to nature should be under-stood dialectically. We relate to nature not externally as a power over it, but dialectically through a unity (not identity) of the natural and social realms. This meant that he was very much alive to the ecological limits of human activity. John Bellamy Foster has argued that his comments on the unintended consequences of earlier attempts to master nature have a very modern, ecological ring to them (Foster et al. 2010):

> Let us not, however, flatter ourselves overmuch on account of our human victories over nature. For each such victory nature takes its revenge on us. Each victory, it is true, in the first place brings about the results we expected, but in the second and third places it has quite different, unforeseen effects which only too often cancel the first. The people who, in Mesopotamia, Greece, Asia Minor and elsewhere, destroyed the forests to obtain cultivable land, never dreamed that by removing along with the forests the collecting centres and reservoirs of mois-ture they were laying the basis for the present forlorn state of those countries. When the Italians of the Alps used up the pine forests on the southern slopes, so carefully cherished on

the northern slopes, they had no inkling that by doing so they were cutting at the roots of the dairy industry in their region; they had still less inkling that they were thereby depriving their mountain springs of water for the greater part of the year, and making it possible for them to pour still more furious torrents on the plains during the rainy seasons. Those who spread the potato in Europe were not aware that with these farinaceous tubers they were at the same time spreading scrofula. Thus at every step we are reminded that we by no means rule over nature like a conqueror over a foreign people, like someone standing outside nature—but that we, with flesh, blood and brain, belong to nature, and exist in its midst, and that all our mastery of it consists in the fact that we have the advantage over all other creatures of being able to learn its laws and apply them correctly. (CW 25, 460–461)

Far from signaling a retreat from the praxis theory of the 1840s to a fatalistic reduction of human history to natural history (Colletti 1972, 69–70), Engels's discussion of the relation of freedom to necessity is best understood as a powerful attempt to locate human agency within nature without subsuming it to nature (Timpanaro 1975, 102; Foster et al. 2010, 262; Ferraro 1992, 161–170). Freedom, from this perspective, is an emergent property that takes its fullest form with the victory of the socialist revolution:

The extraneous objective forces that have hitherto governed history pass under the control of man himself. Only from that time will man himself, with full consciousness, make his own history—only from that time will the social causes set in movement by him have, in the main and in a constantly growing measure, the results intended by him. It is human-ity's leap from the kingdom of necessity to the kingdom of freedom. (CW 25, 270)

The evolutionary underpinning of this argument was most explicitly articulated in Engels's minor masterpiece, *The Part Played by Labour in the Transition from Ape to Man* (1876). This essay, which is arguably the most powerful and certainly the most successful section of *Dialectics of Nature* (Patterson 2009, 84), marks Engels's most explicit exploration of the emergent relationship between cultural and biological evolution through the lens of a critique of Darwin's interpretation of the evolution of modern humans. In *The Descent of Man* (1871) Darwin had argued that the decisive moment in the evolution of humanity occurred with the development of large brains. It was after this, or so he assumed, that other human characteristics of upright gait, free hands, and language evolved. By contrast, Engels suggests that massive brain development followed upon the evolution of an upright gait: "Climbing assigns different functions to the hands and the feet, and when their mode of life involved locomotion on level ground, these apes gradually got out of the habit of using their hands [in walking] and adopted a more erect posture. This was the decisive step in the transition from ape to man" (CW 25, 453). Once the hands of our ape ancestors were no longer primarily used to climb, evolution-ary advantage moved to favor hands that could work tools. From then onward it was only a matter of time before our ancestors' hands evolved into something resembling those of the modern humans. This fact is of terrific importance because it shows that "the hand is not only the organ of labour, it is also the product of labour" (CW 25, 453).

This evolutionary adaptation had profound cultural and biological consequences for the further evolution of humanity. Engels notes that while social man must have evolved from a gregarious forebear, because "labour necessarily helped to bring the members of society closer toge ther . . . men . . . arrived at a point where they had something to say to each other" (CW 25, 455). Labor therefore reinforced existing ten-dencies toward the evolution of social behavior, up to and including the adaptation of the larynx, facilitating the development of language. Finally, labor and language together became the two most important stimuli of rapid brain expansion (CW 25, 456). Increased intelligence and techno-logical know-how subsequently led to the development of a more varied diet. The broadening of our ancestors' diet, in turn, underpinned further expansions of the brain, which then facilitated the conquest of fire and the domestication of livestock (CW 25, 458). The basis for social evolution was therefore the natural evolution of an upright gait. As it happens, as Stephen Jay Gould has pointed out, Engels has been proved right and Darwin wrong on this issue (Gould 1980, 110; cf Parrington 2015, 169; Patterson 2009, 84; Woolfson 1982, 3). Social and natural evolutionary processes from then onward reinforced each other in a positive feedback loop to propel the evolution of our ancestors forward toward our modern form. Engels argued that Darwin's inability to grasp this process was a consequence of the "ideological influence" on his thought, which tended to demean the importance of labor to social history more generally (CW 25, 459; cf Gould 1977, 212; Levins and Lewontin 1985, 58, 70, 253).

It has been suggested that *The Part Played by Labour in the Transition from Ape to Man* confused Darwinian and Lamarckian theories of evolution. In a sense, it would be unsurprising if it were otherwise since Ernst Haeckel, Germany's foremost Darwinian at the time, accepted that acquired characteristics could be inherited. However, I do not think that Engels meant that culturally evolved characteristics could be inherited directly, and certainly his argument need not be interpreted in that way (Foster et al. 2000, 206; Gould 1987, 111). Rather, he posited a dialectical relationship between cultural and natural evolution, whereby an important part of the "natural" environment, within which humans compete for survival, is culturally constructed, such that cultural structures act as part of the context within which natural selection takes place. Consequently, whereas all animals change their environments, human evolution adds something new to the mix: "But animals exert a lasting effect on their environment unintentionally and, as far as the animals themselves are concerned, accidentally. The further removed men are from animals, however, the more their effect on nature assumes the character of premeditated, planned action directed towards definite preconceived ends" (CW 25, 459).

It is a damning indictment of capitalism that even as we become daily more aware of the catastrophic damage we are doing to the environment, the profit motive acts as an absolute barrier to the rational reorganization of society in line with this knowledge. So, while our understanding of the natural environment is expanding, including, through Darwin's contribution, our awareness of humanity's ecological "oneness with nature" and thus of the senselessness of the opposition between "man and nature," Marx and Engels insisted that the experience of nineteenth-century capitalism showed that capitalist social relations acted as a fundamental constraint to the rational regulation of the "metabolic interaction between man and the earth" (Marx 1976, 637; CW 25, 461). And such is the power of this constraint that "classical political economy," precisely because it is "the social science of the bourgeoisie," is unable to see beyond it. According to Engels, it is because "individual capitalists are engaged in production and exchange for the sake of immediate profit" that "only the nearest, most immediate results must first be taken into account." Consequently, so long as a profit is made, capitalists remain effectively unconcerned by the long-term unintended consequences of their actions. Similarly, because classical political economy is rooted in the standpoint of the bourgeoisie, the focus of mainstream economics tends to be on the immediately intended effects of human actions on nature, with unintended consequences of actions relegated to the position of "externalities." The concept of externalities illuminates mainstream economics' failure to understand capitalism as a totality, and its corresponding inability to conceive an adequate solution to the contemporary environmental crisis. Conversely, or so Engels wrote long before the advent of the present environmental crisis, to realize the potential oneness of our relationship with nature demands a new world-view oriented to "a complete revolution in the hitherto existing mode of production, and simultaneously a revolution in our whole contemporary social order" (CW 25, 462–463; Magdoff and Foster 2011, 39–40, 72). So, for Engels, the emergence, on the one hand, of humanity as the most con-scious part of nature, alongside, on the other hand, Marxism's contribution to understanding the alienated form taken by our relationship to nature, leads to the conclusion that socialist revolution is necessary if the positive ecological implications of humanity's unity with nature is to be realized.

12

Toward a Unitary Theory of
Women's Oppression

Engels further extended his defense of revolutionary politics in his next book: *The Origin of the Family, Private Property and the State* (1884). While it is probably true, as Lise Vogel hypothesizes, that this work can be understood as a "silent polemic" against the utopian and reformist implications of SPD leader August Bebel's recently published and enormously influential *Women and Socialism* (Vogel 2013, 102), its main impetus came from Engels's reading of Marx's notes on Lewis Henry Morgan's *Ancient Society*. The first edition of Bebel's book came out in 1879 and was immediately banned under Bismarck's antisocialist laws. The 1883 edition was retitled *Women in the Past, Present and Future* in an unsuccessful attempt to bypass Bismarck's censors. Bebel's book did, however, succeed in its main goal of challenging sexism within the German workers' movement: it went through fifty editions over the next thirty years (nine by the time of the ending of the antisocialist laws in 1890) to become the most borrowed book from workers' libraries over this period (Vogel 2013, 100). These circulation figures reflected an important sea change in opinion across the German left as Bebel's arguments for the common class interests between male and female workers marked an enormous step forward from Ferdinand Lassalle's claim that women should be kept out of the factories (Draper 2013, 235–246). Unfortunately, beyond its critique of contemporary sexism, Bebel's book was marked by a fundamental incoherence: while its theoretical architecture seemed to disbar women's liberation as a real historical possibility, it simultaneously suggested a relatively simple mechanism by which liberation might be realized.

Vogel points out that, despite the close relationship between the two men, Engels wrote nothing that we know of (we cannot be certain because not all of his correspondence has survived) to highlight weaknesses in Bebel's book. And where he did mention the book to Bebel, for instance, in a letter dated January 18, 1884, in which he thanked Bebel for sending him a copy, his brief comment seemed to damn it with faint praise: "Many thanks for your book *Die Frau*. I read it with great interest and there is much in it that is very good. What you say about the development of industry in Germany is particularly good and clear. This is a matter to which I, too, have again been turning my attention of late and I would, given the time, write something about it for the *Sozialdemokrat*" (CW 47, 81). One has only to compare these lines with comments he made in a letter to Kautsky a few months later about Fourier's "brilliant" anticipation of the conclusions of modern anthropology and ethnography to get a sense of his lukewarm response to Bebel's book (CW 47, 132; CW 26, 276). Bebel's book itself opened with the claim that

> from the beginning of time oppression has been the common lot of woman and the labouring man. In spite of all changes in form this oppression has remained the same . . . her position was even lower than his, and even by him was she regarded as an inferior and continues to be so to this day. . . . *Woman was the first human being that tasted bondage, Woman was a slave before the slave existed.* (Bebel 1988, 7)

This transhistorical conception of women's oppression as a brute fact of life would seem to imply that women's liberation could not be imagined except as an abstractly utopian ideal. However, this was not Bebel's conclusion. He suggested that because the social basis for women's oppression lay in the "dependence" of women on men within the family, independence from men would solve the "woman question": "the woman of future society is socially and economically independent; she is no longer subject to even a vestige of domination and exploitation; she is free, the peer of man, mistress of her lot" (Bebel qtd. in Vogel 2013, 106). Vogel is probably right to assume that Engels's decision not to explicitly challenge Bebel's arguments stemmed from his belief that rather than mount a full-scale attack on his book he would be better served writing an alternative and more powerful analysis both of the historical nature of women's oppression and the socialist strategy for women's liberation. Whatever his reasoning,

Engels implicitly countered Bebel's argument by challenging the notion that women's oppression was a universal characteristic of human history by claiming that women had been in a position of rough equality prior to the emergence of agriculture communities, that the family structures through which the oppression of women was reproduced had changed over time, and that the modern proletarian family pointed to the possibility of women's liberation through the struggle for socialism.

Incredibly, even though Engels's book was not based on original research and was written very quickly after reading a relatively narrow range of literature, Randall Collins argues that by historicizing the family and sexual relations *Origin* marked a "pivotal" contribution to sociological theory. Likewise, Carol Gould has described it as "one of the first major contributions to the theoretical analysis and critique of women's oppression" (Collins 1994, 80; Gould 1999, 253). Engels's *Origin* also acts as a powerful challenge to what Martha Gimenez calls the "taken for granted" textbook criticisms of Marxism that tend, absurdly, to find it guilty of "economism, class reductionism, and sex blind categories of analysis" (Gimenez 2018, 82). It is for these reasons that Engels's contribution to developing a historical understanding of women's oppression alongside his revolutionary critique of capitalism ensured that *Origin* became a major point of reference for what Susan Watkins calls "the starburst of original thinking that exploded with the 1970s women's liberation movement" (Watkins 2018, 50). If Engels's reputation waned as feminism morphed from the 1970s women's liberation movement that aimed to "overthrow the existing order" into what Watkins calls "anti-discrimination" feminism whose goal is to "induct women into" that order (Watkins 2018, 11–12), this is less a consequence of its intellectual failings and more a reflection of the narrowing of theoretical and political horizons after the defeats suffered by the workers' movement from the mid-1970s onward (Harman 2008, 583–589).

Among second-wave socialist feminists Rosalind Delmar noted that Engels's book was one of the earliest attempts to theorize "women's oppression as a problem of history, rather than of biology, a problem which should be the concern of historical materialism to analyse and revolutionary politics to solve" (Delmar qtd. in Pelz 1998, 124). Similarly, Karen Sacks called it "the basic Marxist feminist statement" that was "alone in providing a materialist theory—one that sees women's position as varying from society to society, or epoch to epoch, according to the prevailing economic and political relationships of the society," while Michèle Barrett suggested it "provided the starting point of a materialist analysis of gender relations" (Sacks 1982, 97; 1975, 211; Barrett 2014, 48). It was for this reason that Juliet Mitchell could write in 1974 that *Origin* "is probably still the most influential work in the field" (Mitchell 1974, 365). Comparable appreciations of *Origin* continued well into the cultural turn. Thus in 1987 Janet Sayers, Mary Evans, and Nanneke Redclift commented that "Engels is important to contemporary feminists because he offers the possibility of a materialist explanation for women's subordination and attempts to establish a relationship between the ownership of private property and the ideological subordination of women" (Sayers et al. 1987, 1). Although theory's linguistic turn has subsequently tended to marginalize the sort of historical and materialist analysis that Engels pioneered (Ebert 2015, 353), his work continues to act as a significant point of reference for those seeking a materialist account of the changing nature of the family and women's oppression (German 1998; Gimenez 2018; Harman 1994; Vogel 1996). Engels's appeal to these writers is in large part because, as Lynn Chancer and Beverly Xaviera Watkins suggest, his book not only has an "ongoing explanatory resonance," but within it there is also a tight fit between theory and practice (Chancer and Watkins 2006, 26).

Engels's book essentially (and explicitly) functions as a popular recasting through the lens of Marx's ethnological notebooks of Lewis Henry Morgan's pathbreaking study of the route taken from prehistoric foraging communities to the emergence of civilization: *Ancient Society* (1877). Engels noted that though Marx had mentioned Morgan's book to him before his death, the two friends had not discussed it in any detail. Subsequently, he discovered Marx's extensive excerpt notebooks on Morgan, which run to around 150 pages in Lawrence Krader's collection *The Ethnological Notebooks of Karl Marx* (1974). After reading these notebooks Engels spent several months trying to lay his hands on a copy of Morgan's hard-to-find book. Once he acquired a copy he quickly wrote *Origin* between March and May 1884. As it happens, speed of production meant he cut corners. However, it is interesting that on his own account he nonetheless managed to "guess" correctly what had been written in the literature he did not read! While carrying out the research for the fourth edition that he should have done for the first, he confided to Marx's daughter Laura, "I had to read the whole literature on the subject (which *entre nous* I had *not* done when I wrote the book—with a cheek worthy of my younger days) and to my great astonishment I find that I had *guessed* the contents of all these unread books pretty correctly—a good deal better luck than I had deserved" (CW 49, 202; Hunley 1991, 32). The methodological core of the *Origin* is famously expressed in its opening claim that Morgan had rediscovered the materialist conception of history,

> according to [which], the determining factor in history is, in the final instance, the production and reproduction of the immediate essentials of life. This, again, is of a twofold character. On the one side, the production of the means of existence, of articles of food and clothing, dwellings, and of the tools necessary for that production; on the other side, the production of human beings themselves, the propagation of the species. The social organization under which men of a particular historical epoch and a particular country live is determined by both kinds of production: by the stage of development of labour on the one hand and of the family on the other. (CW 26, 131–132)

More than any other passage, these lines have been subjected by Engels's interlocutors to critical scrutiny. The reason is simple enough: whereas *Anti-Dühring* had defended a method for grasping concrete reality as a complex totality constituted through internal relations, this passage seems to suggest a more pluralistic "dual systems" approach: capitalist class exploitation on the one hand and the patriarchal oppression of women on the other as two distinct and externally related aspects of reality.

Commentary on Engels's formulation of the relationship between the oppression of women and the exploitation of workers has informed a myriad of competing interpretations and appreciations of his work. Among German Social Democrats, both Karl Kautsky and Heinrich Cunow criticized Engels's dual system for pointing away from Marxism toward an idealistic conception of historical change (Thönnessen 1973, 38). Socialist feminists, by contrast, have tended to criticize Engels for giving insufficient weight to reproduction within his dual system approach. For instance, Jane Humphries welcomed Engels's denaturalization of marriage and the family but combined praise for his insights with an expression of grave concern about his failure to live up to the potential of the dual systems approach. She suggested that in the "the execution of his analysis" Engels tends to exclude reproduction from his account of society's economic base. Consequently, despite the many insights of his analysis, for him "feminist issues become secondary, and the contradiction between men and women subservient to that between capital and labour" (Humphries

1987, 11). Similarly, Frigga Haug has recently argued that though the dual systems approach laid the basis for a theory of gender, in practice Engels undermined this potentiality by prioritizing the production of the means of existence over the production of human beings (Haug 2015, 48). Juliet Mitchell responded to an earlier iteration of this argument with the claim that "the economic mode of capitalism and the ideological mode of patriarchy" should be understood as "two autonomous areas" (Mitchell 1974, 412). In another classic critique of Engels's thesis, Heidi Hartmann defended a dual systems model as an essential means of making sense of the fact that, despite his claim that socialism would guarantee women's liberation, history had shown that "a society could undergo transition from capitalism to socialism . . . and remain patriarchal" (Hartmann 1981, 4–5, 17). Hartmann substantiated this claim by reference to the experience of postrevolutionary China. This point was also raised by Mary Evans, for whom "the evidence of socialist states suggests that the entry of women into social production without an accompanying change in the ideology of gender and the social organisation of the sexual division of labour institutionalises the double shift that women work." She highlights the fact that "the exclusion of women from public power is as marked a feature of state socialism as it is of capitalism" (Evans 1987, 82–83). Similar points were made by Kate Millett and Shulamith Firestone, who extended aspects of Engels's declared method to subvert his conclusions: the experience of the communist states had shown that patriarchy rather than class exploitation was the fundamental division within modern society (Millett 2000, 174; Firestone 1970, 169; Barrett and McIntosh 1982, 18–19; Barrett 2014, 10–12; German 1998, 63).

Unfortunately, while the dual systems approach is able to make sense of the continuation of women's oppression under (supposedly) communist regimes, it does so at a great cost. Methodological pluralism tends to the kind of theoretical eclecticism that opens a space for "commonsense" ahistorical conceptions of social relations (Ilyenkov 2013). Martha Gimenez points out that Firestone's and Millett's supposed improvements on Engels actually mark a retreat from his insights about the historical character of sexual and marriage relations. Their alternative conception of patriarchy effectively amounts to a warmed-over version of the kind of ahistorical method that Marx and Engels had demolished in *The German Ideology*: "early feminist rejection of Marx's 'economic determinism' led to the production of ahistorical theories of patriarchy" (Gimenez 2018, 346).

In her important contribution to this literature, *Marxism and the Oppression of Women: Towards a Unitary Theory* (1983; second edition 2013), whose subtitle I have borrowed for the title of this chapter, Lise Vogel criticized Engels for opening the door to ahistorical arguments of this sort. She claims that the duality between production and reproduction in his analysis reflects his failure to transcend the weakest aspects of *The German Ideology*: "while Engels underscores the simultaneous emergence of sex- and class-conflict, he never achieves a clear picture of their connection" (Vogel 2013, 137). Vogel suggests that, as in this early text, *Origin* reproduces "a relatively sharp distinction between natural and social phenomena." This in turn led Engels to conceive women's oppression "virtually autonomously" from social production (Vogel 2013, 94, 136). If this approach paved the way to Millett's and Firestone's subversion of his political conclusions, Vogel recognizes that at its best Engels's analysis jars against the theoretical weaknesses of his system, for instance, at those points in the text where he argues that women's liberation might be realized through a combination of women's full participation in public production, the socialization of domestic labor, and the decoupling of the family from its role as an economic unit (Vogel 2013, 137). So, whereas Engels's feminist critics have argued that his analysis suffers from a failure to rise to the level of sophistication of his dual systems theory, Vogel suggests that his theoretical precepts are the weakest aspect of his work, and what is needed is a Marxist account of women's oppression as a specifically capitalist form. She claims that Engels failed adequately to conceptualize women's oppression in relation to Marx's analysis of the reproduction of labor power in *Capital*. Though this criticism of Engels is important, Vogel subsequently seems to have accepted that she had overstated her case.

Thus in "Engels's *Origin*," a reworked version of the chapter on Engels from her 1983 book, Vogel came to agree with Martha Gimenez that, despite Engels's nominal acceptance of the equivalence between production and reproduction, "throughout the *Origin*, as elsewhere, Engels describes the developments in production as fundamentally causal" (Vogel 1996, 144; cf. Gimenez 1987, 39). This is closer to the truth (though Engels did not hold to a simple causal model of historical change), and it underpins his critics' suggestion that his book failed to rise to the level of its preface. Indeed, whatever might be inferred from the preface about the existence of two distinct modes of production, the substance of *Origin* is much less ambiguous: the production of the means of existence is seen

208 Friedrich Engels and Modern Social and Political Theory

to increasingly predominate over the production of human beings as the productivity of labor increases through history. So, the meat of Engels's argument is much more monist than pluralist interpretations of the preface to his book would suggest.

Actually, as Chris Harman and Lindsey German have pointed out, the preface to *Origin* is much less vague than Engels's critics have claimed (Harman 1984, 16; German 1998, 65–66). Within the same paragraph that he makes his claim about two systems he immediately insists on the tendency for the production of the means of existence to predominate over the production of life:

> The social institutions under which men of a definite historical epoch and of a definite country live are determined by both kinds of production: by the stage of development of labour, on the one hand, and of the family, on the other. The less labour is developed and the more limited the volume of its products and, therefore, the wealth of society, the more predominantly the social order appears to be dominated by ties of kinship. However, within this structure of society based on ties of kinship, the productivity of labour develops more and more; with it, private property and exchange, differences in wealth, the possibility of utilising the labour power of others, and thereby the basis of class antagonisms: new social elements, which strive in the course of generations to adapt the old structure of society to the new conditions, until, finally, incompatibility of the two leads to a complete transformation. The old society, based on ties of kinship, bursts asunder with the collision of the newly developed social classes; in its place a new society appears, constituted in a state, the lower units of which are no longer groups based on ties of kinship but territorial groups, a society in which the family system is entirely dominated by the property system, and in which the class antagonisms and class struggle, which make up the content of all hitherto *written* history now freely unfold. (CW 26, 132)

These important lines suggest that Engels did not err in his execution of a dual systems approach because he did not hold one. He argued that changes in family structure were determined by the changing nature of production. Specifically, the turn to agriculture underpinned the emergence of private property, which in turn came into conflict with and eventually led to the overthrow of preexisting egalitarian family structures.

Engels's account of the emergence of private property, states, and women's oppression drew on Morgan's periodization of human history into three main epochs—savagery (foraging), barbarism (agriculture), and civilization (urban). Engels explained the rise of classes, the state, and sexual oppression in the context of the change in the mode of production from foraging through horticulture and on to agricultural and urban societies. He argued that it was only at the point in history when the productivity of labor exceeded that necessary for its own "maintenance" that the exploitation of man by man, and the existence of social classes, became a possibility (CW 26, 163). Developing his and Marx's discussion of the division of labor in *The German Ideology*, he argued that the rough early egalitarian division of labor within the family between (male) hunters and (female) gatherers was slowly transformed into a power relationship as the move to pastoralism dramatically increased the status of men without changing the division of labor within the family. The position of women deteriorated relative to the position of the men in a context where woman's domestic position brought less and less wealth into the household relative to the man's new wealth in livestock (CW 26, 165). Furthermore, with the increased productivity of labor and the existence of surplus product, warfare became endemic as people stole both livestock and other people to use as slaves. Wars over the control of social surplus in turn begat warriors, and this process informed the emergence of a new division of labor: men and women could for the first time become the spoils of war, creating a new class of unfree labor, while a second division arose between more and less powerful men within the victorious groups. Engels argued, "from the first great social division of labour arose the first great cleavage of society into two classes: masters and slaves, exploiters and exploited" (CW 26, 261).

It was at this point in history that the concept of private property emerged to delineate the control by particular individuals over parts of the social surplus. Once private property emerged, the problem of how to reproduce it over generations became a concrete concern. Whereas descent had previously been measured through the mother, now fathers, requiring a mechanism to pass on property to children, demanded sole sexual access to specific women. In this context, the family developed not as a realm of domestic bliss, "which forms the ideal of the present day philistine," but as a property right bestowed upon the man. So, in contrast to the reproductive structure of savage and barbarian groups, the emergence of civilization marked "the overthrow of mother right," which was itself "the world historical defeat of the female sex" (CW 26, 165). After a protracted process, the new inequalities and divisions were solidified, and with the birth of civilization there emerged "a class which no longer concerns itself with production" (CW 26, 265). However, as class exploitation and sexual oppression emerged through history, so too did the struggles against them. In this context, the state grew as a structure needed to stabilize society in the interests of the new ruling class:

> The state is . . . a product of society at a particular stage of development; it is the admission that this society has involved itself in insoluble self-contradiction and is cleft into irreconcilable antagonisms which it is powerless to exorcise. But in order that these antagonisms, classes with conflicting economic interests, shall not consume themselves and society in fruitless struggle, a power, apparently standing above society, has become necessary to moderate the conflict and keep it within the bounds of "order." . . . [However], as the state . . . also arose in the thick of the fight between the classes, it is normally the state of the most powerful, economically ruling class, which by its means becomes also the politically ruling class, and so acquires new means of holding down and exploiting the oppressed class. (CW 26, 269, 271)

By contrast with this powerful critique of the state, Engels praised the Iroquois for their happy existence without a state: "and a wonderful constitution it is, this gentile constitution, in all its childlike simplicity! No soldiers, no gendarmes or police, no nobles, kings, regents, prefects, or judges, no prisons, or lawsuits—and everything takes its orderly course" (CW 26, 202). Eleanor Burke Leacock has argued that "the Iroquois confederacy represents the highest stage of political organisation under the gentile system" (Leacock 1972, 47). It was only as society evolved beyond this level of complexity that statelike formations grew. As late as 1946 V. Gordon Childe, one of the most influential archaeologists of the twentieth century, could write, "the sevenfold division adumbrated by Lewis H. Morgan and refined by Friedrich Engels, with his more comprehensive knowledge of European archaeology, is still unsurpassed" (Childe 2004, 77). While the detail of the various ways in which class divisions and states evolved have long since moved beyond this account—indeed Childe moved to embrace a more multilinear approach by the 1950s—Patterson points out that Morgan's and Engels's importance lay in the fact that they highlighted the novelty both of social classes and states: "the appearance of social-class structures is always linked to the institutions, practices and legal codes of the state, which simultaneously represents the interests of the dominant class" (Patterson 2009, 112). The emergence of states and classes alongside women's oppression marked a profound transformation in human history; albeit, as Ian Hodder points out in his discussion of the archaeological evidence at Çatalhöyük, this qualitative change was underpinned by a gradual and cumulative process of quantitative changes (Hodder 2006, 17–18, 214). And despite the massive strides taken within archaeology and anthropology since Engels's death, Vincente Lull and Rafael Micó have recently commented on the similarities between his account of the emergence of the state and modern processual archaeological models (Lull and Micó 2011, 227).

Eleanor Burke Leacock seems therefore to have been right to argue that "despite its shortcomings, [Engels's *Origin*] is still a masterful and profound theoretical synthesis" (Leacock 1981, 25). If the key insights of the book included Engels's analysis of the historical novelty of both women's oppression within the family and the state as a power over society, among its shortcomings, one that has commanded more attention than it should have, is his claim that the emergence of civilization marked "the overthrow of mother right." Numerous commentators have taken this to imply that Engels conflated matrilineal and matrilocal societies with matriarchal societies. But this is simply not the case. He justified his use of the term "mother right" much more pragmatically: "I retain this term for the sake of brevity. It is, however, an unhappy choice, for at this stage of society, there is as yet no such thing as right in the legal sense" (CW 26, 152). He was, however, on weaker ground when he followed Morgan in assuming that certain forms of familial classifications were fossilized remains of earlier forms of group marriage and promiscuity, and he was probably wrong about the importance of lineages in preclass societies— foraging groups were much too "loose and flexible" to be considered either patrilineal or matrilineal (Harman 1994, 133–134, 111). Moreover, the paucity of evidence led him into the realm of speculation as regards the mechanisms by which family structures changed and states arose. As Simone de Beauvoir pointed out, while she accepted that *Origin* illuminated the historical nature of private property, the family, and the state, Engels failed to elucidate the concrete mechanism by which this change was realized (de Beauvoir 1972, 86–87; Trat 1998, 94; Foreman 1977, 25–29).

Despite these errors and lacunae, Chris Harman has persuasively argued that Engels's "overall picture of the rise of class society is basically correct" as is his claim that "women were not subordinated to men until the rise of classes, that 'the first class antagonism which appears in history coincides with the development of the antagonism between man and woman in monogamous marriage, and the first class oppression with that of the female sex by the male'" (Harman 1994, 113, 129; 2008, 3–31; Woolfson 1982; cf. CW 26, 173; Feeley 2015). Similarly, and despite being more critical of Engels's approach, Stephanie Coontz and Peta Henderson have claimed that "a growing body of evidence supports the broad evolutionary perspective first suggested by Engels: relations between the sexes seem to be most egalitarian in the simplest foraging societies and woman's position worsens with the emergence of social stratification, private property, and the state" (Coontz and Henderson 1986, 108; cf. Bloodworth 2018). Engels may not have located the details of the mechanism by which this change came about, but that this revolutionary change occurred at this moment and that it entailed the emergence of women's oppression, which consequently is best conceived as a historical rather than a universal and natural characteristic of human society, is of the first importance to any strategy aiming at women's liberation.

However, as I noted in my discussion of *Anti-Dühring*, an adequate political challenge to the status quo requires more than an awareness that existing social relations are not fixed parts of our nature. It is also essential to point to the tendencies immanent to the system which point beyond it. This aspect of Engels's analysis in *Origin* is less successful. Specifically, his discussion of the proletarian family is very problematic.

Engels's discussion of the modern working-class family is not, though, without significant insight. If his historical account of changing family forms challenged simplistic accounts of the universality of patriarchy, Michèle Barrett has suggested that "Engels's most important achievement was his perception of materially different relations between the sexes for members of different social classes" (Barrett 2014, 48). Despite formal similarities in family structures across social classes in the nineteenth century, Engels illuminated the very real substantive differences between bourgeois and proletarian families. He was scathing in his critique of the bourgeois family—institutionalized prostitution was how he described the arrangement between a man, who effectively agreed to provide his wife's keep, and a woman, who in return agreed to produce his legitimate heirs. Beneath the platitudes about love, this form of monogamy was a cynical economic contract aimed at the reproduction of private property over the generations. Monogamy in this sense was an "economic unit," and a hypocritical one at that—while it was assumed that men would stray, the penalties for women who did so were severe. So the bourgeois family carried on a tradition of women's oppression going back to the emergence of private property.

The proletarian family, by contrast, had a very different social content. Without property, there was "no incentive . . . [and] no means . . . to make this male supremacy effective" within the working-class family. Similarly, the power of the male as "breadwinner" was diminishing in direct relation to the success of large-scale industry in pulling women into the labor force. And because proletarians had little or no access to the law (it was too expensive), legal prescriptions pertaining to the relations between the sexes had very little impact on their lives. Consequently, the conditions for bourgeois monogamy did not exist within the proletariat. The work-ing-class family "is therefore no longer monogamous in the strict sense, even where there is passionate love and firmest loyalty on both sides." Or rather the proletarian marriage was becoming "monogamous in the etymological sense of the word, but not at all in its historical sense" (CW 26, 179). For Engels then, as the relations that underpinned the oppressive essence of historical monogamy faded, the conditions were emerging for the transformation of the social content of monogamy into what he called "individual sex love" (CW 26, 183)—a condition very different to the ruling-class monogamy that, at its blissful best, amounted to "a conjugal partnership of leaden boredom" (CW 26, 178). He thus imagined non-oppressive and liberated sexual relations as potentially realizing the ideal of monogamy against its reality; and what is more he suggested that this ideal was emerging within the working class as he wrote.

Clearly, there is something to this account of the proletarian family: sexual relations are different when not primarily mediated by concerns about the reproduction of private property. Nonetheless, Engels's sketch of the working-class family is far too optimistic. Barrett comments that "the problems with [Engels's] account of the proletarian marriage are legion" (Barrett 2014, 49). The issue is not, though, that Engels was unaware of the real patterns of oppression within modern families. In a brilliant historical sketch, he suggested:

> In the old communistic household, which embraced numerous couples and their children, the administration of the household,

entrusted to the women, was just as much a public, a socially
necessary industry as the procurement of food by the men. This
situation changed with the patriarchal family, and even more
with the monogamian individual family. The administration
of the household lost its public character. It was no longer
the concern of society. It became a *private service*. The wife
became the first domestic servant, pushed out of participation
in social production. Only the large-scale industry of our time
has again thrown open to her—and only to the proletarian
woman at that—the avenue to social production; but in such
a way that, if she fulfils her duties in the private service of
her family, she remains excluded from public production and
cannot earn anything; and if she wishes to take part in public
industry and earn her living independently, she is not in a
position to fulfil her family duties. (CW 26, 181)

More specifically, he insisted that "the modern individual family is founded
on the open or concealed domestic slavery of the wife," and that "within
the family . . . at least in the possessing classes . . . he is the bourgeois,
and the wife represents the proletariat" (CW 26, 181). Though this latter line became a favorite propagandistic slogan of the German socialist
movement at the turn of the twentieth century, it cannot stand up to
critical scrutiny as a scientific statement about the relationship between
men and women in the family. In fact, it appears innocent of both the
mediated nature of the domestic relationship for upper-class women—for
whom cooks, nannies, cleaners, and the like ensure a life that is a long
way from domestic slavery—and the harshness of conditions experienced
by proletarian women, most of whom have little choice between domestic
slavery and wage slavery; they are compelled to do both.

Engels is, however, surely right to claim that the *possibility* of women's
liberation is predicated upon women's participation within the production
process, which is itself a consequence of large-scale capitalist development:

The emancipation of women becomes possible only when
women are enabled to take part in production on a large,
social scale, and when domestic duties require their attention
only to a minor degree. And this has become possible only as
a result of modern large-scale industry, which not only permits
of the participation of women in production in large numbers,

but actually calls for it and, moreover, strives more and more to reduce private domestic duties to a public industry. (CW 26, 262)

Nonetheless, capitalism is characterized by a contradiction in which industrial growth sucks increasing numbers of women into the labor force while simultaneously demanding that the proper place for women is in the home rearing children. One consequence of this situation is that the potential for women to participate in the collective strength of the working class is limited by an ideology of gender roles within the family.

If capitalism consequently creates the conditions for the possibility of women's liberation, the ideology of gender roles punctures any simple optimism about the realization of this potentiality. With or without private property, working-class families are characterized by oppressive relations that are, if anything, worse than those experienced by the middle classes. In fact, Engels too quickly jumps from a discussion of the proletarian family under capitalism to an overview of its position after a revolution had transformed the means of production from private to social property (CW 26, 182ff.). If this movement underpins his speculative discussion of the sublation of monogamy into "individual sex love," it also meant that he bypassed a proper analysis of the relationship between the proletarian family and capital accumulation.

Vogel points out that because Engels failed to address this issue, he "misses the significance of the working class household as an essential social unit, not for the holding of property but for the reproduction of the working class itself." He also "overlooks the ways in which a material basis for male supremacy is constituted within the proletarian household. And . . . vastly underestimates the variety of ideological and psychological factors that provide a continuing foundation for male supremacy in the working-class family" (Vogel 2013, 88–89, 143–156).

It is certainly true that Engels is at his weakest when discussing the relationship of the modern family to capitalism, and this is perhaps not coincidental given what has been written previously about the weaknesses with Engels's conception of the capitalist value form. The relationship between the modern family and the capital accumulation process is perhaps best understood in relation to the forces that brought the working-class family back from the brink of collapse in the mid-nineteenth century. In a period when industrial capitalism sucked women and children into the labor process, one in four children in Manchester in the 1860s did not live to see their first birthday, and the high death rate among children meant that life expectancy for men in some areas of Salford in the 1870s was as low as seventeen years! If this situation reflected the short-term demands of capital, longer-term requirements depended on some mechanism to reproduce the labor force. This is what Marx called "the absolutely necessary condition for capitalist production." Unfortunately, Marx was terse in the extreme as to the detail of the social reproduction process: "The maintenance and reproduction of the working class remains a necessary condition for the reproduction of capital. But the capitalist may safely leave this to the worker's drives for self-preservation and propagation" (Marx 1976, 716, 718; cf. Foster and Clark 2018). Lindsey German argues that labor legislation in mid-Victorian Britain effectively addressed this issue by reconstituting the working-class family in light of the demands of capital accumulation. These labor laws ensured a steady stream of new workers through a novel structure—the modern nuclear family—that was justified by a nominally natural but in fact modern ideology in which men were accounted breadwinners, while women were housewives whose role it was to bring up the next generation of workers, who in their turn were reimagined as "children" (German 1998, 15–42).

Vogel's book amounts to the most powerful attempt to conceptualize the relationship between the modern working-class family and the capital accumulation process through Marx's concept of the social reproduction of labor power. She suggests there are three aspects to this process. First, the daily reproduction of the direct producers who need food, sleep, clothing, shelter, and so forth. Second, the reproduction of nonproductive members of the working class—the young, old, sick, and so on. Third, the reproduction of the next generation of wage laborers (Vogel 2013, 188). This process implies an inclusive definition of the working class. So, by contrast with the those who define the working class narrowly to include only those involved in wage labor, Vogel insists that, in her broader model, "the working class will be viewed as consisting of a society's past, present, and potential wage-labour force, together with all those whose maintenance depends on the wage but who do not or cannot themselves enter wage-labour" (Vogel 2013, 166). The capitalist form of women's oppression, she argues, has its roots in this process: "It is the provision by men of means of subsistence to women during the childbearing period, and not the sex-division of labour in itself, that forms the material basis for women's subordination in class-society" (Vogel 2013, 153). In so relating the modern family to the process of capital accumulation, Vogel overcame the fundamental weakness of Engels's *Origin* (Vogel 2013, 136). It is not that Engels had not registered aspects of this reality, but rather that he failed to integrate these insights into his broader analysis of the oppression of working-class women under capitalism.

While Vogel is right to claim that because Engels's account of the working-class family does not take account of its position within broader capitalist social relations it fails adequately to underpin a revolutionary solution to women's oppression as an integral part of the struggle for socialism, her contribution to developing a unitary theory of women's oppression (Vogel 1995, 51, 63–65) is somewhat undermined by her suggestion that similar patterns of women's oppression to those experienced in the West were reproduced in such socialist states as China, Cuba, the Soviet Union, and Albania (Vogel 2013, 180–181). Writing in 1983, Vogel was, of course, right about the existence of women's oppression in these states. Where her argument foundered was in characterizing them as socialist in the first place.

Clearly, if socialism reproduced essentially the same form of women's oppression as exists under capitalism—and Vogel effectively naturalized the persistence of gender inequalities in communist states by explaining these as a consequence of "real differences between [men and women], particularly in the area of child bearing"—Firestone and Millett are right to view women's oppression as a distinct and more fundamental division than that between social classes. In fact, Vogel's comments on women's experience of Stalinism fails to match the clarity of Millett's account of the same. For whereas Millett points to the fact that the Stalinist bureaucracy actively chose to push the cost of social reproduction onto women in the family—"Having declined to fulfil its promise of crèches and collective housekeeping, and in view of its experience without them, as well as in view of the priority it put upon industrial projects, particularly armaments, Stalin's Russia preferred to bolster the family to perform the functions the state had promised but did not choose to afford"—Vogel suggests that the Stalinists were merely "unable . . . to confront the problems of domestic labour and women's subordination in a systematic way" (Millett 2000, 174; Vogel 2013, 180).

The problem with this argument is not merely that it tends to deny the agency of the Stalinist bureaucracy. More importantly, it obscures the fact that the Stalinist state bureaucracies were indeed systematic in their approach to the "woman question": systematically reactionary in defense of their own social interests. As Leon Trotsky perceptively suggested in the 1930s, "the consecutive changes in the approach to the problem of the family in the Soviet Union best of all characterize the actual nature of Soviet society and the evolution of its ruling stratum" (Trotsky 1972, 145). Chanie Rosenberg details the transformations from the early progressive attempts by the Russian revolutionaries to socialize child care and other family responsibilities to Stalin's counterrevolutionary decree of 1936, "In Defence of Mother and Child," which "reversed all the gains of the revolution in respect of family law and reintroduced Tsarist prejudices and restrictions," including outlawing abortion and putting "divorce beyond the means of workers' families" (Rosenberg 1989, 94). Herbert Marcuse points to the simple economic rationale for the new laws: in the context of economic and military competition with the West the Stalinist bureaucrats intended to increase economic growth as cheaply as possible (Marcuse 1958, 206–207).

In her important study *Marx on Gender and the Family*, Heather Brown, like Vogel before her, criticizes Engels from a position that effectively accepts the logic of Millett's interpretation of Soviet history. The experience of Russian "Communism," she argues, suggests that "[p]atriarchy can exist without private property. This is evident in working-class families which have little property, and was even the case in societies with state ownership of the means of production such as the Soviet Union and China" (Brown 2013, 54). This is a particularly odd statement given Brown's explicit debt to Raya Dunayevskaya's reading of Marx (Brown 2013, 8). Dunayevskaya may have been a harsh critic of Engels, but she was much more severe in her criticisms of what she called Soviet "state capitalism." This concept is of direct relevance to Brown's discussion of Engels's *Origin* (Brown 2013, 163–176). For Dunayevskaya understood more than most that the Marxist conception of private property cannot be reduced either to Western-type free market economies or to particular patterns of ownership among workers and capitalists: "To Marx, private property is the power to dispose of the labour of others. That is why he is so adamant that to make 'society' the owner, but to leave the alienated labour alone, is to create 'an abstract capitalist' " (Dunayevskaya 1988, 61–62). Such was the situation, Dunayevskaya insisted, in Russia, China, and other supposedly twentieth-century "Communist" states. She argued that beginning with the introduction of the first Five Year Plan in 1928–1929 and culminating in the "bloodletting" associated with the first great Show Trial of 1936 the Soviet Union was transformed into a state capitalist social formation (Dunayevskaya 1988, 215–229). The great strength of Dunayevskaya's and similar conceptions of Russian state capitalism is that they pierce the surface appearance of Russian "Communism" to illuminate its underlying essence as a bureaucratic statist variant of twentieth-century capitalism. In these social formations state planning, far from escaping the system of alienation, was subordinated to it. In the words of Tony Cliff: "The Stalinist state is in the same position vis-à-vis the total labour time in Russian society as a factory owner vis-à-vis the labour of his employees." So, while the economy is "planned," planning is itself oriented to military competition with other countries (Cliff 1974, 202–203).

By conceptualizing Soviet Russia, China, and the like as bureaucratic state capitalist social formations, writers such as Dunayevskaya and Cliff laid the foundations for a reply to Millett's and Firestone's arguments about the links between the struggles for women's liberation and socialism. In his Marxist analysis of women's oppression, Chris Harman attempted, like Vogel, to develop Engels's insights in the direction of social reproduction theory. But against those who suggested that the experience of twentieth-century communism undermined this project, his analysis of the material roots of women's oppression in modern capitalism was framed against the background of the claim that Russia, China, and elsewhere were bureaucratic state capitalist social formations. He argued that whereas Millett and Firestone, among others, insisted that the experience of Russia, Cuba, Vietnam, and China show that "socialism can coexist with women's oppression . . . those of us who recognise that the rise of Stalinism established state capitalism in Russia, do not need to draw this conclusion at all." Indeed, the experience of the Russian Revolution was evidence that the opposite was the case: "the revolution carried through a programme of women's liberation never attempted anywhere else—complete liberation of abortion and divorce laws, equal pay, mass provision of communal child care, socialised canteen facilities and so on." Conversely, it was the Stalinist counterrevolution that brought in its train "the re-imposition of the stereotyped family, anti-abortion laws, restrictions on divorce, and so on" (Harman 1984, 28–29).

Harman's analysis is doubly interesting because his understanding of Russian state capitalism is rooted in Tony Cliff's deployment of Engels's analysis, in *The Peasant War in Germany*, of the tragic position of Thomas Müntzer and the Anabaptists in Germany in 1525. Just as Engels argued that material constraints would have prevented Müntzer from realizing his proto-communist dreams in the sixteenth century had the social movement he led won, so Cliff explained Stalin's counterrevolution as a necessary consequence, once the hope of international revolution had faded with the final defeat of the German Revolution in 1923, of Russia's extreme poverty in the 1920s. As in Germany in 1525, because the material pre-conditions for socialism did not as yet exist, the only historically viable option for Russia was a brutal form of primitive capital accumulation (CW 10, 469–470; Cliff 1974, 149).

By thus conceiving Stalinism as a variant of capitalism, this tradition of Marxism was able to explain the persistence of women's oppression in Stalinist Russia as a variant of women's oppression under capitalism. These writers consequently cleared the way for the kind of unitary theory of women's oppression as a capitalist form originally promised in Engels's *Origin*. Their claim that women's oppression is rooted within the modern family conceived as a unit for the privatized reproduction of labor power overcomes the limitations of Engels's account of the modern working-class family in a way that makes more secure his argument that the struggles for women's liberation and for socialism are two sides of the same coin: "True equality between men and women can, or so I am convinced, become a reality only when the exploitation of both by capital has been abolished, and private work in the home been transformed into a public industry" (CW 47, 312). The analytical power of this way of conceiving the relationship between women's oppression and class exploitation points beyond the descriptive limitations of intersectionality theory without succumbing to the kind of class reductionism feared by so many fem-inist theorists (Blackledge 2018a; McNally 2017, 97–99). Insofar as it does so, it also points beyond the weak (Kantian) moralistic aspects of some contemporary forms of feminism toward the much more powerful neo-Aristotelian ethical humanism characteristic of Marx's work in which politics is conceived as the critical practice that aims to realize human freedom immanent to contemporary struggles against capitalist alienation (Watkins 2018; Blackledge 2012a, 19–43).

This conception of women's liberation opens a space for us to recapture the spirit of Engels's powerful vision of sexual relations in a truly socialist alternative to capitalism:

> Thus, what we can conjecture at present about the regula-tion of sex relationships after the impending effacement of capitalist production is, in the main, of a negative character, limited mostly to what will vanish. But what will be added?

That will be settled after a new generation has grown up: a generation of men who never in their lives have had occasion to purchase a woman's surrender either with money or with any other social means of power, and of women who have never had occasion to surrender to any man out of any consideration other than that of real love, or to refrain from giving themselves to their beloved for fear of the economic consequences. Once such people appear, they will not care a damn about what we today think they should do. They will establish their own practice and their own public opinion, conforming therewith, on the practice of each individual—and that's the end of it. (CW 26, 189)

13

Beyond 1848

Engels's "Testament"

In January 1895 Richard Fischer, secretary of the SPD, wrote to Engels asking him to write a new introduction to Marx's study of the 1848 revolutions, *The Class Struggles in France*. The immediate context of Fischer's request was the introduction of a new antisubversion bill in 1894 that was due to become law in 1895. The party, anticipating a renewed period of illegality, wanted to publish Marx's pamphlet before the new law came into effect (Draper 2005, 232). Despite suffering from terminal cancer, Engels reluctantly agreed to write the piece. He then reluctantly agreed to some editorial changes requested by Fischer that muted its message. In and of itself, there is nothing particularly interesting about this course of events—Engels was responding undogmatically to a request for help from the German party. However, not long after Engels's death Eduard Bernstein attempted to justify his own revisionist break with Marxism by reference to Engels's 1895 introduction. Engels, he suggested, was "so thoroughly convinced that tactics [associated with *The Communist Manifesto*—PB] geared to a catastrophe have had their day that he considers a *revision to abandon them* to be due" (Bernstein 1993, 4). To justify this claim, Bernstein sought to drive a wedge between Engels's essay and his previous writings. He did so by declaring the hastily written and somewhat pruned essay to be Engels's "political testament" (Bernstein 1993, 35). Thus framed, debates around Engels's 1895 introduction have taken on an importance out of all proportion to the essay's significance in Engels's mind. What we do know is that the terminal nature of his illness was kept from him by his friends, so it is more by accident than by design that this essay became his last substantial contribution to the socialist presses before his death (Mayer 1936, 300). Draper is therefore right to point out that "the claim that this was Engels's 'last testament' was nonsense since Engels did not know he was dying" (Draper 2005, 236). More to the point, the general thrust of what Engels wrote was not particularly novel: it was only by taking some of his arguments out of context that he could be labeled a (proto)revisionist (Blackledge 2011a).

Looking back to the postrevolutionary period almost half a century earlier, Engels suggested that while he and Marx had been right to insist that the workers' movement was on the cusp not of a renewed offensive but of a "long struggle" after defeats in 1848, they had not grasped the full significance of this turning point: "the mode of struggle of 1848 is today obsolete in every respect" (CW 27, 510). By contrast with his and Marx's prognosis of the possibilities for future success in 1850, Engels claimed that "history has proved us wrong . . . the state of economic development on the Continent at that time was not, by a long way, ripe for the elimination of capitalist production" (CW 27, 512). If economic boom from the 1850s onward had pushed revolution off the political agenda, Bismarck's introduction of universal male suffrage in 1866 created a new political landscape atop this economic prosperity. Engels argued that the German workers' movement had responded powerfully to this new situation. They had transformed the "franchise . . . from a means of deception . . . into an instrument of emancipation." Universal male suffrage allowed the left to gauge its strength within the working class. Beyond this, suffrage created a space for the left to use

> election propaganda . . . as a means, second to none, of getting in touch with the mass of the people where they still stand aloof from us; of forcing all parties to defend their views and actions against our attacks before all the people; and, further, it provided our representatives in the Reichstag with a platform from which they could speak to their opponents in parliament, and to the masses outside, with quite different authority and freedom than in the press or at meetings. (CW 27, 516)

Universal male suffrage had consequently inaugurated "an entirely new method of proletarian struggle"; it allowed the workers to use "state institutions . . . to fight these very state institutions." Specifically, "workers took part

in elections to particular diets, to municipal councils and to trades courts."
Both through elections and in elected offices the workers' representatives
contested the bourgeoisie: "And so it happened that the bourgeoisie and
the government came to be much more afraid of the legal than of the
illegal action of the workers' party, of the results of elections than of those
of rebellion" (CW 27, 516). So, in a context where, as Engels had been
arguing since 1848, "the old style, street fighting with barricades . . . had
become largely outdated," the SPD showed the world that "the conditions of
the struggle had changed fundamentally" (CW 27, 517). And in a comment
clearly meant as a critique of Blanquism from a perspective informed by
the democratic model of revolution first outlined in *The German Ideology*,
he wrote, "the time of surprise attacks, of revolutions carried through by
small conscious minorities at the head of masses lacking consciousness is
past. Where it is a question of a complete transformation of the social
organisation, the masses themselves must also be in on it, must themselves
already have grasped what is at stake" (CW 27, 520).

These arguments were not new, nor did they imply that he rejected
the idea of revolution. As recently as January 26, 1894, Engels had written
to Filippo Turati that "since 1848 the tactics which have most often ensured
success for the socialists have been those of the *Communist Manifesto*" (CW
27, 438; CW 45, 430). Noting the international lessons to be learned from
Germany, he wrote: "Of course, our foreign comrades do not in the least
renounce their right to revolution. The right to revolution is, after all,
the only *really* 'historical right,' the only right on which all modern states
rest without exception, Mecklenburg [Germany—PB] included" (CW 27,
521). Most importantly, none of this led Engels to believe that a peaceful
transformation to socialism in Germany was likely: "do not forget that the
German empire, like all small states and generally all modern states, is a
product of contract; of the contract, first, of the princes with one another and,
second, of the princes with the people. If one side breaks the contract, the
whole contract falls to the ground; the other side is then also no longer
bound" (CW 27, 517). His expectation was clear enough: the ruling class
would in all likelihood break the contract through the use of counterrevolutionary violence if workers threatened to win a parliamentary majority.
As he wrote three years earlier: "I have never said the socialist party will
become the majority and then proceed to take power. On the contrary,
I have expressly said that the odds are ten to one that our rulers, well
before that point arrives, will use violence against us, and this would shift
us from the terrain of majority to the terrain of revolution" (CW 27, 271).

Similarly, in the 1886 preface to *Capital* he wrote that though the social revolution might be effected entirely by peaceful means in England, Marx "never forgot to add that he hardly expected the English ruling class to submit, without a 'pro-slavery rebellion,' to this peaceful and legal revolution" (Marx 1976, 113). The term "proslavery rebellion" was a reference to the American Civil War: Lincoln had come to power peacefully but only kept power by the most violent of means to suppress the South's proslavery rebellion. Similarly, Engels insisted in a letter to Gerson Trier, December 18, 1889, that "the proletariat cannot seize political power . . . without violent revolution" (CW 48, 423).

The wholly unoriginal nature of the 1895 introduction was, unfortunately, somewhat suppressed by omissions to the essay. These revisions are all the more confusing because the SPD published (almost simultaneously) two versions of Engels's introduction in 1895: an utterly bowdlerized version in *Vorwärts* and an edited (with Engels's consent) version in *Neue Zeit*. The fact that two editions of this essay were published in 1895, and that one of these versions—the *Vorwärts* edition—quickly thereafter became all but unobtainable, has lent itself to a curious situation. Engels's angry response to the publication without his agreement of the *Vorwärts* version has often been misunderstood as an attack on the *Neue Zeit* version. This confusion has in turn clouded the debate over Bernstein's interpretation of the introduction. Bernstein's critics have tended to insist that Engels had disowned the text—this was true of the *Vorwärts* version, but not of the version to which Bernstein referred. Bernstein, by contrast, insisted that the version published in *Neue Zeit* reflected Engels's considered opinions on the topic. This claim was disingenuous, as he knew that Engels had only reluctantly agreed to remove lines that would have made its revolutionary implications more explicit. So, whereas Bernstein's critics made, by and large, honest mistakes (for a recent instance of this, see Kellogg 1991, 166), he was more obviously deceitful in his attempt to reimagine Engels as a forerunner of his own revisionism (Draper 2005, 235–237).

The *Vorwärts* version published by Liebknecht was clearly intended to justify a reformist strategy. Liebknecht excised anything remotely revolutionary from the introduction to effectively vindicate his belief that German capitalism could be overcome by the use of the ballot box alone. When he saw this text, Engels was furious. In a letter to Paul Lafargue he wrote:

> Liebknecht has just played me a fine trick. He has taken from my introduction to Marx's articles on France 1848–50 every-

thing that could serve his purpose in support of peaceful and anti-violent tactics at any price, which he has chosen to preach for some time now, particularly at this juncture when coercive laws are being drawn up in Berlin. But I preach those tactics only for the *Germany of today* and even then with many *reservations*. For France, Belgium, Italy, Austria, such tactics could not be followed as a whole and, for Germany, they could become inapplicable tomorrow. So please wait for the complete article before judging it—it will probably appear in *Neue Zeit*, and I expect copies of the pamphlet any day now. It's a pity that Liebknecht can see only black and white. Shades don't exist for him. (CW 50, 489–490)

The revisions Engels accepted to the *Neue Zeit* version included the removal of a comment referring to "future street fighting" and a rider to a sentence on the use of the parliamentary tactic in which he suggested that "everywhere the unprepared launching of an attack has been relegated to the background." He also agreed to replace the line "what they are fighting for, body and soul" with "what they are coming out for" and remove two lines referring to the "decisive day" and the "decisive combat" (CW 27, 518; 520). Finally, he agreed to excise two substantive passages. First:

Does that mean that in the future street fighting will no longer play any role? Certainly not. It only means that the conditions since 1848 have become far more unfavourable for civilian fighters and far more favourable for the military. In future, street fighting can, therefore, be victorious only if this disadvantageous situation is compensated by other factors. Accordingly, it will occur more seldom at the beginning of a great revolution than at its later stages, and will have to be undertaken with greater forces. These, however, may then well prefer, as in the whole great French Revolution or on September 4 and October 31, 1870, in Paris, the open attack to passive barricade tactics. (CW 27, 519)

Second, he agreed to the removal of the following rider to his comment about the ruling class's probable breaking of its contract with the German people: "as Bismarck demonstrated to us so beautifully in 1866. If, therefore, you break the constitution of the Reich, Social-Democracy is free, and can do as it pleases with regard to you. But it will hardly blurt out to you today what it is going to do then" (CW 27, 523).

Clearly, these excisions were meant to temper Engels's language. Fischer had asked him to make the revisions so as not to give the government an excuse to pass the antisubversion bill. Engels unenthusiastically agreed:

> I have taken as much account as possible of your grave objections although I cannot for the life of me see what is objectionable about, say, half of the instances you cite. For I cannot after all assume that you intend to subscribe heart and soul to absolute legality, legality under any circumstances, legality even vis-à-vis laws infringed by their promulgators, in short, to the policy of turning the left cheek to him, who has struck you on the right. . . . My view is that you have nothing to gain by advocating complete abstention from force. Nobody would believe you, *nor* would *any* party in any country go so far as to forfeit the right to resist illegality by force of arms. . . . However, I bow to your wishes. Well, I can go so far and *no further*. I have done everything in my power to spare you embarrassment in debate. But you would be better advised to adhere to the standpoint that the obligation to abide by the law is a legal, not a moral one . . . and that it ceases absolutely when those in power break the law. (CW 50, 458–459)

With or without these editorial interventions, to read Engels's 1895 introduction as a revisionist text assumes a caricatured interpretation of revolutionary politics. Rosa Luxemburg, for instance, had no doubt that Engels's introduction showed that "democracy is indispensable not because it renders superfluous the conquest of political power by the proletariat but, on the contrary, because it renders this conquest of power both necessary as well as possible" (Luxemburg 1970a, 80–81; 1970d, 409; Tudor 1993, xxiii).

Bernstein's attempt to portray Engels as the first revisionist, by contrast, depends on a conflation of Marxist revolutionary politics with Blanquism. To explain why Engels had not gone further with his revisionism, Bernstein partook in a little barroom psychology. Engels was unable to think through the full logic of his tactical revisionism because had he done so he would have been compelled to "come to terms with [i.e., reject—PB]

Hegelian dialectic" (Bernstein 1993, 36). In *The Preconditions of Socialism* (1899), Bernstein insisted that in their theory of revolution Marx and Engels had failed to transcend the Jacobin legacy and this failure could, in large part, be understood as a consequence of their reading of Hegel. He claimed that Hegelian philosophy was "a reflex of the great French Revolution" and that, insofar as Marxism failed to disentangle itself from this framework, it too remained politically tied to the far-left tendencies associated with François-Noël "Gracchus" Babeuf and Auguste Blanqui that carried forth the Jacobin tradition into the nineteenth century (Bernstein 1993, 36ff.). According to Bernstein, what Marx and Engels learned from these two was a program for the "overthrow of the bourgeoisie by the proletariat by means of violent expropriation" (Bernstein 1993, 37). Bernstein did not believe that Marx and Engels were uncritical of Babeuf and Blanqui. Nevertheless, he insisted that they failed in their attempt to synthesize the "destructive" politics of these early socialists with more modern and more "constructive" tendencies. Bernstein concluded that once the political rights of voting, association, and a free press had been established, the old methods of "political expropriation" were no longer relevant. Emancipation was now to come through "economic organisation" (Bernstein 1993, 41).

As should be apparent from our previous discussion of Engels's critique of Blanqui, Bernstein's argument willfully misrepresents Marx and Engels's politics. They criticized Blanqui for failing to understand that revolutions in the modern world could not be the work of a small elite acting on behalf of the working class but could only come through the self-emancipation of the working class. By conflating these radically different models of revolution, Bernstein's intention was to subvert Engels's concrete articulation of a revolutionary strategy for Germany to his own revisionist ends.

Manfred Steger has argued that Engels opened the door to Bernstein's interpretation because of the ad hoc way in which he attempted to square his commitment to the politics of *The Communist Manifesto* on the one hand with his embrace of political "gradualism" on the other. Steger claims that his interpretation of Engels's mature politics improves over previous attempts at this because it is situated within the political context rather than operating as a simple history of ideas (Steger 1999, 182). But this argument is fundamentally problematic. To justify the (at least partial) validity of Bernstein's interpretation of Engels, Steger implicitly accepts the revisionist interpretation of the "dramatically changed political situation" in which the latter wrote. Indeed, his claim that Engels confused the distinction between evolution and revolution while simultaneously compromising Marxism's unity of theory and practice is dependent upon conflating Marx and Engels's politics with the kind of one-dimensional conception of revolutionary politics that Engels and Marx had spent their lives criticizing.

Engels was writing in a nonrevolutionary situation. But this fact is not particularly interesting. With the exception of 1871, ever since the defeats of the revolutions of 1848 Marx and Engels had lived through a nonrevolutionary epoch. And because the Paris Commune emerged, as Marx noted in a letter of February 22, 1881, as a response to an excep-tional local politico-military crisis rather than a Europe-wide economic convulsion, 1871 could not be considered a revolutionary event in the way of 1848 (CW 46, 66). Hobsbawm might have somewhat overstated the point when he wrote that, while the Commune "frightened the wits out of" the bourgeoisie, it "did not threaten the bourgeois order seriously" (Hobsbawm 1975, 200–201; Blackledge 2012b; 2008a). Nonetheless, it is true that for all its political significance the Commune was a precursor of things to come rather than the potential opening of a European-wide alternative to capitalism in the 1870s. The problem that Marx and Engels had attempted to address since 1850 was how to orient to a future rev-olution in a nonrevolutionary context. To suggest, as does Steger, that Engels's "purely tactical" response to this situation "contributed to the further decline of the status of 'theory' in the SPD and strengthened the role of the instrumentalist party tacticians" is to completely misunderstand the nature both of Engels's theory and of the growing reformism within the SPD.

While Bernstein's arguments did not highlight problems with Engels's theory—his book had little by way of intellectual merits—it did give voice to a real and growing reformist tendency as embodied primarily within the bureaucracy of the German labor movement. More to the point, the tactical instrumentalism of this layer had little to do with the strengths or weaknesses of Engels's theory—its opportunism was, as Rosa Luxemburg highlighted, structural in nature. Among Luxemburg's profound contribu-tions to Marxism, was her outline of the first systematic account of social democratic reformism. She recognized that revisionism was not merely a theoretical error in the context of economic expansion but was deeply rooted in the structure of modern trade unionism. She also insisted that the characteristically capitalist separation between politics and economics was reproduced in the labor movement through the division between parliamentary socialism and simple trade unionism. Both Bernstein's revisionism and Kautsky's increasingly mechanical caricature of Marxism are best understood as attempts to reconcile Marxism to the growing social weight of the structurally conservative labor and trade union bureaucracy (Blackledge 2014a; Luxemburg 1970b, 207–218; Schorske 1983, 16–24, 108, 127; Salvadori 1979, 144).

Engels's Marxism did suffer from an important limitation, but it was not a supposed failure to grasp the theoretical implications of the nonrevolutionary nature of the period in which he wrote. The most important lacuna in his thought in this period related, as previously noted, to his (and Marx's) failure to outline a coherent theory of reformism. This theoretical blind spot arguably informed his response to Fischer's call to tone down the language of his 1895 introduction—Engels was not necessarily wrong to do this (he and Marx had a long history of standing against the kind of sectarian demands for political purism that would have insisted on rejecting Fischer's requests for revisions on principle) but he lacked an adequate framework for judging just how far he should compromise with the SPD because he had no theory of their structural reformism (cf. Stedman Jones 1973, 33–36). Unfortunately, while he continued to insist on maintaining the political independence of the workers' party (CW 47, 532; CW 49, 515; CW 50, 113; CW 27, 440; CW 48, 423), without something like Luxemburg's theory of the structural reformism of the labor and trade union bureaucracy, he was unable to give an adequate answer to the question "independent from what?"

The fundamental problem with Steger's claim that Engels's 1895 introduction amounted to an ad hoc and theoretically incoherent recognition of the nonrevolutionary reality of Germany in the 1890s is that this undialectical way of framing the problem fails to see what Engels saw so clearly. As with Liebknecht, shades of gray do not seem to exist for Steger. The dynamic nature of the system meant a unity between revolutionary and nonrevolutionary phases of development. Contradictions developing from the 1890s onward eventually gave rise to a revolutionary situation in Germany between 1918 and 1923 (Broué 2005, 1–10; Harman 2003, 21–22). The problem Engels addressed in the 1895 introduction was of how to orient to this future situation without succumbing to abstractly propagandistic politics in the present. The solution he posed to this question amounts to, as David Fernbach suggests, the "classic Marxist formulation on the transition from electoral politics to insurrection" (Fernbach 1974, 57).

More specifically, the theoretical architecture of Engels's approach to politics generally and to the relationship between class struggles and geopolitics can usefully be understood in relation to Clausewitz's claim that "tactics teaches the use of armed forces in the engagement; strategy, the use of engagements for the object of the war": "The strategist must therefore define an aim for the entire operational side of the war that will be in accordance with its purpose . . . he will, in fact, shape the individual campaigns and, within these, decide on the individual engagements. . . . The strategist, in short, must maintain control throughout" (Clausewitz 2007, 74; 133). Engels, who believed Clausewitz to be a "star of the first magnitude" (CW 26, 450), understood revolutionary politics in similar terms. His dialectical approach informed his ability to marry revolutionary strategy with extreme tactical flexibility. And his writings from this period evidence his keen ability to maintain a dialectical unity between strategy and tactics through concrete assessments of concrete situations (Callesen 2012). He argued that the problem with the incipient reformist tendencies within the nineteenth-century German workers' movement stemmed from the way that their desire for quick victories in individual engagements meant that these politicians lost sight of the final strategic goal. This approach was, as he wrote in 1891, disastrous: "The forgetting of the great, the principal considerations for the momentary interests of the day, this struggling and striving for the success of the moment regardless of later consequences, this sacrifice of the future of the movement for its present, may be 'honestly' meant, but it is and remains opportunism, and 'honest' opportunism is perhaps the most dangerous of all!" (CW 27, 227). He had made much the same point two decades earlier in a letter to Bebel, June 20, 1873: "there are circumstances in which one must have the courage to sacrifice momentary success for more important things" (CW 44, 512). A decade later, January 25, 1882, he warned Bernstein against the debilitating consequences of following the narrow and petty concerns of local politics:

> Petty conditions engender a petty outlook, so that a great deal of intelligence and vigour is called for if anyone living in Germany is to look beyond the immediate future, to keep his eyes fixed on the wider context of world events and not succumb to that complacent "objectivity" that cannot see beyond its own nose and is therefore the most blinkered subjectivity, even though it be shared by a thousand other such fellow-subjects. (CW 46, 187)

This general approach to revolutionary politics suggested in these passages prefigured Lenin's orientation toward what Lukács called the "actuality of the revolution" (Lukács 1970, 9–13; Blackledge 2019d): it is "only by constantly having the 'ultimate aim' in view, only by appraising every step of the 'movement' and every reform from the point of view of the general revolutionary struggle, is it possible to guard the movement against false steps and shameful mistakes" (Lenin 1961, 74; 1963c, 298). Engels's approach to politics essentially cohered with Lenin's. Against both opportunists on the right-wing of the party and sectarians on its left, Engels defended an approach to politics framed around the claim that "[t]he emancipation of the working class can be the work only of the working class itself" (CW 27, 232). So, while he was scathing in his criticisms of the "opportunism which is gaining ground in large sections of the Social-Democratic press" (CW 27, 226), he was just as critical of those on the sectarian left who confused pseudoradical posturing for real engagement in the movement from below.

Against the reformist tendency within the party he insisted that "the working class can only come to power under the form of a democratic republic. This is even the specific form for the dictatorship of the proletariat" (CW 27, 226–227). More specifically, in his introduction to Marx's *Civil War in France* he reiterated Marx's claim that the Paris Commune had shown that

> the working class, once come to power, could not go on managing with the old state machine; that in order not to lose again its only just conquered supremacy, this working class must, on the one hand, do away with all the old repressive machinery previously used against it itself, and, on the other, safeguard itself against its own deputies and officials, by declaring them all, without exception, subject to recall at any moment. (CW 27, 189)

In 1891 he also published Marx's *Critique of the Gotha Programme* in a deliberate attack on the right wing of the party. This essay included Marx's critique of "the Lassallean sect's servile belief in the state" (CW 27, 92; CW 24, 97), alongside his claim that "between capitalist and communist society lies a period of revolutionary transformation . . . a corresponding period of transition in the political sphere . . . a revolutionary dictatorship of the proletariat" (CW 24, 95). More specifically, regarding participation in a bourgeois government, Engels argued that it would be a mistake for socialists to join such a government as a minority partner within a broader coalition. As he wrote to Italian comrades in 1894:

> After the joint victory we might be offered a few seats in the new government, but always in a minority. This is the greatest danger. After February 1848 the French socialist democrats . . . made the mistake of occupying such seats. As a minority in the government they voluntarily shared the blame for all the foul deeds and betrayals perpetrated by the majority of pure republicans against the workers; whilst the presence of these gentlemen in the government completely paralysed the revolutionary action of the working class which they claimed to represent. (CW 27, 440)

If Engels clearly aimed his comments on the continuing necessity of a revolutionary transformation from capitalism to socialism at the growing opportunist wing of the German workers' movement, he also criticized the abstract sectarianism of the (especially academic) ultra-leftist elements of the party. Commenting on the abstract political pronouncements of one group, he wrote of his disappointment at finding in their paper "a ruthless disregard of all the actual conditions of party struggle, a death-defying 'surmounting of obstacles' in the imagination, which may do all honour to the untamed youthful courage of the writers, but which, if transferred from the imagination to reality, would be sufficient to bury the strongest party of millions under the well-earned laughter of the whole hostile world." Against their radical verbiage Engels insisted that

> their "academic education" . . . does not provide them with an officer's commission and a claim to a corresponding post in the party; that in our party everybody must work his way up; that positions of trust in the party are not won simply through literary talent and theoretical knowledge, even if both are undoubtedly present, but that this also demands familiarity with the conditions of party struggle and adjustment to its forms, proven personal reliability and constancy of character and, finally, a willingness to join the ranks of the fighters—in short, that they, the "academically educated" all in all have much more to learn from the workers than the workers from them.

Of the version of Marxism propagated by these sectarians, he suggested that Marx had foreseen "such disciples" when he said to Lafargue of the French left in the 1870s: "I know only this, that I am not a 'Marxist'" (CW 27, 69–71; Blackledge 2007).

Against both opportunism and sectarianism (and the incoherent combination of the two) Engels is much better understood, in Andrew Collier's words, as a "revolutionary realist" (Collier 1996, 43). He looked reality in the face and, knowing the scale of the task ahead, did everything he could to help the workers' movement prepare for it. The events of 1848 had taught him, among other things, that when the workers meet the army across barricades the army tends to win. To overcome this impossible situation his response was twofold: first, make the movement as big as possible; it is infinitely more difficult for soldiers to control a mass movement of many millions organized across the nation than it is for them to pick off sporadic fighting units. The SPD were doing an admirable job of bringing the working class together into a unified force aimed at taking power. Indeed, they were doing what he and Marx had argued for in 1871:

Considering, that against this collective power of the propertied classes the working class cannot act, as a class, except by constituting itself into a political party, distinct from, and opposed to, all old parties formed by the propertied classes; That this constitution of the working class into a political party is indispensable in order to insure the triumph of the social Revolution and its ultimate end—the abolition of classes; That the combination of forces which the working class has already effected by its economical struggles ought at the same time to serve as a lever for its struggles against the political power of landlords and capitalists—The Conference recalls to the members of the *International*: That in the militant state of the working class, its economical movement and its political action are indissolubly united. (CW 22, 427)

Second, as noted earlier, he also aimed to win the army by winning the mass of soldiers to social democracy. This informed the claim he made in *Socialism in Germany* (1891) that the "German army is becoming more and more infected with socialism" (CW 27, 240). Whatever else might be said of this strategy, and Martin Berger, who labels it Engels's "theory of the vanishing army," is wrong to dismiss it as a "passive doctrine" (Berger 1977, 166–169), the aim of overthrowing from within the armed bodies of men who make up the core of the state apparatus is far more revolutionary than any comparative strategy that aims at avoiding state power. In fact, Gilbert Achcar is right to suggest that this tactical insight was a precursor to Lenin's approach to winning the army in 1914 (Achcar 2002, 82–83). And Engels's outline of a combination of legal and illegal methods to realize the struggle for power of an independent worker's movement remains exemplary:

> How many times have the bourgeois called on us to renounce the use of revolutionary means for ever, to remain within the law, now that the exceptional law has been dropped and one law has been re-established for all, including the socialists? Unfortunately, we are not in a position to oblige *messieurs les bourgeois*. Be that as it may, for the time being it is not we who are being destroyed by legality. It is working so well for us that we would be mad to spurn it as long as the situation lasts. It remains to be seen whether it will be the bourgeois and their government who will be the first to turn their back on the law in order to crush us by violence. That is what we shall be waiting for. You shoot first, *messieurs les bourgeois*. No doubt they will be the first ones to fire. One fine day the German bourgeois and their government, tired of standing with their arms folded, witnessing the ever increasing advances of socialism, will resort to illegality and violence. To what avail? With force it is possible to crush a small sect, at least in a restricted space but there is no force in the world which can wipe out a party of two million men spread out over the entire surface-area of a large empire. Counter-revolutionary violence will be able to slow down the victory of socialism by a few years; but only in order to make it all the more complete when it comes. (CW 27, 240–241)

14

Legacy

At the graveside of his friend and comrade, Engels famously compared Marx to Darwin, claiming that whereas the latter had "discovered the law of development of organic nature," Marx had "discovered" both "the law of development of human history" and "the special law of motion governing the present-day capitalist mode of production" (CW 24, 467–468).

Engels's critics have claimed that these lines illuminate the deterministic and fatalistic essence of his thought. And if some of these critics damn Marx and Marxism by association with these ideas, others have focused their criticisms of Marxism on Engels, who, or so they say, was Marx's greatest mistake.

Nothing could be further from the truth. Through their partnership both Marx and Engels became more and better than they would have been had they acted alone. Of course, Engels's financial support was vital to Marx. But much more important to both men was their intellectual and political comradeship. And while Engels recognized Marx's greater stature, and sacrificed the prime years of his life working for the family business in Manchester, in part, to help finance his comrade while he wrote *Capital*, throughout their friendship both men gained enormously from a constant dialogue through which they deepened and extended the revolutionary standpoint they had first formulated in the mid-1840s. Beyond the simple fact that Marx and Engels liked each other, their relationship worked because Engels was, as he had written of Marx, not merely a man of science who made "independent discoveries . . . in every single field which [he] investigated" but also "before all else a revolutionist" for whom "fighting was his element" (CW 24, 468).

Marx and Engels's revolutionary perspective was first articulated in *The German Ideology* as an attempt to understand the world from the novel perspective of working-class struggles against capitalism. If the dialectical method they subsequently deepened was intended to help make sense both of the novelty and the conflictual essence of our alienated world and the struggles against it, their contribution to the study of history aimed to illuminate the historically evolving material parameters of the struggle for freedom. And by illuminating the parameters of the possible, this method is best understood as a form neither of mechanical materialism nor of political fatalism but rather as a guide to action. This is why Jean-Paul Sartre, for instance, could agree with Engels's interpretation of the relationship between structure and agency (as outlined in a letter to W. Borgius of January 25, 1894):

> the effect of the economic situation is not, as is sometimes conveniently supposed, automatic; rather, men make their own history, but in a given environment by which they are conditioned, and on the basis of extant and actual relations of which economic relations, no matter how much they may be influenced by others of a political and ideological nature, are ultimately the determining factor and represent the unbroken clue which alone can lead to comprehension. (CW 50, 266; cf. Sartre 1963, 31)

This statement, which obviously echoes the opening lines of Marx's *Eighteenth Brumaire* (CW 11, 103), suggests a formal solution to the structure-agency problem that has subsequently been accepted as something like common sense among most serious historians, for whom it has acted as a useful heuristic through which to conceptualize the material determination of creative human agency, praxis. What is more, this conception of agency involves not only the sublation of classical divisions between practice, theory, and technique but also culminated in the claim that there are no fixed divisions between the human and the natural worlds. According to this model, because human agency is materially and socially conditioned, freedom is best understood not in opposition to material necessity but rather through the active comprehension of necessity.

And against Engels's self-deprecating claim that Marx alone had discovered the laws of history and capitalist development, the truth is, as

Marx recognized, Engels made an important contribution to this joint effort. Engels saw the importance of developing a coherent critique of political economy before Marx did, and he started along the road to a coherent theory of history at least as early as his older friend. And while Marx may have gone further, especially in regard to value theory, it remains the case that Engels often led the way and made important independent contributions of his own. For instance, beyond historical materialism and value theory, Engels independently recognized the fundamental importance of working-class agency and was the first to map the strengths and weaknesses of trade unions as institutional expressions, however compromised by the strong conservative tendency of their leaders to limit class conflict to struggles within not against capitalism, of socialism as a real emergent movement from below.

The myth that Engels was Marx's greatest mistake is predicated upon a hopelessly one-dimensional interpretation of Engels's writings, especially *Anti-Dühring* and the *Dialectics of Nature*. Far from evidencing forms of mechanical materialism and political fatalism *Anti-Dühring* was, in the first instance, a political intervention designed to win hegemony for Marxist ideas within the German socialist movement. And, coherently enough, it was and remains a brilliant defense of the form of "practical materialism" he and Marx articulated in 1845–1846. It explicates, in popular fashion, the dialectical method by which they transcended the sterile opposition between idealist (moral) and materialist (causal) conceptions of human agency to make history intelligible for the first time as a really *human* activity.

More to the point, Engels showed that the practical corollary of this new conception of history is an approach to political intervention that is at once organically rooted in a scientific analysis of social reality while simultaneously aiming at the revolutionary transformation of that reality. Thus, in the wake of the defeat of the revolutions of 1848, Engels was at the forefront of attempts to make sense of this new context in a way that avoided the twin errors associated with those who bade their farewells to the left on the one side or who became sectarian moralists on the other. The March and June addresses of 1850, alongside Engels's historical studies of the movements of 1848 and 1525, were intended to make sense of the possibilities for immediate and future socialist activity. Similarly, Engels's studies of military theory and war on the one side and religion on the other were intended to enrich left-wing thought through detailed analyses of the political and ideological aspects of the struggle against alienation. So too were his writings on the art of revolution that especially influenced Lenin's understanding of the insurrectionary moment of the revolutionary process.

Without *Anti-Dühring* the German left risked being lost to Dühring's blathering justification for a retreat into liberalism two decades before Bernstein's first attempts at revisionism. And for all the tragedy of the SPD in 1914, the European left would have been infinitely weaker without it from the 1880s onward.

If Engels's critics seem incapable of reading his use of the word "science" without interpreting it as denoting some form of empiricism or positivism and its corollary a mechanical and fatalistic model of agency, this is their problem not his. Engels was neither an empiricist nor a positivist. And as regards the charge of reductionism, he held to a stratified view of natural and social reality according to which emergent properties at each level could neither be reduced to laws governing the levels below them, nor could the laws through which they operated be understood in an empiricist or positivist fashion. An interventionist conception of politics was the corollary of the fact that social laws operated as tendencies rather than as Humean constant conjunctures. Darwin may well have shown that nature is the proof of dialectics, but Engels understood that neither social evolution nor still less social revolution could be reduced to epiphenomena of natural processes.

Similarly, while his conception of human agency was rooted in an understanding of our natural needs and desires, he also recognized that because our natural essence is social and cultural it is also historical and complex. In *The Origin of the Family, Private Property and the State* he made the first steps toward grasping the concrete truth of this complex and historically determined essence by pointing toward a unitary theory of women's oppression under capitalism through historical accounts of the rise of the family and the state and changing modes of production. In so doing he made fundamental contributions both to political theory, through his historical conception of the state as a transient structure, and to the struggle for women's liberation, through his similarly historicized conception of the family and women's oppression.

That this project was not completely successful is much less import-ant than the fact that it was a pathbreaking attempt at a historical and nonreductive account both of the historical nature of women's oppression and its modern capitalist form. It is in this sense that *The Origin of the Family, Private Property and the State* remains a milestone on the road to a theoretically informed movement for women's liberation as a necessary part of the broader struggle for socialism.

Neither was Engels dismissive of his and Marx's predecessors in the socialist movement. His criticisms of the utopian socialists were always written from a perspective of respect for those giants upon whose shoulders he and Marx stood. The problem with the utopians was the inverse of the problems faced by those Enlightenment philosophers who, by equating human nature with a form of egoistic individualism, failed to comprehend capitalism as a historical form. The utopians, by inverting this image of human nature, were similarly incapable of understanding capitalism as a historical form, albeit one they loathed.

As Engels wrote in the first lines of *Anti-Dühring*, modern socialism presupposed the emergence of the proletariat whose concrete forms of subjectivity acted both as an immanent challenge to egoistic individualism while simultaneously pointing to the historical and sociological roots of the kind of society that reproduced these egoistic relations. In effect, *Anti-Dühring* amounts to a gloss on Marx's method in *Capital*. Engels agreed with Marx that insofar as a critique of political economy is able to grasp social reality as a "totality," it "represents a class, and it can only represent the class whose task is the overthrow of the capitalist mode of production and the final abolition of all classes—the proletariat" (Marx 1976, 732, 98).

This focus on the self-emancipatory movement of the proletariat illuminates the profound break between Marx and Engels's thought and, first, the degeneration of their ideas within the Second International and, second, the subsequent expulsion of the revolutionary content of these ideas by Stalin in his attempt to transform Marxism from a theory of liberation into a justification for tyranny. Between the removal of Bismarck's antisocialist laws and the outbreak of the First World War, the German Social Democratic Party came increasingly to be characterized by a growing gap between its practical opportunism on the one hand and revolutionary rhetoric on the other. This tension was eventually manifest through the party's degeneration into a mere institution of civil society in which politics was reduced to the struggle for a slightly better version of the capitalist status quo (Luxemburg 1970a, 77–78).

Whereas Engels's failure to theorize reformism blinded him to the true significance of the emerging opportunism that he otherwise stood against within the SPD, nothing in his latter writings, including his 1895 introduction to Marx's *The Class Struggles in France*, suggests he broke with revolutionary politics in his old age. Socialist tactics may have evolved but the strategy he propounded was, in essence, the one he and Marx had formulated in the 1840s. Socialism could only come through the self-emancipation of the working class, and though he was certainly not indifferent to the struggles for reforms, Engels insisted that the workers' party's ultimate revolutionary orientation meant that it must maintain its political independence from institutions of civil society.

If this perspective differentiated Engels's Marxism from Kautsky's, a sea of blood separates this vision of socialism from Stalin's violent counterrevolution. To equate Engels's dynamic, humanist, and creative Marxism with Stalin's bastardization of these ideas is frankly crass. That this myth continues to be reproduced in the textbooks says more about the intellectual shoddiness of much academic research on the issue than it does of the substance of Engels's thought. It also illuminates the interests served by this myth. Up until the collapse of the Soviet Union, Stalinist references to Marx, Engels, and Lenin served to justify the Russian dictatorship in the East, while in the West the attempt to equate Marxism with Stalinism functions to justify the liberal critique of Marxism as a form of authoritarianism (Blackledge 2018c). The contemporary left would do well to extricate the real Engels (and Marx and Lenin) from this self-serving nonsense.

Engels's most important contributions to modern social and political theory were made alongside Marx and include the claims that human history can only adequately be understood in relation to natural history, and that human liberation consequently cannot be won except through a revolution that is ecological as well as social and political in scope; that that the bourgeoisie has since 1848 become irreconcilably counterrevolutionary and that since then the working class is the only consistently revolutionary class, albeit that other classes have and will continue to play a progressive part in revolutionary movements; that the capitalist state would be used to crush the workers' movement; that, nonetheless, the workers should not be indifferent to state forms: freedom of association and other such liberal demands were the necessary "elbow-room" within which the workers' movement could grow; that the workers' party therefore needed to intervene in political issues of the day, defending progressive from less progressive policies; but that in orienting to revolution rather than mere reform the workers' party needed to maintain its political independence from liberal critics of capitalism. This form of political practice is ethical in the classical sense of being rooted in a particular form of practice, in this case the, now open, now hidden, real movement of workers against capitalism, but it tends to stand in contradistinction to much contemporary leftist moral discourse whose abstract proclamations often betray the "impotence in action" that Marx and Engels, following Fourier, first challenged and then transcended in the 1840s.

If Engels's misunderstanding of value theory jeopardized this project, it is a relatively easy thing to rescue his defense of revolutionary politics from the reformist implications of his conflation of abstract and concrete labor, once we recognize that his theoretical error related narrowly to value theory rather than to his broader conception of dialectics. This is not to say that there were no malign consequences of this theoretical error: his failure to clearly specify the capitalist form of family is probably not unrelated to this concern. Nonetheless, these weaknesses are as nothing when set against the positive side of his attempt to raise theory to the level of practice. Engels's principled yet undogmatic approach to political practice is a model for the creative development and application of Marxism.

When Engels warned against the appeal of "honest opportunism" in 1891, he hoped the SPD would recognize that, whatever the short-term political and electoral logic of so doing, omitting the concept of the dictatorship of the proletariat from its program could have disastrous consequences for the party in the long run. Because he expected the German capitalist state (indeed any capitalist state) to respond with violence to any serious threat, electoral as much as insurrectionary, to the rule of capital, a socialist party that did not prepare for such an eventuality would be destined to fail the workers' movement at the decisive moment in the class struggle. Theoretical clarity on this point was therefore an essential prerequisite for practical effectiveness.

Unfortunately, the force of Engels's argument was somewhat undermined by the context in which he wrote. In the last years before his death, twenty years had passed since the French workers had vied for political power in Paris, and it was to be the best part of three decades before the German workers would make their own challenge for power at the end of the First World War. Against this background, Engels's orientation to what Lukács called the "actuality of the revolution" appeared increasingly abstract to a generation of activists for whom the SPD's electoralism was becoming an end in itself. In writing of the honesty of the SPD's opportunism, Engels evidenced an awareness both of a tension between the demands of the SPD's day-to-day political activity and the ultimate aim of revolution, and of the way this tension was magnified in a period when the prospects for revolution seemed increasingly distant.

In Britain, a similar tension underpinned the division between (Lib-) Lab parliamentary representatives of the reformist trade union movement and the abstract sectarianism of the nominally Marxist SDF. Engels's critique of the SDF's approach to the mass May Day March of 1891 illuminates his understanding of how revolutionaries should relate to the struggle for reforms. That year's half-million strong May Day Rally had been organized by a committee of "The Legal Eight Hours and International League" chaired by Edward Aveling with Eleanor Marx playing a key role. After the SDF stopped attending the organizing meetings, Engels complained to Marx's daughter Laura Lafargue that

> both here and in America the people who, more or less, have the correct theory as to the dogmatic side of it, become a mere sect because they cannot conceive that living theory of action, of working with the working class at every possible stage of its development, otherwise than as a collection of dogmas to be learnt by heart and recited like a conjurer's formula or a Catholic prayer. Thus the real movement is going on outside the sect, and leaving it more and more. (CW 49, 186)

The vision of socialism as a "living theory of action" that reflects the "the real movement which abolishes the present state of things" framed Engels's (and Marx's) thought from the 1840s onward and served to distinguish their politics from opportunism on the one side and socialist sectarianism on the other. Their refusal to fetishize a correct party-line was intimately related to this approach. The important thing was to be rooted in, and to fight for leadership of, the real movement from below rather than to have a formally correct program. As Engels noted in 1893, the SDF's program was fine, but its policy was hopelessly sectarian. Clearly, it was better to get both the program and the policy right, but, in contrast to many latter-day sectarians, Marx and Engels insisted that the left should prioritize activity within the real movement from below over doctrinal purity. Indeed, Engels's attempt to navigate between sectarianism and opportunism amounts to a classic case study of how revolutionaries should refuse to "sacrifice . . . the future of the movement for its present" without divorcing themselves from the real movement from below in nonrevolutionary situations.

Despite their superficial differences, reformism and sectarianism are united in a static view of workers' consciousness. Whereas reformists and opportunists tend to reify the dominant ideology as reflected in workers'

consciousness in nonrevolutionary periods, sectarians tend simply to counterpose their own "true" consciousness to this real consciousness. Engels's
orientation to the working class was, by contrast, informed both by his
understanding of the *essence* of the working class as a class in conflict with
capitalism and by a strong sense of the dynamic nature of consciousness—in
particular, his belief that socialist class consciousness could emerge through
periods of heightened class struggle but would emerge in an uneven and
fragmentary manner such that Marxists could not afford to hold sectarian
views about, for instance, the initially religious ideas held by workers as
they moved into conflict with the state and capital.

This standpoint presupposed something like the dialectical view of
reality defended and popularized in *Anti-Dühring*. If internally contradictory
relations underpin movement as the essence of reality, the fundamental
problem with both sectarianism and opportunism is a shared failure
to grasp adequately how socialists should relate to the real movement
from below. At a practical level, Engels had evidenced from the 1840s
onward a keen awareness that struggles for reforms were important not
merely because reforms could lead to real and meaningful improvements
in workers' conditions of life, but also because in so doing they could
expand the political space in which workers could grow in consciousness
while simultaneously opening wider political vistas as they began to feel
their power through collective struggles. Indeed, he always insisted that
to advocate revolution while ignoring day-to-day struggles for reforms
amounted to an inversion of, rather than a solution to, the problem of
opportunism-reformism. And, if sectarianism and reformism have material
roots, they also reflect an undialectical frame of mind. Neither sectarians
nor opportunists are able to grasp what Lukács called the "present as a
historical problem" because they tend to reify the distinction between
struggles within the system and struggles against it.

Whatever the limitations of Engels's Marxism, and as we have seen
there were problems with his attempts, for instance, to make sense of
reformism, value theory, nationalism, and the task of formulating a unitary
theory of women's oppression, he nonetheless made a fundamental contribution to understanding the alienated and dynamic nature of the world in
which we live and the politics necessary to overcome this alienated system.
Edward Thompson was right when he wrote that for all Engels's errors,

> when all this has been said, what an extraordinary, dedicated
> and versatile man he was! How closely he followed his own

times, how far he risked himself—further, often, than Marx—in engagements with his contemporary historical and cultural thought, how deeply and passionately he was engaged in a movement which was spreading to the five continents, how generously he gave himself in his last years to the papers of his old friend and to the incessant correspondence of the movement! If we must learn, on occasion, from his errors, then he would have expected this to be so. (Thompson 1978, 69)

If Engels's historical works illuminate the novelty and historical character of capitalism, his philosophical works point to a conception of capitalism as a concrete, ecological totality and underpin the claim that the potential for a radical democratic alternative to this system is immanent to capitalist social relations. In fact, his philosophical works form a unity with his historical and political works that largely succeeds in theorizing working-class self-emancipation as the concrete, systematic, and democratic alternative to capitalism. In our modern neoliberal world that is still dominated by the Thatcherite idea that "there is no alternative" (TINA), Engels's work is more relevant than ever.

Bibliography

CW in parenthetical citations refers to:
Marx, Karl, and Frederick Engels. *Collected Works*, 50 vols. London: Lawrence and Wishart, 1975–2004.

Achcar, Gilbert. 2002. "Engels: Theorist of War, Theorist of Revolution." *International Socialism* 2, no. 97 (Winter): 69–89.

Adamiak, Richard. 1974. "Marx, Engels, and Dühring." *Journal of the History of Ideas* 35, no. 1 (January–March): 98–112.

Anderson, Kevin. 2010. *Marx at the Margins*. Chicago: University of Chicago Press.

Anderson, Perry. 1974. *Lineages of the Absolutist State*. London: Verso.

Anderson, Perry. 1992. *English Questions*. London: Verso.

Arthur, Chris. 1970. Introduction. In Karl Marx and Frederick Engels, *The German Ideology: Student Edition*, edited by Chris Arthur, 4–34. London: Lawrence and Wishart.

Arthur, Chris. 1986. *The Dialectics of Labour*. Oxford: Blackwell.

Arthur, Chris. 1996. "Engels as an Interpreter of Marx's Economics." In *Engels Today*, edited by Chris Arthur, 173–209. London: Macmillan.

Arthur, Chris. 2015. Review of Daniel Blank and Terrell Carver, *Marx and Engels's "German Ideology" Manuscripts: Presentation and Analysis of the "Feuerbach Chapter"* and Daniel Blank and Terrell Carver, *A Political History of the Editions of Marx and Engels's "German Ideology" Manuscripts* at https://marxand philosophy.org.uk/reviews/8023_marx-and-engelss-german-ideology-manuscripts-a-political-history-of-the-editions-of-marx-and-engelss-german-ideology-manuscripts-review-by-chris-arthur/http://marxandphilosophy.org.uk/reviewofbooks/reviews/2015/1846?

Avineri, Shlomo. 1968. *The Social and Political Thought of Karl Marx*. Cambridge: Cambridge University Press.

Barker, Colin, et al., eds. 2013. *Marxism and Social Movements*. Leiden: Brill.

Barrett, Michèle. 2014. *Women's Oppression Today*. London: Verso.

Barrett, Michèle, and Mary McIntosh. 1982. *The Anti-Social Family*. London: Verso.

Bebel, August. 1988. *Woman in the Past, Present and Future*. London: Zwan.

Bender, Frederic. 1975. *The Betrayal of Marx*. New York: Harper.

Benner, Erica. 1995. *Really Existing Nationalisms*. Oxford: Oxford University Press.

Benton, Ted. 1979. "Natural Science and Cultural Struggle: Engels on Philosophy and the Natural Science." In *Issues in Marxist Philosophy, Vol. II: Materialism*, edited by John Mepham and David-Hillel Ruben, 101–142. Brighton: Harvester Press.

Berger, Martin. 1977. *Engels, Armies and Revolution*. Hamden: Archon Books.

Bernstein, Eduard. 1993. *The Preconditions of Socialism*. Cambridge: Cambridge University Press.

Bernstein, Samuel. 1971. *Auguste Blanqui and the Art of Insurrection*. London: Lawrence and Wishart.

Bhaskar, Roy. 1989. *Reclaiming Reality*. London: Verso.

Bhaskar, Roy. 1993. *Dialectic: Pulse of Freedom*. London: Verso.

Bidet, Jacques. 2007. *Exploring Marx's Capital*. Leiden: Brill.

Blackburn, Robin. 2011. *An Unfinished Revolution: Karl Marx and Abraham Lincoln*. London: Verso.

Blackledge, Paul. 2002. "Historical Materialism: From Social Evolution to Social Revolution." In *Historical Materialism and Social Evolution*, edited by Paul Blackledge and Graeme Kirkpatrick, 8–35. London: Palgrave.

Blackledge, Paul. 2006a. *Reflection on the Marxist Theory of History*. Manchester: Manchester University Press.

Blackledge, Paul. 2006b. "What Was Done?" *International Socialism* 2, no. 111: 111–126.

Blackledge, Paul. 2007. "Marx and Intellectuals." In *Marxism, Intellectuals and Politics*, edited by David Bates, 21–41. London: Palgrave.

Blackledge, Paul. 2008a. "English Marxist History." In *Critical Companion to Contemporary Marxism*, edited by Jacques Bidet and Eustache Kouvelakis, 333–351. Leiden: Brill.

Blackledge, Paul. 2008b. "Marxism and Ethics" *International Socialism* 2, no. 120: 125–150.

Blackledge, Paul. 2010a. "Symposium on Lars Lih's Lenin Rediscovered: Editorial Introduction." *Historical Materialism* 18, no. 3: 25–33.

Blackledge, Paul. 2010b. "Marxism, Nihilism and the Problem of Ethical Politics Today." *Socialism and Democracy* 24, no. 2: 101–123.

Blackledge, Paul. 2011a. "Theory and Practice of Revolution in the Nineteenth Century." In *The Edinburgh Critical History of Nineteenth-Century Philosophy*, edited by Alison Stone, 259–277. Edinburgh: Edinburgh University Press.

Blackledge, Paul. 2011b. "Why Workers Can Change the World." *Socialist Review* 364: 9–12.

Blackledge, Paul. 2012a. *Marxism and Ethics*. Albany: State University of New York Press.

Blackledge, Paul. 2012b. "Eric Hobsbawm (1917–2012)." *Socialist Review* 374: 22–24.

Blackledge, Paul. 2012c. "Freedom and Democracy: Marxism, Anarchism and the Problem of Human Nature." In *Libertarian Socialism*, edited by Alex Pritchard, Ruth Kinna, Saku Pinta, and David Berry, 17–34. London: Palgrave.

Blackledge, Paul. 2013. "Left-Reformism, the State and the Problem of Socialist Politics Today." *International Socialism* 139: 25–56.

Blackledge, Paul. 2014a. "The Split in the International and the Origins of War." In *Communism in the Twentieth Century: Vol. II Wither Communism*, edited by Shannon Brincat, 31–56. Santa Barbara: Praeger.

Blackledge, Paul. 2014b. "The New Left: Beyond Stalinism and Social Democracy?" In *The Far Left in Britain Since 1956*, edited by Evan Smith and Matthew Worley, 45–61. Manchester: Manchester University Press.

Blackledge, Paul. 2015. "G.A. Cohen and the Limits of Analytical Marxism." In *Constructing Marxist Ethics*, edited by Michael Thompson, 288–312. Leiden: Brill.

Blackledge, Paul. 2017. "Practical Materialism." *Critique* 47, no. 4: 483–499.

Blackledge, Paul. 2018a. "Social Reproduction and the Problem of a Unitary Theory of Women's Oppression." *Social Theory and Practice* 44, no. 3: 297–321.

Blackledge, Paul. 2018b. "Hegemony and Intervention." *Science and Society* 82, no. 4: 479–499.

Blackledge, Paul. 2018c. "Lenin: Soviet Democracy in 1917." In *Democratic Moments*, edited by Xavier Marquez, 129–136. London: Bloomsbury.

Blackledge, Paul. 2019a. "Historical Materialism." In *Oxford Handbook of Karl Marx*, edited by Matt Vidal, Tony Smith, Tomás Rotta, and Paul Prew, 000–000. Oxford: Oxford University Press.

Blackledge, Paul. 2019b. "Engels's Politics: Strategy and Tactics after 1848." *Socialism and Democracy* (July): 000–000.

Blackledge, Paul. 2019c. "War and Revolution: Friedrich Engels as a Military and Political Thinker." *War and Society* (May): 81–97.

Blackledge, Paul. 2019d. "On Strategy and Tactics: Marxism and Electoral Politics." *Science and Society*: 355–380.

Bloch, Ernst. 1986. *The Principle of Hope*. 3 vols. Oxford: Blackwell.

Bloodworth, Sandra. 2018. "The Origins of Women's Oppression—A Defence of Engels and New Departure." *Monthly Review*, online at https://mronline.org/2018/07/31/the-origins-of-womens-oppression-a-defence-of-engels-and-a-new-departure/.

Boer, Roland. 2012. *Criticism of Earth*. Chicago: Haymarket.

Broué, Pierre. 2005. *The German Revolution 1917–1923*. Leiden: Brill.

Brown, Heather. 2013. *Marx on Gender and the Family*. Chicago: Haymarket.

Callesen, Gerd. 2012. "Engels on Revolutionary Tactics, 1889–1895." *Socialism and Democracy* 26, no. 1 (March): 85–102.

Carver, Terrell. 1981. *Engels*. Oxford: Oxford University Press.

Carver, Terrell. 1983. *Marx and Engels: The Intellectual Relationship*. Bloomington: Indiana University Press.

Carver, Terrell. 1989. *Friedrich Engels: His Life and Thought*. London: Macmillan.

Carver, Terrell. 1998. *The Postmodern Marx*. Manchester: Manchester University Press.

Carver, Terrell. 2010. "*The German Ideology* Never Took Place." *History of Political Thought* 31, no. 1: 107–127.

Carver, Terrell, and Daniel Blank, eds. 2014. *Marx and Engels's "German Ideology" Manuscripts*. London: Palgrave.

Chancer, Lynn, and Beverly Xaviera Watkins. 2006. *Gender, Race, and Class*. Oxford: Blackwell.

Childe, V. Gordon. 1966. *Man Makes Himself*. London: Fontana.

Childe, V. Gordon. 2004. *Foundations of Social Archaeology*. Oxford: Berg.

Claeys, Gregory. 1984. "Engels's Outlines of a Critique of Political Economy (1843) and the Origins of the Marxist Critique of Capitalism." *History of Political Economy* 16, no. 2: 207–231.

Claeys, Gregory. 2018. *Marx and Marxism*. London: Penguin.

Clausewitz, Carl von. 2007. *On War*. Oxford: Oxford University Press.

Cliff, Tony. 1974. *State Capitalism in Russia*. London: Pluto.

Cliff, Tony. 2001. "Engels." In *International Struggles and the Marxist Tradition*, 133–142. London: Bookmarks.

Cohen, I. Bernard. 1985. *Revolution in Science*. Cambridge: Harvard University Press.

Cohen-Almagor, Raphael. 1991. "Foundations of Violence, Terror and War in the Writings of Marx, Engels and Lenin." *Terrorism and Political Violence* 3, no. 2: 1–24.

Colletti, Lucio. 1972. *From Rousseau to Lenin*. New York: Monthly Review.

Collier, Andrew. 1994. *Critical Realism*. London: Verso

Collier, Andrew. 1996. "Engels: Revolutionary Realist?" In *Engels Today*, edited by Chris Arthur, 29–45. London: Macmillan.

Collins, Henry, and Chimen Abramsky. 1965. *Karl Marx and the British Labour Movement*. London: Macmillan.

Collins, Randall. 1994. *Four Sociological Traditions*. Oxford: Oxford University Press.

Coontz, Stephanie, and Peta Henderson. 1986. "Property Forms, Political Power and Female Labour in the Origins of Class and State Societies." In *Women's Work, Men's Property*, edited by Stephanie Coontz and Peta Henderson, 108–155. London: Verso.

Creaven, Sean. 2000. *Marxism and Realism*. London: Routledge.

Cummins, Ian. 1980. *Marx, Engels and National Movements*. London: Croom Helm.

Das, Raju. 2017. *Marxist Class Theory for a Skeptical World*. Leiden: Brill.

Davis, Mike. 2018. *Old Gods, New Enigmas: Marx's Lost Theory*. London: Verso.

de Beauvoir, Simone. 1972. *The Second Sex*. London: Penguin.

Della Volpe, Galvano. 1980. *Logic as a Positive Science*. London: New Left Books.

Draper, Hal. 1977. *Karl Marx's Theory of Revolution, Vol. I*. New York: Monthly Review Press.

Draper, Hal. 1978, *Karl Marx's Theory of Revolution, Vol. II*. New York: Monthly Review Press.

Draper, Hal. 1986. *Karl Marx's Theory of Revolution, Vol. III*. New York: Monthly Review Press.

Draper, Hal. 1990. *Karl Marx's Theory of Revolution, Vol. IV*. New York: Monthly Review Press.

Draper, Hal. 2004. *The Adventures of the Communist Manifesto*. Alameda: Centre for Socialist History.

Draper, Hal. 2005. *Karl Marx's Theory of Revolution, Vol. V*. New York: Monthly Review Press.

Draper, Hal. 2013. *Women and Class*. Alameda: Centre for Socialist History.

Dunayevskaya, Raya. 1988. *Marxism and Freedom*. New York: Columbia University Press.

Eagleton, Terry. 2009. *Reason, Faith and Revolution*. New Haven: Yale University Press.

Eagleton, Terry. 2016. *Materialism*. New Haven: Yale University Press.

Ebert, Teresa. 2015. "Epilogue: Gender after Class." In *Marxism and Feminism*, edited by Shahrzad Mojab, 347–367. London: Zed Books.

Elson, Diane. 1979. "The Value Theory of Labour." In *Value: The Representation of Labour in Capitalism*, edited by Diane Elson, 115–180. London: CSE Books.

Evans, Andrew. 1993. *Soviet Marxism-Leninism*. Westport: Praeger.

Evans, Mary. 1987. "Engels: Materialism and Morality." In *Engels Revisited*, edited by Janet Sayers, Mary Evans, and Nanneke Redclift, 81–97. London: Tavistock.

Feeley, Dianne. 2015. "Marx and the Family Revisited." *Against the Current* 175: 35–38.

Fernbach, David. 1974. Introduction. In *Karl Marx: The First International and After*, edited by David Fernbach, 9–72. London: Penguin.

Ferraro, Joseph. 1992. *Freedom and Determination in History According to Marx and Engels*. New York: Monthly Review Press.

Fine, Ben, and Lawrence Harris. 1979. *Rereading Capital*. London: Macmillan.

Fine, Ben, Costas Lapavitsas, and Dimitris Milonakis. 2000. "Dialectics and Crisis Theory." *Historical Materialism* 6: 133–137.

Firestone, Shulamith. 1970. *The Dialectics of Sex*. New York: Bantam.

Foreman, Ann. 1977. *Femininity as Alienation*. London: Pluto.

Foster, John Bellamy. 2000. *Marx's Ecology*. New York: Monthly Review Press.

Foster, John Bellamy, and Paul Burkett. 2017. *Marx and the Earth*. Chicago: Haymarket.

Foster, John Bellamy, and Brett Clark. 2018. "Women, Nature and Capital in the Industrial Revolution." *Monthly Review* 69, no. 8: https://monthlyreview.org/2018/01/01/women-nature-and-capital-in-the-industrial-revolution/.

Foster, John Bellamy, Brett Clark, and Richard York. 2010. *The Ecological Rift*. New York: Monthly Review Press.

Freedman, Lawrence. 2013. *Strategy*. Oxford: Oxford University Press.

Fromm, Erich. 1966. *Marx's Concept of Man*. New York: Unger Press.

Frow, Edmund, and Ruth Frow. 1995. *Frederick Engels in Manchester*. Manchester: Working Class Movement Library.

Frow, Ruth, and Edmund Frow. 1985. *Karl Marx in Manchester*. Manchester: Working Class Movement Library.

Gallie, W. B. 1978. *Philosophers of Peace and War*. Cambridge: Cambridge University Press.

Gemkov, Heinrich, Horst Bartel, Gerhard Becker, Rolf Dlubek, Erich Kudel, Horst Ullrich, Heinz Helmert, Martin Hundt, Wolfgang Jahn, Rosie Rudich, Wolfgang Schröder, Richard Speed, Inge Taubert, and Walter Wittwer. 1972. *Frederick Engels: A Biography*. Dresden: Verlag im Bild.

Geras, Norman. 1983. *Marx and Human Nature*. London: Verso

German, Lindsey. 1998. *Sex, Class and Socialism*. London: Bookmarks.

Gilbert, Alan. 1981. *Marx's Politics*. Oxford: Martin Robertson.

Gimenez, Martha. 1987. "Marxist and Non-Marxist Elements in Engels's Views on the Oppression of Women." In *Engels Revisited*, edited by Janet Sayers, Mary Evans, and Nanneke Redclift, 37–56. London: Tavistock.

Gimenez, Martha. 2018. *Marx, Women, and Capitalist Social Reproduction*. Leiden: Brill.

Goldmann, Lucien. 1968. *The Philosophy of the Enlightenment*. London: Routledge & Kegan Paul.

Gould, Carol. 1999. "Engels's Origin: A Feminist Critique." In *Engels After Marx*, edited by Manfred Steger and Terrell Carver, 253–260. Manchester: Manchester University Press.

Gould, Stephen Jay. 1977. *Ever Since Darwin*. London: Penguin.

Gould, Stephen Jay. 1980. *The Panda's Thumb*. London: Penguin.

Gould, Stephen Jay. 1987. *An Urchin in the Storm*. London: Penguin.

Gouldner, Alvin. 1980. *The Two Marxisms*. London: Macmillan.

Gramsci, Antonio. 1971. *Selections from the Prison Notebooks*. London: Lawrence and Wishart.

Green, John. 2008. *Engels: A Revolutionary Life*. London: Artery Publications.

Hamilton, Richard. 1991. *The Bourgeois Epoch*. Chapel Hill: University of North Carolina Press.

Hammen, Oscar. 1969. *The Red 49'ers*. New York: Charles Scribner's Sons.

Harman, Chris. 1984. "Women's Liberation and Revolutionary Socialism." *International Socialism* 23: 3–41.

Harman, Chris. 1992. "The Return of the National Question." *International Socialism* 56: 3–61.

Harman, Chris. 1994. "Engels and the Origins of Human Society." In *The Revolutionary Ideas of Frederick Engels*, edited by John Rees, 83–142. London: International Socialism.

Harman, Chris. 2003. *The Lost Revolution: Germany 1918 to 1923.* Chicago: Haymarket.
Harman, Chris. 2008. *A People's History of the World.* London: Verso.
Harris, Nigel. 1990. *National Liberation.* London: I. B. Tauris.
Hartmann, Heidi. 1981. "The Unhappy Marriage of Marxism and Feminism: Towards a More Progressive Union." In *The Unhappy Marriage of Marxism and Feminism,* edited by Lydia Sargent, 1–41. London: Pluto.
Harvey, David. 1996. *Justice, Nature and the Geography of Difference.* Oxford: Blackwell.
Harvey, David. 2010. *A Companion to Marx's Capital.* London: Verso.
Haug, Frigga. 2015. "Gender Relations." In *Marxism and Feminism,* edited by Shahrzad Mojab, 33–75. London: Zed Books.
Haupt, Georges. 1986. *Aspects of International Socialism 1871–1941.* Cambridge: Cambridge University Press.
Heinrich, Michael. 1996–1997. "Engels's Edition of the Third Volume of *Capital* and Marx's Original Manuscript." *Science and Society* 60, no. 4: 452–466.
Henderson, W. O. 1976. *The Life of Friedrich Engels.* 2 vols. London: Frank Cass.
Hegel, Georg. 1952. *Philosophy of Right.* Oxford: Oxford University Press.
Hinton, James. 1973. *The First Shop Stewards Movement.* London: George Allen & Unwin.
Hinton, James. 1983. *Labour and Socialism.* Brighton: Wheatsheaf.
Hobsbawm, Eric. 1962. *The Age of Revolution.* London: Abacus.
Hobsbawm, Eric. 1964. *Labouring Men.* London: Weidenfeld and Nicolson.
Hobsbawm, Eric. 1975. *The Age of Capital.* London: Abacus.
Hobsbawm, Eric. 1998. *Introduction to Karl Marx and Frederick Engels' "The Communist Manifesto."* London: Verso.
Hobsbawm, Eric. 1999. *Industry and Empire.* London: Penguin.
Hodder, Ian. 2006. *The Leopard's Tale.* London: Thames & Hudson.
Hodges, Donald. 1965. "Engels's Contribution to Marxism." *Socialist Register.* 297–310.
Hollander, Samuel. 2011. *Friedrich Engels and Marxian Political Economy.* Cambridge: Cambridge University Press.
Holloway, John. 2010. *Change the World Without Taking Power.* London: Pluto.
Humphries, Jane. 1987. "The Origin of the Family: Born Out of Scarcity Not Wealth." In *Engels Revisited,* edited by Janet Sayers, Mary Evans, and Nanneke Redclift, 11–36. London: Tavistock.
Hunley, Dill. 1991. *The Life and Thought of Friedrich Engels.* New Haven: Yale University Press.
Hunt, Richard. 1975–1984. *The Political Ideas of Marx and Engels.* 2 vols. London: Macmillan.
Hunt, Tristram. 2009. *Marx's General.* New York: Henry Holt & Co.
Ilyenkov, Evald. 2013. *The Dialectics of Abstract and Concrete in Marx's Capital.* Delhi: Aakar Books.
Ilyichov, L. F., Y. P. Kandel, N. Y. Kolpinsky, A. I. Malysh, G. D. Obichkin, V. V. Platkovsky, Yevgenia Stepanova, and B. G. Tartakovsky. 1974. *Frederick Engels: A Biography.* Moscow: Progress.

Jenkins, Mick. 1951. *Frederick Engels in Manchester*. Manchester: Lancashire and Cheshire Communist Party.

Johnson, Carol. 1980. "The Problem of Reformism and Marx's Theory of Fetishism." *New Left Review* 1, no. 119: 70–96.

Jordan, Z. A. 1967. *The Evolution of Dialectical Materialism*. London: Macmillan.

Kapp, Yvonne. 1976. *Eleanor Marx, Vol. II: The Crowded Years 1884–1898*. London: Lawrence and Wishart.

Kellner, Douglas. 1999. "Engels, Modernity, and Classical Social Theory." In *Engels After Marx*, edited by Manfred Steger and Terrell Carver, 163–178. Manchester: Manchester University Press.

Kellogg, Paul. 1991. "Engels and the Roots of Revisionism." *Science and Society* 55: 158–174.

Kiernan, Victor. 2001. *Twenty Years of Europe: The Engels-Lafargue Correspondence 1868–1888*. London: Socialist History Society.

Kircz, Joost, and Michael Löwy, eds. 1998. *Friedrich Engels: A Critical Centenary Appreciation*. Special issue of *Science and Society* 62, no. 1.

Kirk, Neville. 1985. *The Growth of Working-Class Reformism in Mid-Victorian England*. Chicago: University of Illinois Press.

Kitchen, Martin. 1977. "Friedrich Engels's Theory of War." *Military Affairs* 41, no. 3: 119–124.

Korsch, Karl. 1970. *Marxism and Philosophy*. London: New Left Books.

Korsch, Karl. 2015. *Karl Marx*. Leiden: Brill.

Krader, Lawrence. 1974. *The Ethnological Notebooks of Karl Marx*. Assen: Van Gorcum & Co.

Lafargue, Paul. n.d. "Reminiscences of Engels." In *Reminiscences of Marx and Engels*. Moscow: Progress.

Leacock, Eleanor Burke. 1972. Introduction. In Frederick Engels, *The Origin of the Family, Private Property and the State*. London: Lawrence and Wishart.

Leacock, Eleanor Burke. 1981. *Myths of Male Dominance*. New York: Monthly Review Press.

Lebowitz, Michael. 2009. *Following Marx*. Leiden: Brill.

Lefebvre, Henri. 2009. *Dialectical Materialism*. Minneapolis: University of Minnesota Press.

Lenin, Vladimir. 1961. "Persecutors of Zemsvo and Hannibals of Liberalism." In *Collected Works*, 45 vols., vol. 5: 31–80. Moscow: Progress, 1960–1970.

Lenin, Vladimir. 1962. "Against Boycott." In *Collected Works*, vol. 13: 15–49.

Lenin, Vladimir. 1963a. "The Attitude of the Workers' Party to Religion." In *Collected Works*, vol. 15: 402–413.

Lenin, Vladimir. 1963b. "The Three Sources and Three Component Parts of Marxism." In *Collected Works*, vol. 19: 23–28.

Lenin, Vladimir. 1963c. "The Discussion of Self-Determination Summed Up." In *Collected Works*, vol. 22: 320–360.

Lenin, Vladimir. 1964. "Advice of an Onlooker." In *Collected Works*, vol. 26: 179–181.

Lenin, Vladimir. 1966. "Notes of a Publicist." In *Collected Works*, vol. 33: 204–211.

Levin, Michael. 1999. "Carlyle, Engels and 'Feudal Socialism.'" *Studies in Marxism* 6: 71–89.

Levine, Norman. 1975. *The Tragic Deception: Marx Contra Engels*. Oxford: Clio Press.

Levins, Richard, and Richard Lewontin. 1985. *The Dialectical Biologist*. Cambridge: Harvard University Press.

Levitas, Ruth. 1990. *The Concept of Utopia*. Syracuse: Syracuse University Press.

Lichtheim, George. 1964. *Marxism*. London: Routledge and Kegan Paul.

Liedman, Sven-Eric. 2018. *A World to Win: The Life and Works of Karl Marx*. London: Verso.

Lih, Lars. 2006. *Lenin Rediscovered*. Leiden: Brill.

Lobkowicz, Nicholas. 1967. *Theory and Practice*. Notre Dame: University of Notre Dame Press.

Losurdo, Domenico. 2015. *War and Revolution*. London: Verso.

Löwy, Michael. 1993. *On Changing the World*. Atlantic Highlands: Humanities Press.

Löwy, Michael. 1996. *The War of Gods*. London: Verso.

Löwy, Michael. 1998. "Friedrich Engels on Religion and Class Struggle." *Friedrich Engels: A Critical Centenary Appreciation*. Special issue of *Science and Society* 62, no. 1: 79–87.

Lull, Vincente, and Rafael Micó. 2011. *Archaeology and the Origin of the State*. Oxford: Oxford University Press.

Lukács, Georg. 1970. *Lenin: A Study in the Unity of His Thought*. London: New Left Books.

Lukács, Georg. 1971. *History and Class Consciousness*. London: Merlin Press.

Lukács, Georg. 1975. *The Young Hegel*. London: Merlin Press.

Lukács, Georg. 1978. *The Ontology of Social Being: Marx*. London: New Left Books.

Lukács, Georg. 2000. *A Defence of History and Class Consciousness: Tailism and the Dialectic*. London: Verso.

Luxemburg, Rosa. 1970a. "Reform or Revolution." In *Rosa Luxemburg Speaks*, edited by Mary-Alice Waters, 33–90. New York: Pathfinder.

Luxemburg, Rosa. 1970b. "The Mass Strike." In *Rosa Luxemburg Speaks*, edited by Mary-Alice Waters, 153–218. New York: Pathfinder.

Luxemburg, Rosa. 1970c. "The Junius Pamphlet." In *Rosa Luxemburg Speaks*, edited by Mary-Alice Waters, 257–331. New York: Pathfinder.

Luxemburg, Rosa. 1970d. "Speech to the Founding Convention of the German Communist Party." In *Rosa Luxemburg Speaks*, edited by Mary-Alice Waters, 400–427. New York: Pathfinder.

MacIntyre, Alasdair. 1967. *Secularization and Moral Change*. Oxford: Oxford University Press.

MacIntyre, Alasdair. 1995. *Marxism and Christianity*. London: Duckworth.

Magdoff, Harry, and John Bellamy Foster. 2011. *What Every Environmentalist Needs to Know About Capitalism*. New York: Monthly Review.

Maguire, John. 1978. *Marx's Theory of Politics*. Cambridge: Cambridge University Press.

Mandel, Ernest. 2015. *The Formation of the Economic Thought of Karl Marx 1843 to Capital*. London: Verso.

Marcus, Steven. 1974. *Engels, Manchester and the Working Class*. London: Weidenfeld and Nicolson.

Marcuse, Herbert. 1958. *Soviet Marxism*. London: Penguin.

Marcuse, Herbert. 2008. *On Authority*. London: Verso.

Marx, Karl. 1973. *Grundrisse*. London: Penguin.

Marx, Karl. 1976. *Capital*, vol. 1. London: Penguin.

Marx, Karl. 1981. *Capital*, vol. 3. London: Penguin.

Marx, Karl, and Frederick Engels. 1983. *Letters on "Capital."* London: New Park.

Marx-Aveling, Eleanor. n.d. "Frederick Engels." In *Reminiscences of Marx and Engels*. Moscow: Progress.

Mayer, Gustav. 1936. *Friedrich Engels*. London: Chapman & Hall.

McKinnon, Andrew. 2006. "Opium as Dialectics of Religion." In *Marx, Critical Theory, and Religion*, edited by Warren Goldstein, 11–29. Chicago: Haymarket.

McLellan, David. 1969. *The Young Hegelians and Karl Marx*. London: Macmillan.

McLellan, David. 1977. *Engels*. London: Fontana.

McLellan, David. 1979. *Marxism After Marx*. London: Macmillan.

McLellan, David. 2006. *Karl Marx: A Biography*. London: Palgrave.

McNally, David. 2017. "Intersections and Dialectics." In *Social Reproduction Theory*, edited by Tithi Bhattacharya, 94–111. London: Pluto.

Meikle, Scott. 1979. "Dialectical Contradiction and Necessity." In *Issues in Marxist Philosophy*, vol. 1, edited by John Mepham and David Hillel Ruben, 5–35. Brighton: Harvester Press.

Meikle, Scott. 1985. *Essentialism in the Thought of Karl Marx*. La Salle: Open Court.

Meikle, Scott. 1999. "Engels and the Enlightenment Reading of Marx." In *Engels After Marx*, edited by Manfred Steger and Terrell Carver, 83–107. Manchester University Press

Mészáros, István. 1975. *Marx's Theory of Alienation*. London: Merlin.

Millett, Kate. 2000. *Sexual Politics*. Chicago: University of Illinois Press.

Mitchell, Juliet. 1974. *Psychoanalysis and Feminism*. London: Penguin.

Mojab, Shahrzad, ed. 2015. *Marxism and Feminism*. London: Zed.

Moseley, Fred. 2016. Introduction. In *Marx's Economic Manuscripts 1864–1865*, edited by Fred Moseley, 1–44. Leiden: Brill.

Neimanis, George. 1980. "Militia versus the Standing Army in the History of Economic Thought from Adam Smith to Friedrich Engels." *Military Affairs* 44, no. 1: 28–32.

Neumann, Sigmund, and Mark von Hagen. 1986. "Engels and Marx on Revolution, War, and the Army in Society." In *Masters of Modern Strategy*, edited by Peter Paret, 262–280. Oxford: Oxford University Press.

Niebuhr, Reinhold. 1964. Introduction. In *Karl Marx and Friedrich Engels on Religion*, vii–xiv. New York: Schocken Books.

Nimtz, August. 2000. *Marx and Engels: Their Contribution to the Democratic Breakthrough*. Albany: State University of New York Press.

Norman, Richard, and Sean Sayers. 1980. *Hegel, Marx and Dialectic*. Brighton: Harvester Press.

Oakley, Allen. 1984. *Marx's Critique of Political Economy*, vol. 1. London: Routledge and Kegan Paul.

Ollman, Bertell. 1976. *Alienation*. Cambridge: Cambridge University Press.

Ollman, Bertell. 2003. *Dance of the Dialectic*. Chicago: University of Illinois Press.

O'Neill, John. 1996. "Engels without Dogmatism." In *Engels Today*, edited by Chris Arthur, 47–66. London: Macmillan.

Osbourne, Peter. 2005. *How to Read Marx*. London: Granta.

Parkinson, G. H. R. 1977. *Georg Lukács*. London: Routledge.

Parrington, John. 2015. *The Deeper Genome*. Oxford: Oxford University Press.

Patterson, Thomas. 2009. *Karl Marx, Anthropologist*. Oxford: Berg.

Pelz, William. 1998. "Class and Gender: Friedrich Engels's Contribution to Revolutionary History." *Friedrich Engels: A Critical Centenary Appreciation*. Special issue of *Science and Society* 62, no. 1: 117–126.

Perry, Matt. 2002. *Marxism and History*. London: Palgrave.

Petrović, Gajo. 1991. "Praxis." In *A Dictionary of Marxist Thought*, edited by Tom Bottomore, 435–440. Oxford: Blackwell.

Pickard, John. 2013. *Behind the Myths*. Bloomington: AuthorHouse.

Pollock, Ethan. 2006. *Stalin and the Soviet Science Wars*. Princeton: Princeton University Press.

Post, Charlie. 2010. "Exploring Working-Class Consciousness: A Critique of the Theory of the 'Labour Aristocracy.'" *Historical Materialism* 18, no. 4: 3–38.

Prinz, Arthur. 1968. "The Background and Ulterior Motive of Marx's 'Preface' of 1859." *Journal of the History of Ideas* 30: 437–450.

Putnam, Hilary. 1978. "The Philosophy of Science." In *Men of Ideas*, edited by Bryan Magee, 224–239. London: BBC.

Rapport, Mike. 2008. *1848: Year of Revolution*. London: Abacus.

Rees, John. 1994. "Engels's Marxism." In *The Revolutionary Ideas of Frederick Engels*, edited by John Rees, 47–82. London: International Socialism.

Rees, John, ed. 1994. *The Revolutionary Ideas of Frederick Engels*. London: International Socialism.

Rees, John. 2000. Introduction. In Georg Lukács, *A Defence of History and Class Consciousness Tailism and the Dialectic*, 1–38. London: Verso.

Rex, John. 1969. "Friedrich Engels." In *The Founding Fathers of Social Science*, edited by Timothy Raison, 68–75. London: Pelican.

Rigby, S. H. 1992. *Engels and the Formation of Marxism*. Manchester: Manchester University Press.

Robbins, Glyn. 2018. "Engels and the Perennial Housing Crisis." *Critical and Radical Social Work* 6, no. 2: 231–239.

Roberts, Edwin. 1997. *The Anglo-Marxists*. Lanham: Rowman & Littlefield.

Rockmore, Tom. 2018. *Marx's Dream*. Chicago: University of Chicago Press.

Rosdolsky, Roman. 1987. *Engels and the "Nonhistoric" People: The National Question in the Revolution of 1848*. London: Critique Books.

Rose, Steven. 1987. *Molecules and Minds*. Milton Keynes: Open University Press.

Rosen, Michael. 1982. *Hegel's Dialectic and Its Criticisms*. Cambridge: Cambridge University Press.

Rosenberg, Chanie. 1989. *Women and Perestroika*. London: Bookmarks.

Rowthorn, Bob. 1980. *Capitalism, Conflict and Inflation*. London: Lawrence and Wishart.

Rubin, Isaac Ilyich. 1973. *Essays on Marx's Theory of Value*. Montreal: Black Rose.

Rubin, Isaac Ilyich. 1979. *A History of Economic Thought*. London: Ink Links.

Saad-Filho, Alfredo. 2002. *The Value of Marx*. London: Routledge.

Sacks, Karen. 1975. "Engels Revisited." In *Towards an Anthropology of Women*, edited by Rayna Reiter, 211–235. New York: Monthly Review Press

Sacks, Karen. 1982, *Sisters and Wives*. Chicago: University of Illinois Press.

Salvadori, Massimo. 1979. *Karl Kautsky and the Socialist Revolution*. London: Verso.

Sandle, Mark. 1999. *A Short History of Soviet Socialism*. London: UCL Press.

Sandle, Mark. 2007. "Soviet and Eastern Bloc Marxism." In *Twentieth-Century Marxism*, edited by Daryl Glaser and David Walker, 59–77. London: Routledge.

Sargent, Lydia, ed. 1981. *The Unhappy Marriage of Marxism and Feminism*. London: Pluto.

Sartre, Jean-Paul. 1963. *Search for a Method*. New York: Alfred A. Knopf.

Saville, John. 1988. *The Labour Movement in Britain*. London: Faber and Faber.

Sayers, Janet, Mary Evans, and Nanneke Redclift, eds. 1987. *Engels Revisited*. London: Tavistock.

Sayers, Sean. 1980a. "On the Marxist Dialectic." In *Hegel, Marx and Dialectic*, edited by Richard Norman and Sean Sayers, 1–24. Brighton: Harvester Press.

Sayers, Sean. 1980b. "Dualism, Materialism and Dialectics." In *Hegel, Marx and Dialectic*, edited by Richard Norman and Sean Sayers, 67–143. Brighton: Harvester Press.

Sayers, Sean. 1996. "Engels and Materialism." In *Engels Today*, edited by Chris Arthur, 153–172. London: Macmillan.

Schäfer, Gert. 1998. "Friedrich Engels: Builder of Closed Systems?" *Friedrich Engels: A Critical Centenary Appreciation*. Special issue of *Science and Society* 62, no. 1: 35–47.

Schorske, Carl. 1983. *German Social Democracy, 1905–1917*. Cambridge: Harvard University Press.

Semmel, Bernard. 1981. *Marxism and the Science of War*. Oxford: Oxford University Press.

Sheehan, Helena. 1985. *Marxism and the Philosophy of Science*. Atlantic Highlands: Humanities Press.

Siegel, Paul. 1986. *The Meek and the Militant*. London: Zed.

Silberner, Edmund. 1946. *The Problem of War in Nineteenth-Century Economic Thought*. Princeton: Princeton University Press.

Sperber, Jonathan. 2013. *Karl Marx: A Nineteenth-Century Life*. New York: Norton.

Stanley, John, and Ernest Zimmermann. 1984. "On the Alleged Differences Between Marx and Engels." *Political Studies* 32: 226–248.

Ste. Croix, Geoffrey de. 1983. *The Class Struggle in the Ancient Greek World*. London: Duckworth

Stedman Jones, Gareth. 1973. "Engels and the End of Classical German Philosophy." *New Left Review* 79: 17–36.

Stedman Jones, Gareth. 1977. "Engels and the Genesis of Marxism." *New Left Review* 106: 79–104.

Stedman Jones, Gareth. 1982. "Engels and the History of Marxism." In *The History of Marxism*, edited by Eric Hobsbawm, 290–326. Brighton: Harvester Press.

Stedman Jones, Gareth. 1983. *Languages of Class*. Cambridge: Cambridge University Press.

Stedman Jones, Gareth. 2016. *Karl Marx: Greatness and Illusion*. London: Penguin.

Steedman, Ian. 1977. *Marx after Sraffa*. London: Verso.

Steger, Manfred. 1996. Introduction. In Eduard Bernstein, *Selected Writings of Eduard Bernstein*, edited by Manfred Steger, 1–29. Atlantic Highlands: Humanities Press.

Steger, Manfred. 1999. "Friedrich Engels and the Origins of German Revisionism." In *Engels After Marx*, edited by Manfred Steger and Terrell Carver, 118–196. Manchester: Manchester University Press.

Stepanova, Yevgenia. 1985. *Engels: A Short Biography*. Moscow: Progress.

Stirner, Max. 2005. *The Ego and His Own*. Translated by Steven Byington. New York: Dover.

Thomas, Paul. 2008. *Marxism and Scientific Socialism*. London: Routledge.

Thompson, Edward. 1978. *The Poverty of Theory and Other Essays*. London: Merlin.

Thönnessen, Werner. 1973. *The Emancipation of Women*. London: Pluto.

Timpanaro, Sebastiano. 1975. *On Materialism*. London: Verso.

Trat, Josette. 1998. "Engels and the Emancipation of Women." *Friedrich Engels: A Critical Centenary Appreciation*. Special issue of *Science and Society* 62, no. 1: 88–105.

Trotsky, Leon. 1958. *Diary in Exile*. London: Faber and Faber.

Trotsky, Leon. 1971. *Military Writings*. New York: Pathfinder.

Trotsky, Leon. 1972. *The Revolution Betrayed*. New York: Pathfinder.

Tucker, Robert. 1961. *Philosophy and Myth in Karl Marx*. Cambridge: Cambridge University Press.

Tudor, Henry. 1993. Introduction. In Eduard Bernstein, *The Preconditions of Socialism*, xv–xxxvi. Cambridge: Cambridge University Press.

Tudor, Henry, and J. M. Tudor, eds. 1988. *Marxism and Social Democracy: The Revisionist Debate 1896–1898*. Cambridge: Cambridge University Press.

Vogel, Lise. 1995. *Woman Questions*. New York: Routledge.

Vogel, Lise. 1996. "Engels's *Origin*." In *Engels Today*, edited by Chris Arthur, 129–151. London: Macmillan.

Vogel, Lise. 2013. *Marxism and the Oppression of Women: Towards a Unitary Theory*. Chicago: Haymarket.

Vollgraf, Carl-Erich, and Jurgen Jucknickel. 2002. "Marx in Marx's Words?" *Journal of Political Economy* 32, no. 1: 35–78.

Vygodski, Vitali. 1973. *The Story of a Great Discovery*. Berlin: Verlag Die Wirtschaft.

Walicki, Andrzej. 1995. *Marxism and the Leap to the Kingdom of Freedom*. Stanford: Stanford University Press.

Watkins, Susan. 2018. "Which Feminisms?" *New Left Review* 109: 5–76.

Wayne, Mike, and Diedre O'Neil. 2013. "The Engels Project." *Film International* 11, nos. 3–4: 6–10.

Weeks, John. 1981. *Capital and Exploitation*. Princeton: Princeton University Press.

Wheen, Francis. 1999. *Karl Marx*. London: Fourth Estate.

Whitfield, Roy. 1988. *Frederick Engels in Manchester*. Manchester: Working Class Movement Library.

Wolf, Eric. 1987. "The Peasant War in Germany: Friedrich Engels as Social Historian." *Science and Society* 51, no. 1: 82–92.

Wood, Ellen Meiksins. 1986. *The Retreat from Class*. London: Verso.

Wood, Allen. 2004. *Karl Marx*. London: Routledge.

Woolfson, Charles. 1982. *The Labour Theory of Culture: A Re-examination of Engels's Theory of Human Origins*. London: Routledge and Kegan Paul.

Zelený, Jindřich. 1980. *The Logic of Marx*. Oxford: Blackwell.

Index

www.ingramcontent.com/pod-product-compliance
Lightning Source LLC
Chambersburg PA
CBHW030350270326
41926CB00009B/1043